Modern Critical Views

Edward Albee

African American
  Poets Volume I

American and Can-
  adian Women
  Poets, 1930–present

American Women
  Poets, 1650–1950

Maya Angelou

Asian-American
  Writers

Margaret Atwood

Jane Austen

James Baldwin

Samuel Beckett

Saul Bellow

The Bible

William Blake

Jorge Luis Borges

Ray Bradbury

The Brontës

Gwendolyn Brooks

Elizabeth Barrett
  Browning

Robert Browning

Italo Calvino

Albert Camus

Lewis Carroll

Willa Cather

Cervantes

Geoffrey Chaucer

Anton Chekhov

Kate Chopin

Agatha Christie

Samuel Taylor
  Coleridge

Joseph Conrad

Contemporary Poets

Stephen Crane

Dante

Daniel Defoe

Charles Dickens

Emily Dickinson

John Donne and the
  17th-Century Poets

Fyodor Dostoevsky

W.E.B. Du Bois

George Eliot

T. S. Eliot

Ralph Ellison

Ralph Waldo Emerson

William Faulkner

F. Scott Fitzgerald

Sigmund Freud

Robert Frost

George Gordon, Lord
  Byron

Graham Greene

Thomas Hardy

Nathaniel Hawthorne

Ernest Hemingway

Hispanic-American
  Writers

Homer

Langston Hughes

Zora Neale Hurston

Henrik Ibsen

John Irving

Henry James

James Joyce

Franz Kafka

John Keats

Jamaica Kincaid

Stephen King

Rudyard Kipling

D. H. Lawrence

Ursula K. Le Guin

Sinclair Lewis

Bernard Malamud

Christopher Marlowe

Gabriel García
  Márquez

Cormac McCarthy

Carson McCullers

Herman Melville

Molière

Arthur Miller

John Milton

Molière

Toni Morrison

Native-American
  Writers

Joyce Carol Oates

Flannery O'Connor

Eugene O'Neill

George Orwell

Octavio Paz

Sylvia Plath

Edgar Allan Poe

Katherine Anne
  Porter

J. D. Salinger

Jean-Paul Sartre

William Shakespeare:
  Histories and
  Poems

William Shakespeare:
  Romances

William Shakespeare:
  The Comedies

William Shakespeare:
  The Tragedies

George Bernard Shaw

Mary Wollstonecraft
  Shelley

Percy Bysshe Shelley

Alexander
  Solzhenitsyn

Sophocles

John Steinbeck

Tom Stoppard

Jonathan Swift

Amy Tan

Alfred, Lord Tennyson

Henry David Thoreau

J. R. R. Tolkien

Leo Tolstoy

Mark Twain

John Updike

Modern Critical Views

Kurt Vonnegut

Alice Walker

Robert Penn Warren

Eudora Welty

Edith Wharton

Walt Whitman

Oscar Wilde

Tennessee Williams

Thomas Wolfe

Tom Wolfe

Virginia Woolf

William Wordsworth

Richard Wright

William Butler Yeats

Modern Critical Views

MOLIÈRE

Edited and with an introduction by
Harold Bloom
Sterling Professor of the Humanities
Yale University

CHELSEA HOUSE PUBLISHERS
Philadelphia

Library of Congress Cataloging-in-Publication Data

Moliére / edited and with an introduction by Harold Bloom.
    p. cm. – (Modern critical views)
    Includes bibliographical references and index.
      ISBN 0-7910-6335-6 (alk. paper)
      1. Moliére, 1622-1673--Criticism and interpretation. I.
Bloom, Harold. II. Series.

PQ1860 .M553 2001
842'.4--dc21   2001047213

Chelsea House Publishers
1974 Sproul Road, Suite 400
Broomall, PA 19008-0914

http://www.chelseahouse.com

Contributing Editor: Elizabeth A. S. Beaudin

Contents

Editor's Note   vii

Introduction   1
  Harold Bloom

General
Mise En Scène and the Classic Text   5
  Jim Carmody

The Comic at Its Limits   27
  Gérard Defaux

Molière, La Fontaine, and Authority   35
  James F. Gaines

"Introduction" in *Molière:* A Collection of Critical Essays   45
  Jacques Guicharnaud

Mime   59
  W. G. Moore

Dom Juan
Dom Juan's Equal Opportunity Rivalry   69
  Michael S. Koppisch

Dom Juan   77
  Robert McBride

Le Bourgeois gentilhomme
Rehearsal and Reversal in *Le Bourgeois gentilhomme*   107
  Ronald W. Tobin

L'Ecole des femmes
Parody in *L'Ecole des femmes*   123
 H. Gaston Hall

Le Médecin malgré lui
Restructuring a Comic Hero of Molière: *Le médecin*   137
malgré lui
 Joseph I. Donohue, Jr.

Le Misanthrope
Le Misanthrope: philosophical implications   145
 Peter H. Nurse

Legal Elements in *Le Misanthrope*   163
 David Shaw

Tartuffe
Love in *Tartuffe*, Tartuffe in Love   175
 Jules Brody

Le Tartuffe   183
 Andrew Calder

Chronology   207

Contributors   209

Bibliography   211

Acknowledgments   215

Index   217

Editor's Note

My Introduction reconsiders Moliere's bruising of theatrical limits in *Dom Juan* and *Le Misanthrope*, while contrasting him with Shakespeare's even more radical experimentation.

Jim Carmody, attempting to correct the disciples of W.G. Moore, tries to undo the concept of Molière as a "Classical Author," while Gerard Defaux sees Molière as seeking to heal his audience, in the mode of the optimistic humanism of the Counter-Reformation. James F. Gaines invokes the fabulist La Fontaine as a complementary master of the very kinds of authority that Molière exemplified.

Jacques Guicharnaud, dean of Molière critics, sees the dramatist as an artist of "frenzied struggles" controlled by his comic vision, while W.G. Moore establishes Molière the actor as the master of mime and mask, who kept close to the clarity of unchanging character in his roles.

Dom Juan is judged by Michael S. Koppisch essentially to be an sequel to *Tartuffe*, since *Juan* is equally low-minded, after which Robert McBride studies the ironies by which Molière distances himself from the libertine.

Le Bourgeois Gentilhomme, a sublime satire on social elevation, is viewed by Ronald W Tobin as culminating in the spectacle of Mamamouchi Jourdain imposing an absolute order, while H. Gaston Hall analyzes the parodistic element in *L'Ecole des Femmes*.

Le Medecin malgre lui, is regarded by Joesph I. Donohue, Jr. as rehabilitating its comic hero, after which we receive contrasting perspectives on *Le Misanthrope*, with Peter H. Nurse pursuing its philosophical implications and David Shaw investigating the legal aspects of the play.

Tartuffe concludes this volume with rival readings by Jules Brody and Andrew Calder. For Brody, the theme of hypocrisy washes away illusory love while, in Calder's analysis, the play centers upon its satire of religious casuistry.

Introduction

After Shakespeare, Molière, more than Racine, disputes Ibsen's eminence as the prime creator of European drama. The best starting-point for regarding Molière I learned long ago from Jacques Guicharnaud: our lives are romances, farces, disgraces so that we have to embrace bad faith lest we doubt ourselves.

Is that the inner drama of Molière's *Dom Juan*? I myself dissent from the two readings of *Dom Juan* offered by this volume, but then I have never encountered an interpretation, or a performance of *Dom Juan* that persuaded me. Molière, who played the role of Sganarelle, got into more than his usual trouble with moralists, both secular and religious, with this ambiguous drama. In conjunction with *Tartuffe*, *Dom Juan* cost Molière the last sacrament and an unsanctified burial. During the playwright-actor's life, he suffered threats and consequent anxieties, though his great patron, the Sun-King, Louis XIV, protected him to a considerable degree.

Goethe delighted in *Dom Juan*, as in the rest of Molière, and one sees why: Molière's irony is already Goethean. Dom Juan is hardly the free spirit he presents himself as being. Anticipating Bryon's Don Juan as well as Goethe's Faust, Molière's Dom Juan is remarkably passive: his career has become accidental, though he continues to run for election (as it were) to the eminence of Super-Seducer, and he seeks votes everywhere, as though he doubts his own mythic status. Though he proclaims his autonomy, he himself belies it, since to maintain yourself as a living legend is a considerable exhaustion. Entropy threatens the Great Lover, and yet he persists, though with increasing irony. He knows that he acts in a contradictory fashion, but exults in the uniqueness of what he does. At the same time, he shows less and less interest in enjoying his female victims, if "enjoyment" is at all an accurate category in regard to his erotic project.

Molière, subtle and deep beyond devising, makes Dom Juan the most sympathetic figure in the play, certainly more so than the tricky

1

Sganarelle. And yet the dramatist limits our sympathy: the diabolic seducer is not at all diabolic, and endlessly suffers the cost of confirmation. If I were directing the play, I would find a Bill Clinton look-alike for the role of Dom Juan (I should say that I voted twice for Clinton, and wish I could help elect him for a third time). There can be no rest for Dom Juan, for he is the victim of his myth, and he would become the equivalent of an aging rock-star or ex-president if he fortunately did not achieve a sublime punishment at play's end.

Dom Juan's entire project is blasphemous, not because of its dubious sexuality, but because God is the ultimate rival, the more successful seducer. The pragmatic enmity of God, the greater celebrity, is what redeems the hero-villain from nihilism, and confers aesthetic dignity upon him. Nowhere else in Molière does anyone die; Shakespearean deaths on stage were considered barbarous by most of the French. When Juan is swallowed up by hellfire, we have a unique moment in French theater, up to that time. But *Dom Juan* is a singular play: what genre is it? Molière transgresses the limits of comedy in this work, as though he had become impatient with the conditions set for his exercise of his art.

Dom Juan cannot change, but then nobody in Molière can change, a condition in which they have more in common with Dante's characters than with Shakespeare's. But Dante knows the truth; Molière knows only that truth is evasive and elusive, while Shakespeare is too intellectually large and imaginatively wealthy to allow much relevance to truth.

What is the truth about Alceste in that most exuberant of all non-Shakespearean comedies, *The Misanthrope*? He is the most complex character in Molière, who acted the part, whereas he avoided the role of Dom Juan, just as he played Orgon rather than Tartuffe. In some respects, Alceste is a comic Hamlet, but then so is Hamlet. There are large differences: Hamlet has a considerable sense of humor, is as fierce towards himself as he is severe to others, and is too great to risk an absurd quest. And yet Alceste is a strenuous satirist, like Hamlet, and like Hamlet he has the aesthetic dignity of being authentically outraged by his society's corruption. Molière again bruises the limits of comedy by giving us a hero both impossibly absurd and yet admirable, who resists all moralization you might be tempted to turn against him.

Perhaps Alceste fails as a lover, but so does Hamlet. No great satirist has survived marriage, and Alceste's greatness is almost too palpable for comedy, however outrageously he speaks and behaves. It is totally inaccurate to pair him with Dom Juan, because Alceste does not solicit your favor nor ask you to confirm his metaphysical existence by your suffrage. Eric Bentley shrewdly notes that *The Misanthrope* is an exception to all theatrical rules, just as *Hamlet* is. Alceste's ideas matter a great deal, like Hamlet's and Molière goes against his own dramatic wisdom in allowing Alceste's mind to transcend the world of the play. Falstaff is so witty that the two parts of *Henry IV* cannot contain him, but Shakespeare knew that to allow Falstaff into *Henry V* would destroy that play. Alceste flees the salon, into whatever metaphorical solitude, because his passionate will threatens the play's ability to sustain itself as comedy.

JIM CARMODY

Mise En Scène and the Classic Text

Since the 1949 publication of Will Moore's seminal book, *Molière: A New Criticism*, English-speaking critics of Molière have accepted the premise that Molière's texts should be interpreted in the context of the theater. In France, René Bray's 1954 book, *Molière: homme de théâtre*, exerted a similar kind of influence. Although Moore and Bray were pursuing very different, even fundamentally opposite, intellectual agendas, they agreed that the *theatrical* aspects of the plays had been far too long ignored, and that when interpreting Molière's writings, scholars should remember that Molière wrote for the theater.

As a corrective, Moore offered a reading that discussed some of Molière's major plays under such rubrics as "Mime," "Mask," and "Scene," thus creating a prototype for what has come to be known as "metadramatic criticism." Moore's readings of individual plays, however, are less sensitive to the material aspects of performance than they appear to be. Although he advocates a consideration of Molière's plays as works written for the theater, Moore is principally interested in the elucidation of Molière's *morale*, like those critics who precede him and whose methods he contests. In his discussion of *Tartuffe*, for example, Moore remarks that Molière wore a mask while performing some of his roles, then goes on to discuss *Tartuffe* as a play about the unmasking of Tartuffe. In the course of this discussion, Moore

From *Rereading Molière:* Mise en Scène from Antoine to Vitez. ©1993 University of Michigan.

turns an actor's *commedia* mask into a metaphor without exploring the connection between Molière's use of *commedia* masks in performance and Moore's own description of the "unmasking" of Tartuffe, and without acknowledging that neither Molière nor the other actors wore masks during performances of *Tartuffe*. Instead of investigating Molière's writings as the product of a historically specific artistic and cultural practice, he devotes his attention to the philosophical issues that the critical tradition had already identified in the plays.

Rather than address the material aspects of theatrical production, Moore affirmed the importance of studying Molière's aesthetics as the best means of arriving at an appreciation of the playwright's ethics, an emphasis that encouraged scholars to turn their attention to the text itself after a long period of focusing on Molière's personal life. The frequent, often explicit, linking in recent decades of aesthetics and ethics in the titles of books and articles on Molière indicates the extent of Moore's influence. Following his example, writers employ terms such as *actor, mask,* and *scenic space* to discuss what they take to be the ethical issues raised by Molière's dramaturgy; like Moore, they, too, never discuss actual actors, masks, or scenic spaces. For Moore and those who have adopted his methods, the language of the theater provides a range of useful metaphors that enables a metadramatic critique of a range of issues. It is important to note, however, that these are precisely the same issues that earlier generations of *moliéristes* had discussed using different vocabularies.

A recent book by Nathan Gross, one of the prominent ethics/aesthetics critics of the 1980s, reveals the extent to which the methodology pioneered by Moore continues to ignore the material aspects of performance. In *From Gesture to Idea: Esthetics and Ethics in Molière's Comedy*, as the title of his book implies, Gross selects "gesture" as his theatrical point of reference:

> Each of these essays . . . develops from the observation of a specific detail of language and gesture, more apparent in a staged performance than in reading of the printed text, into an exploration of the underlying ethical values that the play in question urges upon an audience's attention. . . . These gestures recur within episodes of plot arranged in parallel cycles. Organization of the dramatic text . . . guides the spectator's pleasurable response; it furnishes a series of contexts that allow him, by virtue of his knowledge of similar earlier incident, vocabulary, and gesture, to anticipate the comic protagonist's behavior and to appreciate ironies of situation and language.

Although he refers to gestures that are "more apparent in a staged performance than in a reading of the printed text," Gross never discusses actual performances. And although the details that interest Gross could indeed be made apparent in performance, he does not take into account the very real possibility that individual directors might choose to ignore, alter, or even suppress those details.

While an individual actor may perform gestures such as those indicated by Gross, it is unlikely that any performance would provoke on the part of the spectator the kind of systematic moral reflection that Gross finds in Molière's plays. The dramatic text (synonymous here with the printed text) may guide the reader's "pleasurable response," but the spectator is not sitting in the theater reading a book. The spectator's experience of a play is quintessentially different from that of a reader. Whereas the reader can suspend the flow of action to consider and reconsider whatever strikes his or her fancy, rereading the same passage or passages in whatever order seems most productive, the spectator can see a mise en scène only once. Whatever limited kind of "rereading" is possible in the theater, it simply cannot be the same as that which the reader takes for granted. Unlike the reader, the spectator cannot stop the performance to consider the ethical implications of a single gesture, line, exchange of lines, or sequence of events; in other words, the spectator cannot perform any of the analytical operations that Gross's reading fundamentally depends on in the time frame allowed by performance. It is useful to remember, too, that the vast majority of spectators are not professional humanists and do not pay very much attention to the kinds of ethical considerations that this kind of criticism claims to find *systematically* explored in these plays. This is not to say that a spectator with the angle of vision of an ethics/aesthetics critic such as Gross will not be able to discern in a certain mise en scène the very pattern he or she has already identified in the play. Clearly, there are many directors who approach Molière's text looking for precisely the kind of patterning of behavior that interests Will Moore and Nathan Gross.

I shall return to the question of Molière's *morale* in later chapters. What is important, for the moment, is not whether the ethics/aesthetics critics have anything of value to contribute to Molière's studies (they do); what I want to contest is their claim to be dealing with Molière in the context of the theater. What Gross has to say about the repetition of gesture is valid but only in the most general, abstract way. The gestures that Gross describes are not performed by a living actor on a stage before a live audience, although Gross's discussion probably draws on unacknowledged performances that he has attended. Like other ethics/aesthetics critics, and like other scholars who adopt a metadramatic mode of commentary, Gross never addresses the question of which kind of mise en scène he has in mind.

Is he thinking of a realist or nonrealist, modernist or postmodernist mise en scène? Or does he have in mind the kind of classical mise en scène that offers a judicious blend of "classical" acting values and suggestions of contemporary "relevance"? Does he, for instance, prefer Jouvet's *Tartuffe* or Planchon's, Vilar's *Dom Juan* or Chéreau's, and for what reasons? Like most literary scholars, Gross is far more comfortable citing a printed document than a theatrical performance, even though the failure to deal with actual theatrical performances calls his critical methodology into question.

It is useful to remember, however, that the work of Moore, along with that of the critics who have investigated the fields of research that he opened up, is itself determined by the discursive practices within which it emerges and which gives it its specific forms. Molière scholars such as Moore are first and foremost devoted to the humanist study of literature. Consequently, their work on the writings of Molière and on the cultural production of seventeenth-century France reflects the interests of that discipline. As a result, in their professional writings they inevitably privilege the text over theatrical performance, no matter how much they may appreciate and take pleasure in attending performances of Molière's plays. The fact that Molière scholars have, relatively speaking, almost entirely ignored the *comédies-ballets* (almost half of Molière's plays) for over three and a half centuries is perhaps not irrelevant in this context.

Like other ethics/aesthetics critics who take their lead from Moore, Gross avoids any discussion of the material aspects of the theater. René Bray, on the other hand, researched the working habits and environments of seventeenth-century French theater that he believed conditioned, if not actually determined, Molière's development as actor, director, company manager, and playwright. In place of detailed readings of individual plays, Bray offered what was, in effect, a revisionist historiography of French seventeenth-century theater. Bray thus opened up lines of inquiry that have led not only to significant shifts in perspective in Molière studies but also in studies of the work of other dramatists and theaters of the period.

Bray's work is perhaps less frequently quoted that Moore's for a number of reasons. In the first place, Bray offers few interpretive comments on individual plays in his *Molière: homme de théâtre.* (The Bray and Scherer edition of the plays, while listed in many bibliographies, is also seldom discussed.) In the second place, and more significantly, Bray undertakes a sustained assault on the humanist tradition of reading Molière as a *moraliste.* With considerable energy, he contends that Molière is not a systematic thinker and that no significant moral philosophy can be deduced from a reading of the plays. He devotes an entire chapter to posing the question, "Is Molière a Philosopher?" a question he answers unequivocally with a resounding "No." Unsurprisingly, Bray's rejection of Molière as a moral philosopher made his work difficult to assimilate into discussions of the interrelationships between Molière's ethics and aesthetics. Ironically, while his work provided scholars with potentially valuable insights into the practices of the French theater industry during Molière's lifetime, none of the scholars interested in developing a "theatrical reading" of the plays has been willing to set aside his or her interest in Molière's moral philosophy. It is not surprising, therefore, that Laurence Romero, in his 1974 survey of Molière's criticism, offers the disappointing assessment that Moore's and Bray's most important contribution has been that they persuaded critics to look for Molière's thought in the entire play and not simply in the speeches of the *raisonneur*.

Bray's questioning of the kind of philosophically oriented humanistic research that has consistently informed Molière studies (the revelation and explication of Molière's moral "philosophy") emerges as a radical break not only with almost every element of established Molière criticism but also with the humanistic discipline of dramatic criticism itself as it had been practiced until that time. (Indeed, Bray's critique of traditional Molière criticism may perhaps be seen in retrospect as being somewhat akin to poststructuralist critiques of the Author.) Bray insisted on the purely theatrical origin and destination of Molière's text. No satisfactory understanding of those texts could be arrived at, he believed, in the absence of an understanding of the signifying practices within which they emerged.

In *La Formation de la doctrine classique en France*, Bray made substantial contributions to our understanding of classical dramaturgy as it evolved in the real world of seventeenth-century France. Subsequently, other scholars turned their attention to the day-to-day realities of Molière's theater, notably Georges Mongredien and Roger Herzel. In addition to his *Daily Life in the Theatre at the Time of Molière*, Mongrédien published in 1965 the first anthology of seventeenth-century French documents relating to Molière. Herzel produced a number of influential articles on Molière's stagecraft prior to his 1981 book, *The Original Casting of Molière's Plays*. Other scholars have significantly increased our understanding of seventeenth-century theater architecture and scenography. Along with Henry C. Lancaster's monumental history of French classical drama and Jacques Scherer's equally exhaustive *La Dramaturgie classique en France*, this research provides us with a better understanding of Molière's work as actor, director, and company manager—and how that work formed the context for his playwriting. While this research has resulted in significant gains in our understanding of the theater of Molière and his contemporaries, it has also reminded us, time and again, of how very few accounts exist of the performances of Molière's plays.

As an author, Molière was influenced as much by his director's imagination as by his actor's experience; while his experience as an actor nourished his ability to create rich, theatrical characters, his experience as a director taught him to think in terms of the interplay of character, décor, and spectator. Molière's contemporaries acknowledged him as a superbly talented and innovative director. Donneau de Visé, for example, one of the first commentators on *School for Wives*, complimented Molière on the degree of aesthetic control manifested in his mise en scène, remarking that Molière had set a new standard: "Never was a play so well performed with so much attention to detail; each actor knows exactly how many steps to take and every wink is measured". While Molière's experience as a performer undoubtedly helped him create effective scenes between characters at both the moment of writing and the moment of staging, it is his directorial imagination that gave birth to the complex, hybrid form of the *comédie-ballet*. A mixture of different modes of theatrical performance that combines verbal, musical, scenic, and choreographic elements, the *comédie-ballet* demonstrates Molière's ability to think in terms of what the modern era calls the poetry of the stage.

Indeed, much of the scholarly disinterest that has greeted the *comédies-ballets* over the years can be attributed to the fact that Molière's texts quite obviously do not provide an adequate sense of the scenic life of these plays. Accordingly, the texts of the *comédies-ballets* have been relegated to the same secondary status as opera librettos or the "books" of musicals. It is hardly surprising that such creations should have been denied critical approval in the doctrinaire neo-Aristotelian climate of French neoclassicism, or that subsequent generations of scholars and theater artists should have felt embarrassed by the nonliterary (i.e., nonverbal) elements of Molière's texts. Nevertheless, the fact that Molière was capable of creating such works for the stage, often at alarmingly short notice, suggests that his theatrical imagination was directed toward creating works of theater principally at the level of performance or mise en scène. In other words, we can see Molière as the author of two quite distinct texts, the verbal text and the scenic text, only one of which has survived.

At a distance of more than three centuries, it is unlikely that we will ever be able to reconstruct Molière's original mise en scène in anything but the most fragmentary manner; it is therefore possible to propose only the most conjectural readings of Molière's writings in the context of seventeenth-century theater.

Unfortunately, we know very little about the day-to-day work of seventeenth-century theater artists: we do not know how plays were rehearsed, what the acting values were, or what the production values were.

What little we know about production values has been gleaned from sources such as Mahelot's *Mémoire*, seventeenth-century graphic reproductions of décors or scènes from a relatively small number of plays, and the manuals of scenography by experts in scenic illusion. Our information about acting styles, especially Molière's personal technique, is considerably less reliable than the documents on scenic practices, for it is based on comparisons with the extravagantly rhetorical style associated with the tragedians of the Hôtel de Bourgogne, a style about which we know equally little. While Molière was praised for the "natural," realistic quality of his acting, we should not assume that those who praised him shared our modern notions of naturalistic or realistic acting. If Molière was praised for being "natural" onstage, more "lifelike" than his tragedian colleagues at the Hôtel de Bourgogne, he was also simultaneously acknowledged as the most gifted *farceur* of his time, applauded for his extraordinarily flexible facial expressions and talent for grotesque silliness.

If we do not possess sufficient information to discuss Molière's plays in Molière's own stagings, it is possible to consider Molière's work in the context of twentieth-century mises en scène, as many of the most influential mises en scène have been relatively well documented. Fortunately, we have not only critical accounts of the different performances but also texts written by directors and their collaborators that shed considerable light on the problematics of staging French classic drama in this century. No single book, however, can hope to discuss all of the important productions of every Molière play. Perhaps no single book can even hope to undertake a comprehensive discussion of every significant production of one of the major plays. Rather than trying to focus on the entire oeuvre or on every important production of a single play, this book focuses on productions of two plays that proved to be turning points in the twentieth-century staging of Molière's plays. *The School for Wives* and *Tartuffe*. The productions in question are André Antoine's and Jacques Arnavon's 1907 *Tartuffe*, Arnavon's 1936 notebook production of *The School for Wives*, Louis Jouvet's 1936 *School for Wives*, Roger Planchon's two productions of *Tartuffe* in the 1960s and 1970s, and Antoine Vitez's Molière tetralogy of 1978.

These productions are not, by any means, the only important Molière productions of this century, nor are the directors who staged them the only individuals who have achieved significant results with the plays in question. These productions are, however, representative of the best stagings of Molière in this century. More significantly, perhaps, they represent key moments in the history of French theater: each of these productions marks an important development in the ways that plays from the classical period were staged in France. Indeed, I hope to show that, taken together, these productions reveal an almost century-long exploration of the status and identify of "the classics" in twentieth-century French theater. These productions also reveal an abiding interest in exploring the ever-shifting understanding of the "Grand Siècle" as a value in modern and contemporary French culture.

This book, then, is an attempt to take up the challenge of Bray and Moore in a new way by writing about Molière's plays, not in the context of a generalized notion of the theater but, rather, in the context of specific moments of theatrical production. The following chapters offer a synthesis of theater history and dramatic criticism. They attempt a necessarily partial reconstruction of certain productions as a way of examining how Molière has been "read" in the French theater during this century.

The mises en scène that are the focus of this book are the products of a response both to the individual plays in question and to the extraordinarily complex cultural identity of Molière himself. In a sense these directors respond as much to what Molière represents as to the scripts he wrote. Their individual responses are themselves products of the forces of French culture (forces that collide with one another as often as they coalesce) operating within the theatrical and other artistic spheres at a given moment; the same mise en scène may, accordingly, appear conservative from one perspective and revolutionary from another. I have not attempted to map out all of the forces that may have operated on any one of the productions I shall be discussing but have, instead, chosen to concentrate on a nexus of issues: the relationship between director and playwright as manifested in directors' attitudes to the classic text; developments in directors' strategies for adapting the dramaturgy and scenography of the 1660s to the aesthetics of the twentieth century; and developments in directors' responses to the ideologies of "fidelity" and "realism".

Molière, Classical Author

The director's goal is the creation of a mise en scène that his or her contemporaries will find theatrically compelling. In order to create a theatrically compelling mise en scène of a play by Molière, the director must first address two related problems: he or she must find a means of reconciling Molière's seventeenth-century dramaturgy with the poetics of contemporary mise en scène; he or she must also find a satisfactory way of addressing the cultural status of Molière's play as a classic, for the play is being revived in the modern theater precisely because it is a classic. In short, a compelling mise en scène of a classic text must contain both a theatrically exciting performance of the drama in question and a persuasive treatment of the play's identity as a classic.

Since Molière's text exists as a material product of a certain place and time (Paris in the 1660s), the director must choose how to explore the relationships between the text and the society in which it was created, a relationship that is complicated by the double identity of the play as both a script and a recognized literary classic. Whereas the script is but one element, however important, of the technology of the theater, the mere fact of the play's publication as a book by an important author immediately "elevates" the play to what literary scholars have regarded as the higher cultural status of Literature. (It is useful to remember that theater scripts need not take the form of a book. Molière's actors never read the complete text; instead, each actor was given a "side" or copy of his or her own part only, a practice that continued into the present century.) Molière's scripts are products of seventeenth-century French theater; Molière's "classic plays," on the other hand, are as much, if not more so, products of more recent periods of French and other cultures. As classics of French culture, they have been identified as containing timeless truths about the human condition, truths that are fixed for the reader, and the spectator in perfect models of dramatic form. But this notion of the classic is not a seventeenth-century one. For Molière's contemporaries, the "classics" were Greek and Roman. Although Molière and other artists of his day were consciously attempting to create their own art based on Greek and Roman models, they did not label themselves Neoclassicists. That labeling occurred much later.

Molière's status as a classic author has significantly influenced the direction of both Molière studies and productions of his plays. This influence is perhaps best seen in the tendency to treat Molière's comédies as serious dramas and to pay a great deal less attention to his farces and comédies-ballets. Since tragedy as a genre has traditionally been seen as representing a higher level of aesthetic and indeed moral achievement, scholars have tended to privilege the more serious, darker aspects of Molière's drama. Similarly, generations of directors have shown a marked preference for a "tragic" Molière.

Theater is an ephemeral art and, as such, is notoriously difficult to describe and evaluate. Productions not only eventually end their runs and literally disappear forever, but as every theater artist acknowledges, no two performances are ever alike. The published text, however, remains as a permanent trace of the original production and becomes available to each successive generation of readers and potential directors. In a culture that prizes the "timelessness" of the work of art, it is not surprising that the book of the play has superseded the performance of the play as the privileged mode of being for the dramatic work of art. Indeed, until the advent of the theatrical avant-garde at the end of the last century, the relationship between dramatic literature and its performance onstage was relatively unproblematic. With the rise to prominence of the stage director, however, the staging of the production, which I shall be referring to from a semiotic perspective as the scenic text, eventually came to rival the playwright's text as a focus of interest.

For the scholar of drama, the written text understandably remains the primary source of interest, and he or she usually tends to consider both performance and scholarship as sharing a common goal—producing the most convincing, "faithful," or otherwise satisfactory interpretation of the text. Theater artists and spectators, however, are not primarily interested in the written text. As a playwright, actor, and director, Molière wrote his texts with the knowledge that they were to be used as only one element among many that would go into the preparation of a performance. The institution of dramatic literature notwithstanding, theater scripts are not written to be read outside the theater: the potential for performance dictates the content of every line, the shape of every scene, and the identity of every character. Even the plays of Jean Racine, which are generally acknowledged as the greatest literary achievements of seventeenth-century France, were written to take advantage of the possibilities offered by a specific kind of theatrical performance. Arguing for the primacy of performance over text even in the case of an apparently literary theater such as Racine's, Bernard Dort writes:

> On the surface, it seems to be a theater that is exclusively a theater of text. Few, if any, stage directions. Racinian tragedy seems never to have had any existence other than literary. But that is obviously not correct. In fact, the exact opposite was true. The text existed only to fulfill the requirements of an already existing form: the form of tragic performance. And the *palais à volonté* of the Hôtel de Bourgogne was more than a mere décor; it was, properly speaking, a symbolic location, the very image of how a certain society saw itself. The text did nothing more than furnish the ingredients for a ritual that these individuals produced for their own pleasure.

Dort's semiotic analysis of the theatrical event is usefully comprehensive in that it avoids restricting "theatrical performance" to the narrow sense of what transpires on the stage. Instead, he proposes that we examine plays and their performances not only as purely aesthetic events abstracted from the influences of the cultural and political environment but also as responses to an identified, socially circumscribed desire. In the case of Racine, Dort suggests, the playwright was responding to the desire of a certain segment of the aristocracy to see its own experiences figured on a tragic scale.

Like Dort, theater semioticians see all scripts as, in part, responses to the signifying potential present in theatrical performance during a given period. In *The Semiotics of Theatre and Drama*, for instance, Keir Elam writes:

> Since, chronologically, the writing of the play precedes any given performance, it might appear quite legitimate to suppose the simple priority of one over the other. But it is equally legitimate to claim that it is the performance, or at least a possible or "model" performance, that constrains the dramatic text in its very articulation.

The script, then, need not be seen as a writing that exists before the performance but, instead, as a writing that is completed in performance. In a 1985 article, "Theatrical Performance," Marvin Carlson has suggested that we should see the relationship between script and performance not in terms of an adaptation, a translation, or a realization but, rather, in terms of a Derridean complementarity.

Surprisingly enough, semioticians often neglect to consider what actually happens to the script in the theatrical production process: the script (especially an unproduced script) that remains unchanged by the rehearsal process is the exception, not the rule—the dialogue the actors read at the first rehearsal is rarely the dialogue heard by spectators at the first performance. The script, then, represents a certain provisional conception of the dramatic potential of the stage itself, for the playwright begins work with an acquired store of theatrical experience and an acquired knowledge of the conventions of the contemporary theater; the script comes into being in the context of that knowledge.

Although Roland Barthes did not explicitly consider the question of the theater script, his celebrated distinction between work and text provides a valuable perspective on the question. Indeed, Barthes's notion of the text as intertext, as a fabric "woven entirely with citations, references, echoes, cultural languages . . . antecedent or contemporary, which cut across and through it in a vast stereophony," applies equally well to both the script and the mise en scène that eventually subsumes it. It is Barthes's intertextual view of both the script and its mise en scène that informs the following chapters.

In the theater, the author's intention is that the script be used to create something else (given a choice, most living playwrights will choose to be performed rather than understood). Certainly, one can legitimately question the effectiveness of the ways in which the script has been used, just as one can express reservations about the ways in which a certain actor or a certain kind of lighting instrument has been used. The semiotic view of the creative process in the theater should, therefore, not be understood as a means of devaluing the contribution of the playwright; rather, it should be seen as a recognition of the many different sources of creativity that combine to make an effective piece of theater.

This view of the relationship between script and mise en scène has important consequences for the study of what Jonathan Miller calls the "subsequent performances" of plays by Molière or any classic dramatist. If the script comes into being as a kind of proposal for the way the "cybernetic machine that is the théâtre," to borrow Barthes's image, can be made to function at a given moment in time, it makes no sense to ask whether or not the mise en scène has been faithful to the intentions of the author. More productive questions will address the mise en scène, the play-in-performance, as a complex montage of different signifying systems. Furthermore, this understanding of the nature of the script reminds us that the physical realities of the theater, the personalities and skills of the performing and scenic artists, the economic health of the various theatrical and cultural institutions, as well as the tastes and opinions (aesthetic, moral, or political) of the spectators and critics provide more than a mere abstract context for the creation of the play. In fact, the play emerges from a dialectical interplay between the playwright and each of these environments. In the case of the classic playscript, these environments are precisely what have been stripped away by the passage of time, leaving behind only the "book." As Bernard Dort reminds us, once the passage of time has separated the printed text from the cultural and theatrical conditions from which it initially emerged, insisting on fidelity to the text becomes unproductive:

> One can never, dramaturgically, get away from performance. Cut off from its environment and extracted from the theatrical form in which it was to be realized, a classical text can come to life again only in another form. Let us not speak any more of being faithful to the classics or of betraying them; let us speak about the uses we make of them, uses that will never be truly productive unless they acknowledged their necessary infidelity.

Instead of pursuing a fidelity to "the classic," which amounts to privileging the book, Dort directs our attention to the demands of performance, reminding us of its inevitably contingent nature. Performance occurs only at specific moments and in specific locations, and because it depends on its immediate context for its significance as a cultural event, that immediate context often assumes priority over the classic text, notwithstanding the all too familiar and almost inevitable rhetorical gestures on the part of directors who suggest the contrary. Directors typically speak about their work in one or more of the following ways: as attempts to locate hitherto unsuspected meanings in the text; as attempts to present the author's thinking on issues that, in the director's estimation, are of compelling relevance in today's world; as attempts to realize the author's dramatic and theatrical ideas as fully as possible. Each of these positions appears to subject the director and his associates to communicating an already existing set of meanings. Indeed, with few exceptions directors present themselves as being faithful, first and foremost, to the author's "vision." Such rhetoric, as Dort reminds us, has served to obfuscate the actual practice of directors in the theater. In the course of the following chapters, I shall be considering the ways in which each director articulates a personal understanding of "fidelity" to Molière as well as looking at the notions of "Molière" to which he will attempt to be faithful.

Even though he wrote plays for himself and other members of his company to act, Molière, like other playwrights of the period, prepared his scripts for publication, recognizing that his work would be read and enjoyed as dramatic literature by his contemporaries. When he prepared scripts for publication during his own lifetime, Molière assumed, as a result of his readers' familiarity with his mises en scène and conventions of the theater of the time, that his readers would be capable of mentally theatricalizing his printed words. Three centuries later, however, Morlière's readers are no longer aware of the conventions of seventeenth-century theater that provided a frame of reference for Molière's printed text. The linguistic, social, and theatrical conventions adopted (or undermined) by Molière are no longer familiar to us; indeed, Molière may have consciously exploited conventions of which we remain ignorant. Instead, we read his plays in the context of our own experience of twentieth-century theater and in the context of what we *imagine* theatrical performance in the seventeenth century to have been like.

Each of the productions discussed in the following chapters forges a kind of aesthetic compromise between a three-hundred-year-old play and a specifically contemporary theatrical practice. These accommodations between the classic and the contemporary result in the creation, by the director, of a new text, a mise en scène that merges the dialogue of the classic script and a contemporary scenography in the moment of performance. Enveloped in the new mise en scène, the familiar script takes on a new array of possible meanings, meanings that are directly generated by the juxtaposition of the familiar script and its traditional interpretations with a new scenography. The new mise en scène alters the contours of what we imagine we know by creating a fresh set of scenic images that recontextualizes the well-known characters and dramatic events of the classic play. In addition, the new staging often fashions radically different identities for these familiar characters. (Roger Planchon's suggestion, for example, that there exists a homosexual attraction between Orgon and Tartuffe represented a somewhat startling departure from the accepted stage tradition.) The contemporary mise en scène of a classic play may, therefore, be seen as an event in which the past is confronted by the present, the already known becomes the unknown, established interpretations are overturned, and familiar cultural and moral values are contested.

The mise en scène of a Molière play can be seen as a reflection of the individual director's theoretical understanding of the nature of the neoclassical text and of its relationship to the director's culture, of which the critical, scholarly, and performance traditions constitute important parts. Planchon's production of *Tartuffe*, for instance, offers a detailed scenographic evocation of the political and cultural turbulence of Louis XIV's reign that frames the action of the play in an unprecedented way. Planchon's new setting represents a significant departure from the conventionally calm, balanced, and rational neoclassical aesthetic that informs conservative mises en scène of this play. He thus uses his production of *Tartuffe* to offer a revisionist, critical view of the Grand Siècle itself.

Antoine Vitez responds differently to the Grand Siècle and uses his mises en scène of seventeenth-century dramatic texts, both comic and tragic, to explore the extent to which these monuments of French culture, texts that are taught every year in both primary and secondary French schools, are essentially foreign, even indecipherable in terms of their aesthetic form and content to French men and women of the late twentieth century. Vitez thus takes a position completely opposed to that of Antoine's collaborator, Jacques Arnavon, who argues that Molière's thought remains unambiguously present to the reader in his scripts, even for twentieth-century directors or readers. Whereas Arnavon believes that Molière's work communicates to people of every period and is therefore a classic by virtue of its readability (*lisibilité*, in Barthes's sense), Vitez believes that the play's classic status is precisely what blinds us to its real nature as a text is no longer (re)readable but only (re)writable (what Barthes calls *scriptible*).

The following chapters investigate the attitudes of a number of French directors to Molière's classic texts while considering those attitudes in the context of their responses to the theatrical culture of their various periods (ranging from 1907 to 1978) as well as their individual senses of the general purpose of the theater institution itself. Each of these directors is distinguished not only by the extent of his influence on subsequent generations of directors in France but also by the degree to which his work on Molière is carried out in a self-conscious manner. Each sees his work as both creative and critical: creative in the sense that he is involved in the making of new productions; critical in the sense that his new production articulates a response both to Molière's script and to the received traditions of interpretation as manifested onstage and in the writings of theater critics and scholars. Indeed, each in turn comments, in his mise en scène, on the work of his predecessor. Planchon's productions of *Tartuffe*, for instance, constitute a particularly trenchant critique of the interpretations of both Antoine and Jouvet while, at the same time, showing how much he has learned from these two directors. In a similar vein, Vitez explicitly identifies his tetralogy of Molière plays as a critical response to the kind of "socializing mise en scène best represented by Planchon".

Staging the Classic Text: Evolutions in Theory and Practice

The study of the mise en scène of Molière's plays in the present century must inevitably involve some study of the career of the stage director during the same period. It is a commonplace of theater history that the last hundred years or so have been the era of the director. Edward Braun, for instance, begins his account of the history of the stage director with Saxe-Meiningen and Antoine, although he acknowledges that these two men borrowed extensively from the staging innovations of the Romantic and Realist theater. André Antoine, acknowledged by many as the very first modern stage director, shares Braun's sense of the director as a creature of the modern theater. In 1903 he wrote: "Mise en scène is a newborn art, and nothing, absolutely nothing before the last century, before the theater of intrigue and situation, determined its coming into being."

Most theater historians offer accounts strikingly similar to Braun's: without exception, they assume that the rise to power of the director during the last hundred years or so is tied to the theater's increasingly sophisticated attempts to recreate offstage reality onstage. Such histories invariably see the director as the figure of authority who emerged to impose order on the chaos of proliferating innovations in both scenography and dramaturgy, a kind of super-*régisseur*. The director's rise to power, however, can also be related to the director's emergence as an *auteur* figure of comparable stature to the playwright. From yet another perspective, the history of this same emergence could be related to the rise of the scenographer, or the visual poet of the stage, to a stature equivalent to that enjoyed by the dramatist and the actor in earlier periods.

I use the term *scenographer* here (rather than stage or scenic designer) to draw attention to the graphic, textual nature of the design elements of theatrical performance as well as to call attention to the primacy of the visual text in modern performances of plays from the classic repertorie. It goes without saying that no mise en scène of a classic text in this century has achieved distinction in the absence of a compelling and often innovative scenography. Certainly, the illusionist scenography of the Baroque theater attracted crowds of admiring spectators to the theater, but nobody has suggested that such visual entertainments ever achieved the cultural status accorded to the leading actors and writers of that period. In the last hundred years, however, mise en scène has become as valued a cultural product as the play itself. In the case of classic plays, the director's staging of the play has increasingly attracted the spectator's and critic's focus away from the playwright and the actor, the traditional centers of attention in the theater. Indeed, Planchon has suggested that the prominence of the twentieth-century director is a result of the emergence of a certain notion of the classic and, paradoxically, that our ideas about the classics have in turn been greatly affected by the interventions of the director:

> The emergence of the classic brings with it the birth of the dubious character. He presents himself as a museum curator; leaning on Molière and Shakespeare, he levers himself into a position where he is running the whole show. We may lament the fact, but the two things are linked: the birth of the classic gives power to the theatre director. In his hands the great theatres of the world become museums and justify their existence by producing *Oedipus*, *Hamlet* or *The Miser*. A museum curator "restores" works and puts them on show. And this is where the ambiguities begin.

This brief excerpt from Planchon's preface to the 1986 Livre de Poche edition of *L'Avare* (The Miser) echoes many of the concerns of the present study.

In the eyes of Bernard Dort, founding editor of France's two most important postwar theater periodicals, *Théâtre Populaire* and *Travail Théâtral*: "The history of theatrical practice in France, at least during the period that concerns us [1945–60], could well be written in terms of a number of major productions of classic texts rather than in terms of the first productions of new plays". Although Dort's focus is the fifteen-year period immediately following World War II, his comment might equally well be applied to the entire postwar period for two reasons. First, the most prominent French directors have devoted a substantial portion of their energies to the staging of classic texts. Second, and perhaps more significantly, these directors have also achieved considerably more recognition for their work on classic texts than for their work on the first productions of new contemporary plays. Although Vilar, Planchon, and Vitez, for example, all directed the first productions (and acclaimed revivals) of plays by respected contemporary playwrights, their reputations as stage directors (rather than as artistic directors of their respective theaters) rests on their work with plays from the classic repertoire. In the period prior to World War II, however, directors' reputations rested equally on their work with new and classic texts. Both Antoine and Jouvet, for example, established their reputations with productions of new plays and did extensive work with classic plays only in the latter part of their careers.

Before directors as we know them today first appeared on the scene of theater history, their predecessors in the early nineteenth century began to rethink the ways in which they set about the staging of classic texts. The impulse to reconsider the established practice of the preceding two centuries finds its origins in the death of the ancient régime following the French Revolution and in the new aesthetic of Romanticism that ushered in the nineteenth century. In "Les Classiques au théâtre ou la métamorphose sans fin," Dort describes three different notions of the classic, each of which corresponds (although not rigorously) to a period in history. In the seventeenth and eighteenth centuries, Dort writes, the classic was seen as an "old" play that had, by virtue of its continued popularity, remained in the repertory. Such plays were performed as if they were no different from the "new" plays of the day. Theater artists felt no need to differentiate between the old and new, Dort suggests, because classics were by definition timeless and could therefore be treated as if they had just been written.

One factor that made the play's age relatively unimportant for eighteenth-century theater artists was that eighteenth-century dramaturgy was not greatly different from that of the previous century. Similarly, eighteenth-century mise en scène differed very little from seventeenth-century mise en scène. For all intents and purposes, then, seventeenth-century plays presented few problems of technique or comprehension to the eighteenth-century theater artists who performed them or to the eighteenth-century spectators who attended those performances. (A similar situation obtains in our own period, when the naturalist/realist dramaturgy and scenography of the late nineteenth century differ so little from their counterparts of today.)

Dort suggests that with the beginnings of modern mise en scène in the nineteenth century, the classic came to be seen as a cultural product of a different place and time. As a result, artists staging old plays no longer felt able to treat the classics as if they were essentially no different from the plays of their own time. Now that the classics were identified with the past ("the past" emerged in this period as a theme in its own right), directors and designers became obsessed with researching and representing their historical context onstage. Dort cites the familiar examples of directors such as von Meiningen, Antoine, and Stanislavski sending researchers to Rome to learn about the Forum and other Roman locations for productions of *Julius Caesar*. Like their Romantic predecessors earlier in the century, such directors assumed that the classic play's sociocultural context was that of the time and place in which the dramatic action was nominally located, not that of the culture that produced the play itself. They felt that because the action of *Julius Caesar*, for instance, was set in Rome, *Julius Caesar* was a play "about Rome." That *Julius Caesar* is more a play about Elizabethan England than imperial Rome is a relatively recent perception that owes a great deal to the ongoing critique of realist representation that has played such a large role in the artistic and intellectual life of this century.

Although late-nineteenth- and twentieth-century theater artists were aware of the many technical ways in which texts from the classic period were unlike those produced by their own contemporaries, they nevertheless seem to have sensed no radical cultural otherness in those classic texts. Certainly, for all their awareness of the difficulties of staging Molière's three-hundred-year-old plays, Antoine and Jouvet both felt that they shared with Molière in a common culture. Dort suggests, however, that shortly after World War II the theater's relationship to the classic entered a third phase, as theater artists began to recognize the extent to which those classical texts were products of a theater and a culture quite different and far removed from their own. From this estranged perspective on the classic text, directors began to develop new interpretive strategies that have a great deal in common with the strategies of philosophers and literary theorists engaged in modernist and postmodernist critiques of representation.

In "Le Jeu des classiques: réécriture ou musée?" Anne Ubersfeld focuses on this third phase of the theater's response to the question of staging the classic text. For the purposes of her essay, she defines a classic as a text that was "not written for us" and needs to be "adapted for our ears". Ubersfeld investigates the choice of interpretive strategies available to contemporary directors living in this third phase. She distinguishes two different ways of reading and interpreting the classic text: the director (and the scholar too) can either read the text in the conventional manner (*lire*) or disturb those conventions (*délire*). (Ubersfeld's distinction between *lire* and *délire* recalls Barthes's distinction between work and text: we read a work [*lire*] whereas we "play" with a text [*délire*].) Reading in the traditional manner (*lire*), according to Ubersfeld, implies a reliance on a set of ideologically determined assumptions rooted in a bourgeois appropriation of the cultural production of the Grand Siècle, an appropriation, she points out, that was initiated by Voltaire in his *Siècle de Louis XIV*. Ubersfeld enumerates these assumptions:

> 1) The classics are eternal because they speak to us about the unchanging nature of human passions and human character; 2) their truth is of a psychological nature, a psychology that is concerned with individuals, or more exactly, autonomous subjects; 3) their beauty stems from their formal perfection, [making them] absolute models, a universal system of reference.

The productions discussed in subsequent chapters offer particularly fruitful examples of directors wrestling with these assumptions.

Reading in the traditional manner inevitably raises what Dort calls the question of the "impossible fidelity" of the mise en scène, as such a reading assumes that there is indeed something to which the mise en scène must be faithful. Each of the directors whose work is discussed in the following chapters believed that he was being faithful to Molière. As we shall see, however, both "fidelity" and "Molière" mean something quite different in each case. Though each director claimed a certain degree of authenticity in his interpretation, he in fact staged his own ideas about the text and its sociohistorical or cultural context. Indeed, following Dort and Ubersfeld, I shall be arguing that the director can only stage ideas *about* the classic text. Rather than investigate how closely individual directors hew to Molière's intentions, I shall be looking at how the directors have adapted Molière's classic text to their own needs as twentieth-century theater artists.

New Scenographies for Old: Recoding Molière

In their discussions of the various strategies directors have employed for dealing with the "otherness" of the classic text, Dort and Ubersfeld display a clear preference for what they call "historicization" (a concept borrowed from Brecht). For Dort, the key element of a historicization consists in making the classic text's historically determined difference the "center of gravity" of the contemporary mise en scène:

> While respecting the letter of the work, it is a matter of reinserting it in its historical and social context, and of restoring,

to the stage and for today's audience, that unity created by the staging. It is not a matter of attempting, as Antoine did a little naïvely, to reconstitute "the performance of the Cid in 1637" on the stage of the Odéon, but of performing both the play and the distance that separates us from it and from the society from which it emerged and which it reflects in its own manner—indeed, to make of that distance the center of gravity of the performance.

Each of the mises en scène discussed in the following chapters reveals just such a self-conscious attempt at a reconstitution that reflects the director's own vision of Molière's period and/or the status of the Grand Siècle in twentieth-century French culture.

Ubersfeld, for her part, discusses historicization in a more explicitly semiotic manner. She suggests that the director's primary responsibility in staging a play that "was not written for us" is to translate what she calls the "scripted unspoken" (*non-dit textuel*) of the earlier period into its contemporary equivalent. The director is thus faced with a semiotic problem of considerable magnitude. But the problem is even more complicated, for, as Ubersfeld points out, the classic text has itself acquired with the passage of time a range of connotations that have to do with its status as a cultural object:

> The director's task is to find an equivalent for connotations that have become evanescent. . . . The twentieth-century spectator imposes on the text connotations that are those of his own personal culture—not to mention connotations that originate from his cultural relationship with the object itself. The classic [text], read "in class," imposes connotations of its "imaginary" monumentality.

Ubersfeld is not, however, as her examples will clarify, proposing that we see the director as a kind of supertranslator who can master the cultural and theatrical codes of two distinct historical periods and, through the medium of mise en scène, convey a cultural "message" of some complexity across history. Like Dort, she believes that directors can best deal with the "scripted unspoken" by introducing what she calls "a mimetic frame" into the mise en scène.

As examples of what she considers mimetic frames that effectively historicized some of Molière's classic texts, she cites Planchon's representations of Orgon's house and George Dandin's farm. In his celebrated 1960s production of *George Dandin*, Planchon showed the farm workers toiling in Dandin's farmyard during the action of the play. He thus juxtaposed the behavior of the Dandins and their in-laws with the spectacle of their workers sweating at their labor. Although Planchon's scenography provides a historically accurate rendering of life in a seventeenth-century farmyard, Molière's text makes no reference to Dandin's employees working in the farmyard, nor did Molière's own mise en scène attempt to recreate Dandin's "real-life" environment onstage. But Planchon did not feel obliged to restrict himself to representing only what was explicitly mentioned in Molière's text. In fact, he chose to stage what Molière's text remained completely silent about, to frame Molière's text in a way that would have been quite literally unimaginable in Molière's theater. Planchon elected to juxtapose a theatrical fable with a scenographic evocation of a historical reality; he elected to historicize. In doing so, Planchon made Molière's text signify in a new way. By framing Molière's comic action with images of backbreaking physical labor, Planchon used Molière's play to draw our attention to aspects of life in the Grand Siècle that Molière's classic text never addressed.

Historicization is a means of encouraging the spectator to focus on the way in which the action is framed scenographically as much as on the action itself. It is achieved by creating scenic images that the spectator will recognize as representing something other than location of the events of the play in the conventional realist manner. In other words, the spectator is encouraged to recognize that the scenography presents a narrative of its own. Planchon calls this scenographic narrative an *écriture scénique* (literally, "scenic writing"). The scenic writing, in Planchon's conception, is a narrative that does not illustrate or realize the play as those processes have traditionally been understood. Planchon developed his concept of *écriture scénique* in response to the experience of seeing Brecht's work with the Berliner Ensemble on their second visit to Paris in the 1950s. Planchon writes:

> The lesson of Brecht is to have declared that a performance combines both dramatic writing and scenic writing; but the scenic writing—he was the first to say this and it seems to me to be very important—has an equal responsibility with the dramatic writing. In fact any movement on the stage, the choice of a color, a set, a costume, etc., involves a total responsibility. The scenic writing has a total responsibility in the same way as writing taken on its own: I mean the writing of a novel or a play.

Thus, in historicized mise en scène, the spectator is not encouraged to locate the meaning of the play solely in the interactions of the playwright's characters or in the realism-based interactions of character and milieu; instead, the spectator is encouraged to investigate the possible significances of apparent discontinuities between the mise en scène and the classic text.

GÉRARD DEFAUX

The Comic at Its Limits

Molière died late in the evening of 17 February 1673, only hours after having played the title role in his last play, *Le malade imaginaire* (1673; *The Imaginary Invalid*). Some contemporary accounts declare that he felt the first twinges of the fatal attack onstage, during the burlesque and satirical coronation of Argan as "novus Doctor." What his life of endless trials, tribulations, mournings, failures, and betrayals had been unable to do, his death—cast by circumstances into a symbolic and legendary dimension— accomplished. It took the convulsions of agony to smother the laughter in Molière's throat.

Until the very end Molière remained passionately committed to the theater. Refusing to cancel the final performance lest he deprive "fifty poor workers who have only their daily wages on which to live", he carried his concern for his art to the point of making himself the director of and actor in his own death scene. Like his tricksters Mascarille and Scapin, he was such a "clever handler of motive and plot" that he wanted to be certain not to flub his exit. When he wrote *Le malade imaginaire*, Molière knew that his own illness was not at all imaginary, that his days were numbered. Openly constructing his ballet-comedy on the model of his previous works, he reused the fundamental structures and mechanisms of *Tartuffe* (1664–1669), *Les femmes savantes* (1672; *The Learned Ladies*,) and *Le bourgeois gentilhomme*

(1670; *The Would-be Gentleman*) and borrowed dialogues and themes from *Dom Juan* (1665), *L'amour mèdecin* (1665; *Love Is the Best Doctor*), and *Les fourberies de Scapin* (1671; *That Scoundrel Scapin*). Thus *Le malade imaginaire*, with its therapeutic profession of faith—only laughter allows man to accept his mortal condition, cures him from the fear and anxiety of dying—sums up Molière's thought and art; as his comic will and testament, the play worthily crowns his exemplary career as an apologist, poet, and theoretician of theater.

In the 17th century only Pierre Corneille, the jealous and influential father of French "classical theater," had a longer career than Molière. After the miseries and financial ruin of his first troupe, the Illustre-Théâtre (1643–1645), Molière and his associates, the Béjart family, left Paris and spent a dozen arduous years traveling the roads of Languedoc and southern France. In 1658 they returned to the capital, where they competed with the established theatrical companies of the Marais and the Hôtel de Bourgogne. By then Molière was already a complete athlete of the theater, an actor, director, and manager who had also composed some farces and two large-scale comedies of intrigue, *L'étourdi, ou les contre-temps* (1654; *The Blunderer, or the Mishaps*) and *Dépit amoureux* (1656; *The Amorous Quarrel*). But it was during the years in Paris (1658–1673), with his troupe solidly installed in the Palais-Royal theater, that, as "court jester," protégé of the king, and popular author, Molière wrote, staged, and performed his masterpieces.

This lifelong total involvement with the theater undoubtedly provides the best explanation for the riches and diversity of Molière's work, for its astonishing powers of metamorphosis and renewal. He deliberately exploited all existing forms and genres, giving them a soul, a meaning, and a vigor they had previously lacked: farce, with *La jalousie du Barbouillé. Le docteur amoureux. Le médecin volant* (before 1658; *The Jealousy of Barbouillé, The Amorous Doctor, The Flying Physician*), *Les précieuses ridicules* (1659; *The Precious Damsels*), and *Le médecin malgré lui* (1666; *The Physician in spite of Himself*); three-act comedy, with *L'école des maris* (1661; *The School for Husbands*), *George Dandin* (1668), and *Les fourberies de Scapin*; tragicomedy, with *Dom Garcie de Navarre* (1661); mythological fantasy with stage machinery in *Amphitryon* (1668); the court *divertissement*, with *La princesse d'Elide* (1664; *The Princess of Elide*), *Mélicerte* (1666), *La pastorale comique* (1666; *The Comic Pastoral*), *Les amants magnifiques* (1670; *The Magnificent Lovers*), and *Psyché* (1671)—this last written in collaboration with Corneille and Philippe Quinault, with music by Jean-Baptiste Lully—and, above all, the great five-act classical comedy in verse, as well as its variant in prose, a brilliant list of masterpieces including *L'école des femmes* (1662; *The School for Wives*), *Tartuffe*, *Dom Juan*, *Le misanthrope* (1666; *The Misanthrope*), *L'avare*

(1668; *The Miser*), and *Les femmes savantes*. Thanks to the unequaled splendors of *Psyché*, Molière also contributed significantly to the birth of the French opera. Finally, after an apparently fortuitous experiment with *Les fâcheux* (1661; *The Bores*), he created an entirely new type of spectacle, the ballet-comedy—a hybrid that, according to Hali, a character in *Le Sicilien, ou l'amour peintre* (1667; *The Sicilian, or Love Makes the Painter*), "dabbles a bit in music and in dance," adding the pleasures of the senses to those of the text. Of these Molière offered to the king, in his châteaux at Chambord and at Saint-Germain, or to his Paris public at the Palais-Royal, such dazzling masterpieces as *Monsieur de Pourceaugnac* (1669), *Le bourgeois gentilhomme, La comtesse d'Escarbagnas* (1672), and *Le malade imaginaire*.

Overall, then, a corpus of more than thirty plays, twenty-nine of them written after the troupe settled in Paris. Between 1658 and 1673, for fourteen full theatrical seasons, Molière wrote an average of two plays per year (three in 1661, 1664, 1666, 1668 and 1671). This productivity is even more remarkable given the difficulties that ceaselessly battered him throughout the years, suffering and disappointment in his private life mingling with every sort of professional problem to undermine his ever more fragile health: in 1663 Corneille and the rival troupe of actors at the Hôtel de Bourgogne dragged him into a public quarrel over the merits of *L'école des femmes*; the following year the church and the "devout faction" obtained a prohibition of public performances of *Tartuffe* that would last five years; his wife deceived him; Racine betrayed him; in 1667 he was so ill that he had to close his theater for a while, and rumors of his death circulated through Paris; and in 1672, a final test, the king abandoned him, granting Lully the directorship of the Royal Academy of Music and the monopoly of all music productions in the kingdom. In each case Molière fought back with verve and wit, knowing that his best response to jealous rivals was to continue to please his public with new plays; knowing that his dependency on subsidies from the crown required him to honor the commissions he received from the king for the Carnival or for nuptial, military, or holiday celebrations; and knowing, above all, that he must continue to produce for his actors, who depended on him for their livelihood.

These constraints, considered with the amazing diversity of Molière's works, give the impression of an author driven by obligation, who produced his work in haste under multiple pressures. This image led interpreters to envisage each of his comedies as a discrete unit, and the corpus as a random succession of forms, lacking cohesion as well as spirit. Molière was taken to be a writer under too much pressure to think, to meditate on his art and on humanity, a creator whose only concern was to make us laugh. No more.

In the 1960s American critics overturned this interpretation. A series of brilliant analyses of the great trilogy, *Tartuffe*, *Dom Juan*, and *Le misanthrope*, returned Molière to his proper place as a "highly conscious literary artist", as a dramatist for whom creation constantly "moves beyond itself into self-consciousness". He was recognized not only as a great comic poet—certainly, with Rabelais, the greatest in French literature—but also as a strong theoretician of the comic who was in perfect control of his work from beginning to end and who never conceded to circumstances any more than he had to. Viewed in this light, Molière's creation regained its coherence and internal dynamism. It was at last considered, not as a fortuitous succession of discrete moments, but as a living and continuous fabric in which "no individual work, perhaps, can be properly understood in isolation from the whole, any more than one movement of a sonata can stand apart from the whole sonata". Critics perceived that Molière's work conformed to an evolutionary process that was both necessary and deliberate—a movement, a temporal and organic metamorphosis, that, passing through the deep and decisive crisis caused by the prohibition of *Tartuffe* in 1664, led him from classical humanist comedy to the total spectacle of the ballet-comedy.

In a first major period, running from *Les précieuses* to *Tartuffe* and *Le misanthrope*, Molière fashioned a kind of comedy modeled essentially on Terence and the dramatic theories nurtured on Aristotle's *Poetics*. He himself sketched out the theory of this genre in two little one-act plays in prose, both produced in 1663 as a reply to those who were criticizing *L'école des femmes*: *La critique de L'école des femmes* (*The School for Wives criticized*) and *L'impromptu de Versailles* (*The Versailles Impromptu*). During this period Molière was following prevailing classical tastes, rules, and prejudices. Although Corneille's tragic heroes were beginning to show signs of fatigue around 1660—the dramatist had by then reigned supreme for more than twenty years—tragedy remained the noble genre, the only genre, along with epic, able to elevate the writer to the level of the ancients; comedy, though it could make the king and the Paris bourgeoisie laugh heartily, was still considered a bagatelle, unworthy of an author's primary attention. In fact it was not as a writer of farces or as a "mocker of mores" but as a hero of tragedy that Molière set out in 1658 to win over the king and Paris; Pierre Mignard's famous portrait shows him dressed as a Roman emperor. All the work of his early years, from *Sganarelle, ou le cocu imaginaire* (1660; *Sganarelle, or the Imaginary Cuckold*) to *Dom Juan*, and including *Dom Garcie de Navarre* (1661) and *L'école des femmes* (a "burlesque tragedy"), reflects a deep nostalgia for the tragic. Unable to satisfy his desire to be Alexander the Great, Sertorius, or Pompey, because his fate was laughter, Molière became Sganarelle and Arnolphe. Yet his purpose remained lofty: he aimed to achieve in and for comedy the dignity and respectability that it still lacked, to have it recognized as a genre that was, if not superior, at least equal to tragedy. This is why Corneille, still more than Terence, can be considered the true father of classical comedy: a comedy modeled on tragedy—with five acts, alexandrine lines, respect for the *bienséances* (decorum) and the rules of dramatic composition—that would lead Molière to the incomparable greatness of *Le misanthrope*.

As a sister of Cornelian tragedy, classical comedy rapidly assumed the somewhat affected posture of an irreproachable, upright lady. Primarily a woman of the world, she aimed to please by her virtues, her reason, and her convervatism. Steeped in *honnêteté* (honorability), in perfect harmony with the dominant social ideology, she presented herself as strictly orthodox, as conforming in all respects with the expectations of the day. Her greatest quality was perhaps an elaborate "naturalness." In her urbanity and proper modesty, she made only the most traditional of claims: to be a mirror, an image or representation, an imitation of everyday life. Unlike tragedy, which too often veered into the extraordinary and the marvelous, her concern for truth led her to paint "according to nature," to show humanity "as it is," to put onstage portraits that resembled the originals so closely that the latter could not but recognize themselves. This commitment to "realism" allowed comedy to proclaim its utility, to recall that "the theater is the school for man," that it had "a great capacity for correction" (preface to *Tartuffe*, 1669). If comedy was, as the church claimed, a vivid and therefore dangerous description of the passions, it was also "a severe lesson in keeping them in check." Hence Molière's proud declarations on vindicate himself, especially with regard to *Tartuffe*: the responsibility of comedy, its duty, was to correct humanity while entertaining it. Nothing improves humanity better than the depiction of its faults. Vices are hit hard when exposed to universal laughter. People put up readily with remonstrances, but not with mockery. They are willing to be wicked, but not to be ridiculous.

This realist and moral comedy, which showed people their vices and their follies in order to cure them, was imbued with the optimistic humanism of the Counter-Reformation. As Molière's mouthpiece—presumably Jean Donneau de Visé—remarks in the *Lettre sur la comédie de L'imposteur* (1667; *Letter on the Comedy of The Impostor*), comedy treats human beings as *naturally* sensitive to reason, and thus as capable of seeing their errors and correcting them; it places this rational being in an eminently comfortable and reassuring world, a world in which common sense and *honnêteté* rule, in which laughter is the collective expression of reason and moral health, a legitimate weapon serving a triumphant justice and welfare. The ridiculous characters of these comedies—from Cathos and Magdelon through Sganarelle, Arnolphe, and Orgon, to Tartuffe—all amply deserve the public correction that is inflicted on them; they all appear, in the light of the social norm that, through the complicity of comedy, judges and condemns them, as laughable aberrations. Their singularity isolates them irremediably. It excludes them from the polite and conformist world of *honnêteté*—from a world watched over by the king, with his benevolent, just, and lucid gaze.

This poetics enables Molière to rise to the rank of Secretary of State for the Ridiculous, and comedy to take its place alongside tragedy as an estimable genre—a "respectable woman," as Molière dubbed her in the preface to *Tartuffe*. But no theoretical statement accounts satisfactorily for Molière's actual practice. And his conformist outlook and praise of orthodoxy were only a facade. From the beginning, Molière's supposedly "respectable woman" was in fact an irreverent soubrette who took unacceptable liberties. Her "natural" demeanor was often condemned for tending toward grotesque caricature and sinking into the obscene, the improbable, or the ludicrous. It was no longer Terence's urbanity—his *sermo moratus*—that controlled comedy, but Plautus' *vis comica* (comic force) and buffoonery. *L'école des femmes* already possessed all the elements necessary to make clergymen wonder just how far this daring newcomer would go. Molière's comedy had a provocative tendency to pry into everything and respect nothing. When it went so far as to strip Tartuffe of his mask of false piety, Molière's laughter crossed into the realm of public scandal: comedy assumed the dimensions of an affair of state. Aristotle and Cicero had confined the domain of ridicule to the narrow limits of *deformitas* and *turpitudo sine dolore*, physical deformity and moral ugliness, allowing no feelings of horror, misery, or pity. Molière, in contrast, exposed the most unbearable defects, the most monstrous vices; with Tartuffe and Dom Juan, he invited his audience to laugh at a hypocrite and at an "evil lord"; with Harpagon, he put onstage a character who was indeed, "of all humans, the least humane". With Molière, the comic no longer had any limits; it became something universal, a point of view on the entire human condition.

The magnitude of the *Tartuffe* affair prompted Molière to question systematically the principles and the comic mechanisms on which he had been relying. *Dom Juan*, his following play, reflects the first stage of this process: through the libertine's ironic gaze, Molière puts society, its language, its hypocrisy, and its false values, on trial. A year later *Le misanthrope* goes a step further, staging the trial of laughter and moral comedy—his own trial. Alceste's incurable "illness" is his desire to "correct the world', his belief that people are receptive to and capable of correction, and his presumptuous righteousness in judging and censuring the vices of his century. If society has no right to laugh, then comedy has no right either to blame or to pass judgment. In this world, justice and reason simply do not exist. There is no norm, and no truth. We are all fools to some degree, and all equally incorrigible. Rediscovering Erasmus' vision in *Moriae Encomium* (1511; *Praise of Folly*), comedy here abandons its educative and moral claims: as Alceste's friend Philinte says to him, "the world will not be changed by your efforts, you know". The only option, then, is to adjust, to make accommodation with this universal folly that no one can avoid, to transform it into a spectacle, to make it a pleasure, a pretext for the triumph of festivity and amusement. Far from wishing to "cure" the would-be gentleman and the imaginary invalid of their errors, of their blindness and folly, Molière's late comedies make them kings of the Carnival—blossoming, euphoric, happy fools, living in world of fantasy. Whereas moral comedy had treated human vice and virtue from a social perspective, Molière's new comedies do not envision humanity's weak and barren nature in terms of moral value, but in terms of *being* or *existence*. Their perspective is less ethical than both aesthetic and metaphysical. The alternation, in *Le malade imaginaire*, of Argan's somber mania with the various onstage *divertissements* is emblematic of this new trend. Molière's simultaneous shift, after the crisis of *Tartuffe*, toward a pessimistic vision of humanity and a comic wisdom made up entirely of lucid awareness and acceptance, did not impose a dampening, prudential mark on his dramaturgy. On the contrary, his new, disabused conception of comedy proved to be amenable to this renewed theatrical experimentation in the ballet-comedy after 1666. With this charitable sister whose laughter, far from seeking to punish, was primarily benevolent and consoling, he was able to expand the theater's resources, anticipating the search for a total spectacle that Pierre Caron de Beaumarchais would pursue a century later.

In 1673, when Molière expired, the great classical genres were also dying. After Racine's *Phèdre* (1677; *Phaedra*) tragedy would fade away. As far comedy, it survived in the works of a few imitators of varying talent: Charles Dufresny (1648–1724), Jean-François Regnard (1655–1709), Florent Dancourt (1661–1725), and Alain-René Lesage (1668–1747). But none of them, not even Lesage, managed to revitalize a genre that Molière had brought to perfection. Not until Pierre Carlet de Marivaux, Pierre Caron de Beaumarchais, and Denis Diderot would Molière have successors worthy of his genius. The end of the "great century" was instead marked by the success of Lully and the opera. On the fate of comedy after Molière, then, we can hardly differ with the judgment of Nicolas Boileau, who in 1677 evoked the departed Molière in his seventh *Epître (Epistle)* addressed to Racine:

> With Molière lovable comedy was laid low,
> Sought in vain to recover from such a rude blow,
> For to stand in his shoes she was now too late.
> Such was our classical theater's fate.

JAMES F. GAINES

Molière, La Fontaine, and Authority

When the Revolution had decided to turn the former Eglise Ste-Geneviève into a pantheon for heroes of liberty, equality and fraternity, they went searching for the bones of Molière and La Fontaine to place in proximity to those of Rousseau. Having duly exhumed what they thought were the playwright's remains, they were eventually disappointed when forensic analysis revealed the bones to be mainly those of an adolescent female. Those mortal spoils were later deposited in the Père Lachaise in what many think is Molière's tomb, but in reality is only a cenotaph to the author of *Tartuffe*. Perhaps Molière's spirit, which had already been savaged in the *Lettre à D'Alembert sur les spectacles*, was frightened off by the eerie, torch-bearing hand that emerges from Jean-Jacques's monument in the Pantheon. It is true that one of Rousseau's followers, Fabre d'Eglantine, fulfilled his master's ideology by writing a "continuation" to *Le Misanthrope* in which the fawning and feigning aristocrat Philinte in justly put down by a Jacobin version of Alceste. Possibly, the philosophical generation had been excessively influenced by posthumous and dubious anecdotes about the "real" Molière, such as the stories related in Grimarest's biography, where Molière reads his scripts to the charwoman for critique and tosses coins from his carriage to the poor.

From *Papers on French Seventeenth Century Literature* 27, no. 53 (2000). © 2000 Gunter Narr Verlag Tübingen.

By a strange coincidence, La Fontaine was to become a kind of post-mortem Siamese twin to Molière, joined both in spirit and in archaeological fact. Although official records duly recorded the 1693 interment of the "Butterfly of Parnassus" in the Cimetière des Saints-Innocents, the fabulist's friend abbé Olivet was away from Paris at the time La Fontaine died, and he erroneously recorded that he had been buried instead in the Cimetière Saint-Joseph, in the exact spot where Molière had been laid to rest 20 years earlier. Consequently, the grave robbers of 1792, hoping to get a double helping of *philosophes* for their pains, simply scooped up twice as many bones. The supposed remains of La Fontaine thus followed the path of disappointment along with Molière's through various depositories, all the way to the Père Lachaise. In any case, a re-examination of the portrayal of authority in the works of Molière and La Fontaine shows it to be far more nuanced and ambiguous than Rousseau could ever have approved of, or perhaps even understood.

The libertarian reputation of Molière at the time of the Revolution was due not so much to the author's works as to over a century of glosses, evaluations, and comparisons by the likes of Voltaire, Marmontel, and La Harpe, who were eager to name and claim him as a *philosophe avant la lettre*. After all, the most arguably anti-authoritarian of his plays, *Dom Juan*, was not even available in its original, provocative text, but only in Thomas Corneille's edulcorated versification. Molière's ambiguous protagonist had been further displaced by Mozart's operatic hero, who undertakes his mission of seduction from the standpoint of universal freedom, rather than from the interplanetary application of "Playboy Philosophy" described in Act Two of the Molière text. An examination of the plays shows that nobility is by no means a clear and easy target. True, the playwright in unsparing in his ridicule for the Arnolphes, Dandins, and the Messieurs Jourdain and de Pourceaugnac who would usurp an aristocratic rank to which they are not entitled. Molière flouts parasitic nobles such as the Dorante of *Le Bourgeois gentilhomme* and the Vicomte of *La Comtesse d'Escarbagnas*. To the joy of Voltaire, he likewise lashes out at obvious *petits maîtres* like Acaste and Clitandre of *Le Misanthrope* and the Marquis of the *Critique de l'école des femmes*. But at the same time, other nobles, such as Dorante of the latter play, a very different Clitandre in *Les femmes savantes*, and the almost-gentleman Cléonte in *Le Bourgeois gentilhome*, deliver both justifications of court life and a positive exemplum of their order.

Dom Juan himself is, after all, a noble, and if he has negative aspects, these can hardly be attributable to a blind adherence to the prerogatives of class. Perhaps such victims as Elmire, the unknown bride about to be abducted at end of Act One, and the peasants Charlotte and Mathurine richly deserve and secretly long to have their bodices ripped by a handsome *chevalier*. But it is clear that the motivation for this pattern of seduction and abandonment is strictly personal. According to Dom Carlos and Dom Louis, it is also strictly contrary to the codes of the aristocracy. Even if we accept Dom Juan's implication that he is doing everyone else a favor by obeying the call of nature, that does not silence the crowds of unsatisfied women and their relatives who are pursuing him. It takes a reading that ruthlessly disregards history to proclaim Molière's Dom Juan a revolutionary hero, not that such readings are by any means rare.

A more in-depth picture of Molière's view of authority emerges when one compares him with his contemporary and fellow skeptic, La Fontaine. A reading of the *Fables* first helps to set Molière in context by distinguishing three levels of authority: ethical (corresponding to family and community), political (corresponding to institutions and their monarchical framework), and epistemological (corresponding to the more abstract authority of Truth itself).

In terms of ethical authority, Molière's critical and skeptical stance is made very clear as early as the first Sganarelle plays, and even more explicitly in *L'école des femmes*. Arnolphe's ridiculous assertion of masculine hegemony ("La femme est en effet le potage de l'homme . . . Du côté de la barbe est la toute-puissance") is undermined throughout the play, despite the protagonist's attempts to provide a religious underpinning with the reading of the *Maximes du mariage* in Act Three. These totalitarian notions of authority are echoed in many forms throughout Molière's theater. Orgon's desire to arrange marriage to spite his children, Alceste's fantasy of seeing Céliméne reduced to nothing so that she would owe him everything, Monsieur Jourdain's effort to transcend domestic contingencies through instant *anoblissement*, and Argan's threats to confine his daughters in a nunnery are facets of a common urge to power. Even in the rarer cases when familial authoritarianism is invoked in a good cause, as in *Les Femmes savantes*, where Chrysale attempts with much bluster to control his wife's excesses, they inevitably end in failure. The alternative to authority, usually a kind of natural and indulgent generosity, is frequently vague, since it must more often than not be coaxed out with deception. Only in *L'école des maris* does the sustained contrast between Sganarelle and his brother Ariste give any definition to the workings of a positive domestic authority.

On the other hand, Molière's treatment of political authority is not always what one might suspect. Though the hierarchical prerogatives of the sword and the robe are much discussed, it is almost always from the perspective of usurpers such as Arnolphe, Dandin, and Pourceaugnac, or from that of laughable challengers, such as the putative intellectuals of *Les*

Femmes savantes or the doctors of *Le Malade imaginaire*, who would substitute *lèse Faculté* for *lèse majesté*. The periodic defenses of the court by well-bred spokesmen in several plays culminate in the final act of *Tartuffe*, with its encomium of Louis XIV. It is true that the description of the king as an enemy of abuse who can read into the very hearts of men holds the promise of his power as a reformer rather than as a rank authoritarian. Indeed, many royal acts that in retrospect seem clearly and uniquely designed to extend personal authority, including the *recherches de noblesse* and the suppression of elective municipal offices, were successfully marketed during Louis' reign as reforms.

It is intriguing that La Fontaine weighs his presentation of authority quite differently from Molière, giving a very ample treatment of political authority and much less than one would expect on ethical authority. Some might argue that this is because of the fact that his home life was a disaster, involving an arranged marriage that went sour and led to a separation of goods with his spouse. Instead of the rigors of conjugal power struggle, he apparently favored the relatively comfortable and non-contingent status of a professional guest in the households of Fouquet, the Bouillons, the *duchesse* d'Orléans and Mme de la Sablière. But this difference can also be explained on a thematic level by the greater importance La Fontaine gives to epistemological authority in his discussions.

A fable as basic as "Le Loup et le chien" lays the groundwork for his approach to the high price of accepting authority, for the wolf not only flees when he realizes the meaning of his well-fed cousin's collar, but *"il court encore."* The same master who provides meat and a warm, comfortable hearth imposes his will and his restrictions when and how *he* chooses, making the random contingencies of forest life suddenly look more desirable. Read on a slightly different plane, the same poem can be understood as an allegory of the disadvantages of domestic entanglements, especially since Madame La Fontaine's main complaints against her husband aimed apparently at his romantic wanderings. The hearth is, after all, the building block and microcosm of civilization, as Rousseau illustrated in his Discourses, and the collar of marriage may be more frightening for many men than that of serfdom or servitude. As in "Le Rat de ville et le rat des champs" any advancement in luxury or commodity is more than outweighed by its price in fear: "Fi du plaisir / Que la crainte peut corrompre." Another fable that suggests a similar double reading on the domestic and institutional fronts is "L'Œil du maître". Here the stag who almost succeeds in hiding among the cattle is sometimes seen as a figure of the outsider trying to find a refuge in the lower depths of society, only to be flushed out by the monarchical owner who is more greedy and more observant than his flunkees. By adding to

Phaedrus's commentary the line, "Quant à moi, j'y mettrais encor l'œil de l'amant," La Fontaine moves the inquisition from the allegorical stable and the law courts to the bedchamber, and the reader is tempted to finish the conversion of this terror by changing the gender of the lover to *l'amante*.

Plenty of other fables rest on a more uniquely political basis, including "Le Loup et l'agneau" and "Les Animaux malades de la peste". The former of these is so politically rooted, in fact, that it denies the relevancy of epistemological truth. Accused first of muddying the wolf's drinking water and then of slandering him, the lamb successfully shows the falsehood of these accusations, only to be lumped by the wolf into a vast guilty category, "Vous, vos bergers et vos chiens," and summarily eaten. Politeness and truth mean nothing when greed and appetite have already fixed on a violent end. As Marie-Odile Sweetser observes, "There always exists, with La Fontaine, in allegorical form or close to reality, a monster whose ignorance, stupidity, and brutality comes to destroy the balance and harmony of nature cultivated by humans who, through intelligence and labor, try to guarantee abundance and happiness". In "Les Animaux malades de la peste," one finds not merely a single privileged and predatory bully, but an allegory of the entire royal court, where all the meat-eaters are equated with nobles and manage to disculpate, themselves of the sin that has allegedly brought pestilence among the animal kingdom. Only the *roturier* Donkey, who is ignorant of the Clintonesque casuistry displayed by the Lion and the Fox, confesses to a crime not shared by other members of the elite. Although his crime of stolen grass only measures "la largeur de ma langue," it is enough to make him an apt scapegoat for his superiors. No wonder La Fontaine concludes, "Selon que vous serez puissant ou misérable, / Les jugements de Cour vous rendront blanc ou noir." The deliberate double sense of *Cour* as law-court and royal court implicates the entire monarchical superstructure in a pattern of abuse.

One salient feature of the treatment of abuse of authority in La Fontaine is that it functions mainly in the singular. The individual lamb, donkey, or pigeon is always a possible target, but there is no species-wide ethnic cleansing in the *Fables*. A possible explanation for this phenomenon is found in "Jupiter et les tonnerres". Angered at the misbehavior of his human subjects, Jove sends Mercury to summon the cruelest of the Furies from Hell to punish them. But when Alecton, thrilled with her commission, threatens to send the entire human race to the underworld, the king of the gods cancels his order, and insteads flings a thunderbolt in the general direction of a particular "peuple perfide." Even this Cruise Missile from Olympus miscarries and lands in the wilderness, since "Tout pere frappe à côté." Charged with replenishing the arsenal of the Not-So-New World Order,

Vulcan forges two different types of lightning: one merely strikes the clouds or the mountains, the other (no doubt a "smart" thunderbolt) never misses its mark. La Fontaine makes clear the moral aim of this tale to the rulers of nations:

> Ô vous, Rois, qu'il voulut faire
> Arbites de notre sort,
> Laissez entre la colère
> Et l'orage qui la suit
> L'intervalle d'une nuit.

La Fontaine shared in the punishment of his former patron Fouquet by suffering a brief internal exile in Limoges with his kinsman Jannart, and his association with the lord of Vaux would haunt him later in his quest for a seat on the Academy. However, the Limoges episode gave rise mainly to a series of rather nonchalant letters to his wife, filled with glowing touristic accounts of the cuisine, sights, and ladies of the western countryside. It is clear that La Fontaine considered himself and his clan lucky to have avoided further royal wrath. By giving way like the reed in "Le Chêne et le roseau", La Fontaine felt that individuals could preserve their chances of survival and even prosper.

This explains the considerable amount of encomiastic discourse in the *Fables*. As early as the first book, one finds a very positive portrayal of the French monarchy in "Le Dragon à plusieurs têtes et le Dragon à plusieurs queues". Ostensibly a shot at the Holy Roman Empire and its rich but disunited princelings by an ambassador of the autocratic Ottoman Empire, the actual target of this piece is more timely and closer to home. It is clear that the centralized power of the many-tailed dragon, who manages to cross over the hedge and spread terror, while his many-headed counterpart stays innocuously on his side of the divide, is actually a figure of Louis XIV. French armies had successfully crossed the Rhine and threatened not only the declining Empire, but the new Evil Empire of the Netherlands, whose many-headed democracy was far worse than the oligarchical Electors of old. La Fontaine merely joins the chorus of voices, including other skeptics such as Molière and Boileau, who hailed Louis's victories as triumphs for civilization.

Another example of this political deference to absolutism is found in "Les Membres et l'Estomac". The carefully chosen language of this parable aims squarely at both the British Parliamentary Revolution under Cromwell and the nearly simultaneous Fronde Parlementaire in France, events which traumatized the childhood of Louis XIV. The organs and limbs that rebel against the authority of Messer Gaster are specifically labeled as "pauvres gens" and "mutins" before they realize the error of their ways. The fabulist goes on to state explicitly, "Ceci peut s'appliquer à la grandeur royale."

Indeed, La Fontaine evokes the specter of a uniquely *roturier* revolt by enumerating the Artisan, the Merchant, the Magistrate, the Farmer, and the Soldier as the mutinous elements who had sought to enfranchise themselves. His additional historical reference to Menenius and the rift between the Roman Senate and plebes only reinforces the warning against empowering the Third Estate.

Nevertheless, La Fontaine's concessions to royalty share with Molière an emphasis on the practical benefits of centralized power, as perceived by the authors. For La Fontaine, absolutism offers security from foreign danger and domination, shown in the single-headed dragon, and material prosperity symbolized by Messer Gaster's ability to keep the life blood flowing into the various parts of the body. In the fifth act of *Tartuffe*, Molière, through the personality of the Exempt, argues that absolutism provides another kind of security, ensuring justice for the individual when the institutions meant to mete out that justice become permeated with corruption and self-interest. Molière and La Fontaine share a distrust of social institutions based on their skeptical doubts about the ability of human nature to adhere to collective ideals in the face of private temptations. Presiding over this spectacle of fallen humanity, the King, like Pascal's notion of God, is alone capable of transcending human limitations. It is only several years after the playwright's death, with the 1678 edition of the *Fables* and behind a protective dedication to Mme de Montespan, that La Fontaine will seriously begin to question this faith in the overriding virtue of Bourbon monarchy. In the first six books of the *Fables*, as in the 1669 version of *Tartuffe*, absolutism was still seen more as a solution than as a problem.

Molière and La Fontaine also travel parallel paths on the issue of epistemological authority, but with somewhat different outcomes. This is not surprising, given that they were both strongly influenced by skeptical thought. Molière's friendship with the family of La Mothe Le Vayer, followers of the Gassendian branch of "mitigated" skepticism, is well proven, especially by the poem he wrote to console the elder philosopher on the loss of his son, possibly a schoolmate of the playwright. Molière's adventure into translating the Roman philosopher Lucretius was very likely a fruit of this association. His friends Chapelle and Bernier were strongly influenced by Gassendi's Latin treatises, and these men were also well acquainted with La Fontaine. La Fontaine's application of Gassendi's skeptical ideas on representation of reality is reflected in fables almost too numerous to mention here. For a very thorough development of this epistemological dimension, I invite the interested researcher to consult the treatment of "Le Songe d'un habitant du Mogol" in the recent book by Charles Darmon.

Perhaps the clearest demonstration of the relativity of truth in Molière's canon lies in *Le Mariage forcé*. In this *comédie-ballet*, a middle-aged

Sganarelle first consults his friend Géronimo, then the contradictory philosophers Pancrace and Marphurius, and finally a couple of gypsy fortune tellers to find out if he should marry the flirtatious Dorimène. Though Pancrace and Marphurius represent the diametrically opposed schools of Aristotelian philosophy and radically skeptical Pyrrhonism, they reveal themselves equally incapable of giving a practical answer to Sganarelle's admittedly silly question. A similar effect is produced in La Fontaine's "Le Meunier, son fils, et l'âne", where each advisor with whom the miller and his son fall in gives a different opinion on how they should treat the mule they plan to sell. Elderly people say the miller should ride the donkey, instead of carrying him, as they had been doing. Younger neighbors say the son should ride. Animal lovers say the humans should both walk, while penny-pinchers scold the men for wasting good shoe leather when they can take advantage of an idle animal. In frustration, the miller finally decides to ignore all this contradictory advice and follow his own whim, and La Fontaine concludes, "Il le fit, et fit bien." Molière's protagonist is not so lucky, for by first insisting on his inclination to become engaged and then following the gypsies' tardy warning about the dangers of cuckoldry, Sganarelle manages to incur all the expenses and humiliation of a bad marriage and to be beaten for his hesitation as well. Perhaps the lesson is that if one imposes one's own epistemological authority, one must prepare for the consequences and be indulgent, a philosophy La Fontaine seems to have followed in his own life.

Of all of Molière's many characters to suffer from epistemological anguish, none is more troubled than Sosie in *Amphitryon*. Mercure manages to usurp the servant's very identity, undercutting any possible certainty of truth by Cartesian or other means. Though Sosie attempts to counter Mercure's claim in worthy Gassendian terms by objecting, "Je ne pois m'anéantir pour toi, / Et souffrir un discours si loin de l'apparence," he is forced to conclude, "Tout cet embarras met mon esprit sur les dents, / Et la raison à ce qu'on voit s'oppose". Of course, Sosie's dilemma is rooted in a fundamentally political situation, since Jupiter has taken advantage of his *seigneurie* to adopt Amphitryon's very image and make love to his wife, Alcmène. Perhaps the most extreme epistemological irony is that, having technically succeeded, Jupiter cannot really take off his mask and enjoy his trick, since Alcmène refuses to admit to his existence except as her beloved but absent husband. By using the power of sexual consent, she achieves much the same result as what Mercure was able to impose only with a stout stick and a beating.

For his part, La Fontaine goes on to explore several other issues of epistemological authority, including the dangers of accepting illusion as truth. "La Laitière et le pot au lait" illustrates this danger very well. The milkmaid, involved in what many would consider a very justifiable plan for increasing her capital, loses what she has through lack of attention to the specifics, a phenomenon La Fontaine links to all humans "Autant les sages que les fous." The "flatteuse erreur" can lift us to unknown heights, but when it deflates due to some random contingency, we are left as "gros Jean comme devant." The *roturier* tone of the last line is more than an instance of *captatio benevolentiae* on the part of the fabulist; it is a reminder of the social bottom line in any authoritarian structure.

Based particularly on the later fables from Book Seven on, I would have to take issue with Pierre Boutang's contention that they were written as an education for the king. While this may have been an earlier goal, the increasingly mature La Fontaine seems ever more apt to view things from the perspective of the underdog. A good precedent is already established in Book Six by "Le Vieillard et l'âne". The donkey in this fable, who has been allowed a rare moment of leisure in the pasture, refuses to mobilize with his master and flee the approaching enemy troops, since it would only mean enforced labor in the pack train, and for him all servitude is alike, "Notre ennemi, c'est notre maître." It is true that the fabulist tempers this grim, almost Randian view of existence by stressing mutual dependence and interplay in some poems. However, even then it is almost always presented from a defensive, negative point of view, as in "Le Cheval et l'âne" and "L'Oiseleur, l'autour et l'alouette". The former shows that when the horse refuses to share some of the burden of his companion, he is eventually punished by fate, for when the donkey dies, he must carry all the original load, plus the donkey's hide! Compassion is shown as a reasonable, but not necessarily obvious alternative to the natural urge to care only about one's self. The bird trapper in the second poem is likewise trying to supply his natural appetite by luring skylarks with a mirror. One lark manages to pull away, only to fall into the talons of the raptor. When the stronger bird, intent on plucking its victim, is caught in the hunter's net, it pleads to no avail that it has never troubled the man, for the Oiseleur replies, "Ce petit animal / T'en avait-il fait davantage?" Thought apparently teaching the golden rule, this fable turns it entirely around into an inexorable cycle of violence, where the plea for mercy is turned down by a devouring force even more guilty of destruction than the lucky-but-unlucky hawk. The lesson of compassion is only a witty pretext for someone who could just as easily have resorted to the *raison du plus fort* that always seems to wait in the wings. As Sosie and Sganerelle discover, the only real way to deal with authority is to try diligently to stay out of its way. In a very un-Revolutionary tone, La Fontaine recommends a similar retreat from power. In "Les Obsèques de la lionne", he derides the Court as a "Peuple caméléon, peuple singe du maître / . . .

gens . . . de simples ressorts." If one insists on being as independent as the stag in the fable, who will not weep for his dead queen, one must be as capable as he is in the matter of hypocrisy. For he only avoids the avenging teeth of King Lion's killers by spinning a tale worthy of Tartuffe, saying the Lioness's saintly spirit forbade him to shed tears. This type of deception will not abolish or shift authority, but may serve to quell it:

> Amusez les Rois par des songes,
> Flattez-les, payez-les d'agréables mensonges,
> Quelque indignation dont leur cœur soil rempli,
> Ils goberont l'appât, vous serez leur ami.

For the would-be *raisonneur*, too proud or too righteous to play this dangerous game, the only alternative is to speak from afar or not at all— advice which, in the spirit of seventeenth-century intellectual *contestation*, neither Molière nor La Fontaine could bring himself to follow.

JACQUES GUICHARNAUD

"Introduction" in Molière: A Collection of Critical Essays

Probing the mysteries of a vocation is not our intention here. Besides, in Molière's case such an undertaking would be hopeless: we have no diary, no more or less fictionalized autobiography, no memoirs to provide the elements of a psychobiography or an existential analysis. Grimarest *La Vie de Monsieur de Molière*, curious as it may be (Molière confiding his personal torments, his turbulent friendship with Chapelle, and so on) was published in 1705, thirty-two years after Molière's death, and is thus considered extremely questionable by most modern scholars. The other rare pieces of evidence from his contemporaries are all of a polemical nature and, consequently, partial.

Actually, what we have to go on is one simple reality: the presence in France in the second half of the seventeenth century, of a complete man of the theater—actor, leader of a theatrical company, playwright—recognized as such by his contemporaries, transmitted as such by an almost continuous tradition, and obviously shown to be such by his works.

Here, then, are the facts: at a time when actors were more or less outside the law, Jean-Baptiste Poquelin, the son of a good bourgeois family, gave up the security and respectability of the legal profession, at about the age of twenty, renouncing the right to succeed his father as "upholsterer by appointment of the King" (true, he later assumed the title), in order to throw

From *Molière: A Collection of Critical Essays*. © 1964 Prentice-Hall, Inc.

himself body and soul into the mad adventure of the boards. We know nothing about how came to make that choice. Had he limited himself to writing, like Corneille or Racine, we might fancy that we understood. But he began by taking the extraordinary plunge of becoming an actor, and when later he set about writing, he did so mainly to fulfill his possibilities as an actor.

To be sure, the venture was not so novel as it would at first appear. Valdemar Vedel, in his *Molière*, rightly reminds us that the acting profession, while still hazardous and fraught with danger, was not so discreditable about 1650 as it had been in the past, and that the tragedian Montfleury, among others, had also forsaken a bourgeois career at the bar to give himself to the stage. But if Molière is not the only one on the list, he leads it because of his obstinacy and the scope of his enterprise.

For this was, above all, a case of obstinacy. It is one thing to say no to succeeding one's father; it is another to persist under the worst conditions, never returning to eat the fatted calf. We know that in 1643 he and the Béjart family founded the "Illustre Théâtre". Although that name still calls up wonders, we must not forget that it turned out to be lamentable undertaking, doomed to failure by its participants' lack of experience and the competition of the large companies, those of the Hôtel de Bourgogne and the Hôtel du Marais. That failure meant debts, prison (Molière did time in Le Châtelet in 1644), and finally, collapse. One might say "cherchez la femme," and no doubt she would be found in the person of Madeleine Béjart. The classic (or rather, romantic) story of the young man of good family seduced by an obscure actress? Perhaps. But it was more the choice of a profession, against all comers. And a definitive choice. Love may have weighed down the scale, but there is still no doubt that Molière needed the theater as much as the Béjarts needed an energetic and learned young companion. More than Molière's loves, what counts is the constancy of the group to which he belonged—a group which, despite the inevitable upheavals and desertions, was to hold together in adversity as well as in success.

When we say that the Illustre Théâtre collapsed, we mean that the undertaking, not the group, fell apart, for Molière and the Béjarts together joined another company, that of Gros-René, in 1645. And it took but four years for Molière to become its leader. Yet it was exile—in other words, the provinces. Thirteen years in the provinces: can one "imagine," along with René Bray, "that those long years, the years of his beautiful youth, were the happiest of his life?" No doubt the troupe grew, the receipts came in, and success smiled on Molière; in addition, an illustrious protector, the Prince de Conti, was found. But the provinces are the provinces; even Lyons, the troupe's home port, although a rich and Italianized center for more than a century, was—in the eyes of a Parisian such as D'Assoucy—merely a "beautiful village". And the Prince de Conti forsook Molière, becoming devout and at the same time his worst enemy. Indeed, it would seem that those years were years of struggle and apprenticeship, with one impatiently awaited goal: the return to Paris.

It was during those thirteen years that Molière discovered a means of survival: writing. He had once studied seriously at the Jesuit Collège de Clermont; he knew how to wield a pen. One can imagine that he and his friends were weary of feeling ill at ease in plays written by others, plays that were common property as soon as they were published, since there was no copyright. On the other hand, the audience reacted favorably to improvisation modeled on the Italians, to spontaneous witticism. Little more was needed to tempt Molière into writing plays "to order". In other words, Molière began to write comedies not because he had some profound message (satirical or philosophical) to communicate to the world, but because he was able to stock up on jokes, gestures, and situations that "worked" with his audience every time, given his troupe's ability and, mainly, his own. *L'Étourdi*, the first absolutely authenticated text, is a series of "actor's numbers" and, particularly, as René Bray has shown, a "vehicle" entirely conceived to show Molière's talents.

Yet there is more to *L'Étourdi*: it is also a "written" comedy, and well written at that. Combined with Molière's sense of the needs and immediate possibilities of an itinerant troupe was his obvious sense of the *dignity* of comedy. Molière the writer put himself into the service of Molière the actor and his comrades, but without ever stooping: he manipulated the alexandrine; he chose to be a servant in good taste. And doubtless, at heart, he wanted to be known as a good writer, as he was already known as a good clown—having failed to fulfill his early dream of being a good tragedian, an ambition he was wise enough to renounce. He had to survive, to please, to adapt to the possibilities of the material he found, but he did it with esthetic dignity. Son of the manufacturing bourgeoisie, Molière was to try, through-out his career, to reconcile his clients' pleasure with his dignity as a craftsman.

To continue the metaphor, one sees, during those years in the provinces, a dual apprenticeship: knowledge gained of the raw material of comic humor (farce), and an ability to manufacture quality products, although more or less "copies". Molière was never to lose sight of the former, and he was to eliminate the imitative nature of the latter. On his return to Paris, it was with farce that he attracted attention; and it was finally by elevating the element of farce in comedy, by introducing it into great literature, that he produced his "masterwork", in a craftsman's sense of the word: *L'École des femmes*.

We are somewhat surprised today at the great wave of hostility provoked by that comedy. At first sight, nothing could be more innocent than the actual scenario, the tradition of which goes back to antiquity: a young slave girl is stolen away by the young leading man from the old fogy who was keeping her to himself. The play was a pretext for stage effects, with juicy roles for Molière and his best pupil, Lagrange. The ill temper of the minor writers, the prudes' reaction to Molière's private life, the pedants' indignation in the face of some twisting of the rules—all that is not enough to explain the violence of the response. With *L'École des femmes*, a comedy of substance fell on the heads of the Parisian public of 1662, most unexpectedly.

First of all, the play was unlike anything ever performed before. Beneath a well-known and respected form (five acts in verse) lurked a content that was very strange indeed—half farce and half chit-chat—with an obvious disdain for the canons of the comedy of intrigue; and such discord seemed like cheating. That portion of the public which likes to come upon the same reliable patterns in the theater has always been shocked by novelty or invention of any kind. On a deeper level the innovation here consisted in displacing the comedy's center of interest: to be sure, the ridiculous mask is a pretext for "interesting action" (the machinations of Horace and Agnès, Arnolphe's counterattacks), but that action is no longer an end; it is a means, a tool to chip the mask and finally shatter it. And that cannot be done without exploiting to the utmost the characters' traits, just as the grotesques of farce were exploited to the utmost, with a kind of relentlessness that is troubling— or astonishing: for what is more astonishing than the fact that Molière creates a victim whom he obviously wants to destroy and whom at the same time he makes particularly tough? On an even deeper level, such an ambition is dangerous. The comedy, of course, remains literature, but it is no longer literature about literature: originally the cuckold of farce or the jealous lover of the comedy of intrigue, Arnolphe no longer reflects his literary sources but, rather, ourselves. Relatively speaking, he is, to his sources, what Ubu would be to Monsieur Perrichon.

The premiere of *L'École des femmes* (1662) was a theatrical event of as much importance as that of *Le Cid* (1636) and certainly more than that of *Hernani* (1830). Its repercussions can be felt in all the good comedies of the eighteenth century and in the bourgeois genres of the nineteenth, and they continued their course from *Ubu Roi* to the theater of Ionesco in the twentieth, with detours by way of the Boulevards and Jean Anouilh. With *L'École des femmes*, a comic synthesis took place. The fixity of the mask of farce, which suddenly becomes three-dimensional, is the comic counterpart of fate or tragic destiny. Not by chance has J.D. Hubert recently called this play "a burlesque tragedy". In other words, instead of being simply an imaginary *romanesque* world (and its charms are not to be disdained) or conferring on the spectator that absolute superiority of witnessing an exhibition of dehumanized marionettes, comedy suddenly assimilates its diverse pasts and, without repudiating them even when it parodies them, makes our life into a farce and farce into our life: the romanesque quality becomes a true poetic solution, not a mere literary device. With *L'École des femmes*, the spectator finds himself in both the imaginary and the real, literature and life; he is torn apart, as he should be in the theater—pulled out of himself toward the innocent delights of theatrical illusion and at the same time thrown back on himself to the reality of his basic instincts. He has to deal with the contemptible masks of the traditional stage, but the *papier-mâché* of the mask has become flesh, while keeping its original shape and colors. Such transmutation is painful for the audience.

Contemporary playgoers often disparage Beckett or Ionesco by saying: "All that's old hat. One can see the same thing in any Parisian music hall or at any Irish or British vaudeville". Or: "The 'absurd' dialogue of that team of American Negro comedians is worth all of Ionesco's dialogues". Or: "The two cronies in *Waiting for Godot* are merely a mixture of all the cronies of English farce". In *L'école des femmes* (and this essay is too short to go back to *Les Précieuses* ridicules). Molière was the Beckett or Ionesco of his time. By fully exploiting the possibilities of the traditional "number"' he obliged the spectator to recognize, in the clown on stage, both the convention and himself. He submitted his audience to the transition from entertainment to true theater in an intolerable leap.

This was done by means of a certain realism within the unreality. Enough details are given so that Arnolphe, the hero of *L'École des femmes*, is immediately recognizable as a typical French bourgeois of the seventeenth century, a bourgeois in general, and—still more generally—man, to the extent that he is a possessive creature. Representative of a caste at a given moment of history, symbol of a class at any moment of history, and image of a permanent dimension of man in any class at any moment, Arnolphe justifies certain of Sartre's theories on the meaning of literature: it is through specific and historic embodiments that one reaches, if not absolute, at least lasting, truths.

The "truth" of Arnolphe is a priori that of the masks of farce: fixity. A mask is sculptured once and for all, fixed for the duration of the play. If one removes the mask and transposes the lines of the artificial face to the character's psychology, manners, and human attitudes, one then has what the French call a "caractére". A *papier-mâché* mask is communicated from one generation of actors to another. Harlequin, with his black mask and motley, has been the same for at least three centuries, laying eggs and wielding the bat. The counterpart to that tradition is Arnolphe's snicker when he is certain that he has found the recipe against being cuckolded. But although Harlequin, when he is now revived, remains an esthetic delight and even a reminder of the essence of theater, Arnolphe is truer, while just as stylized: Harlequin speaks to us of theater; Arnolphe speaks to us of man. And many men do not like being spoken about.

Arnolphe and Agnès face to face prove that there is no universality outside a concrete and historic embodiment. Once that point is accepted, the critic can profitably study the play. He finds that it deals with tyranny in the face of natural spontaneity, with a desire to change the world in the face of the need for the consent of others, and so forth. Yet all that, in the abstract, is not new. Moreover, in fictional literature and in farce, what normal spectator does not accept a bias in favor of spontaneity and consent? But when asked to consider a three-dimensional cuckold, he balks because at that moment the cuckold becomes identifiable with the spectator, who himself is, and knows he is, three-dimensional—or more simply, the spectator finds himself cuckolded.

Cuckolded and tyrannical and blind and victimized and, on occasion, unhappy. And, in addition, he is asked to laugh at it all—that is, at himself. It is one thing to ask the spectator to laugh at a masked and hunchbacked cuckold with a false goatee and dressed in tights; it is another to present him, by means of the same comic devices, with a potential cuckold, wearing a quite normal beard and dressed, like the spectator, as a bourgeois (a little out of fashion and with a bit too much green, perhaps), without a mask, and physically "real" (perhaps a little too stocky, but so, after all, was Molière).

No, the attack on *L'École des femmes* was not unjustified. Apart from the vicious or personal details, such as the accusation of incest flung at Poquelin himself, and over and above the vulgarity of the *grand siècle*, it showed that comedy, for the first time, was dangerous: it no longer involved some conventional other person but, in the very terms of the convention, the spectator himself.

Have we spoken at too great length about that "touching little farce?" Not really, for whoever reads Molière's works chronologically, amused by *L'Étourdi*, delighted by *Les Précieuses ridicules*, esthetically satisfied by *L'École des maris*, is struck by the innovation of *L'école des femmes*. Molière had up to then struggled to make a living. From that point on, he was also to struggle for his own identity and for the rights of the comic genre: his literary and theatrical apprenticeship was over.

Of course, Molière continued to write entertainments for the court, which in themselves are admirable, charming, poetic. Modern critics are right to bring them back into high esteem: Molière was an organizer of the pleasures of his century, and perhaps the best of them. All periods, even the most tragic, have their free and easy joys, without which no portrait of them would be complete. But if Molière had not existed, some Benserade would have taken his place, with almost as much talent.

In any case, such entertainments should not be disregarded. In them Molière, a complete man of the theater, gave free rein to his imagination; besides, they allowed him to rely more or less on royal protection, thanks to which he was able to explore *high* comedy. For while he was creating *La Princesse d'Élide, L'Amour médecin, Mélicerte,* and *Le Sicilien,* he was also writing the first *Tartuffe* (and fighting to have it performed), *George Dandin, Dom Juan, Le Misanthrope,* and *L'Avare,* as well as *Le Médecin malgré lui* and *Amphitryon.* Those were the five years (1664–69) in Molière's career which crowned his life: from forty-two to forty-seven, even though physically ill, he was in full possession of his art, but at the same time had not "hardened" into a specific image of himself. Thirteen plays in five years is not bad. Out of those thirteen plays, nine are still performable before an inexperienced public, and are performed, which is still better.

What endures is the element shown by that gift of absorption and transmutation revealed by *L'école des femmes.* To take only the established masterpieces of that period (*Tartuffe, Dom Juan, Le Misanthrope, L'Avare*) or the near-masterpieces (*George Dandin, Amphitryon, Le Médecin malgré lui*), all modern critics are agreed that such plays are based on the farcical and the romanesque: two poles of the imaginary which Molière never forgot. His genius was to bring them together without producing a burlesque *a là* Scarron (which would have meant sacrificing the romesque tot he fancical), and from that conjunction, as if from some electrical apparatus, to generate a spark: that of true comedy. At the meeting point of those two poles of the imaginary, thanks to a twist whose force came from experience of the world, the imaginary, while keeping its own dimensions, became the mirror of life. Essentially unrealistic, like all poetic works, Molière's major plays of that period show that everyone's life is a romance, a farce, a disgrace. Their effect might be compared to what would happen if, in a Mack Sennett movie, when a clown throws a cream pie, that pie—by some miracle of film technique—should splash on the faces of all the spectators. The devout, the wellborn, the lovers, the husbands become indignant: they have just been told that they are hypocritical or stupid, ridiculous or cuckolded. Unreality invades reality. The spectator doubts himself—or rather, he is led into a state of bad faith to avoid doubting himself.

For Molière's works of that period are one of the strongest provocations ever presented on the French stage. As their means of expression is laughter, the spectator of the time eased his bad conscience by affecting scorn. Even today one still hears the phase "l'infâme Molière"; in the same spirit the Vichy government tried to ban *Tartuffe*, and Francois Mauriac has used questionable documents to confront Molière with God.

Yet there is great generosity in Molière, shown in his gift for laughter, open laughter devoid of hypocritical sentimentality as well as of indulgence. Arnolphe, Orgon, and Alceste are funny. Even the hateful quality of Harpagon or Tartuffe may provoke laughter which liberates, but which also brings about recognition of man as a creature defined by his passions. The characters are forces, or the meeting point of forces, which live in illusion and mistake their specific determinism for free will. Nothing is funnier than a character in Molière who says "I want . . ." with all the ardor of a Cartesian "généreux," whereas it is not *he* who wants, but *something* in him, something the opposite of his freedom. This misunderstanding with oneself is the source of a drama which goes round in circles—the drama of mania; but such maniacs are quite simply caricatures of ourselves to the extent that we live according to our passions.

One may reject, philosophically, this vision of man. By the same token, one must also reject Racine. But here the question is less one of philosophy than of drama. In repeated meetings of one consciousness with another, each bound by its own mirage, its own desire, and therefore impervious to others, the characters constantly bounce one against the other, and their growing and reciprocal exasperation is paralleled in us. To be sure, there are tormentors and victims, madmen and so-called reasonable men, and we side with the victims against the tormentors, with the reasonable against the mad. But an obstinacy in reason which comes close to mania, despite its defeats, and a stubbornness of the victims in defense of their "normal" appetites, makes them such creatures of passion that it seems no more than a happy chance that their desires are in keeping with the norms of society.

We are alluding here, of course, to the young lovers of Molière's comedies: we find them likable because they consent to each other. Consent can be found in *L'Avare* and *Tartuffe*, but is altogether missing from *Dom Juan*, and exists between Éliante and Philinte, in *Le Misanthrope*, only because of the latter's complete vacuity—as if, at that particular moment in his career, Molière had finally discovered that a man can only consent to another to the extent that he is not a "creature defined by his passion"—that is, to the extent that he stops being a man.

Are Molière's works a comedy of character? A catalogue of unconscious mannerisms, observed in real life or borrowed from tradition, and linked with a conventional or new notion of a "type"? At first sight, yes.

But if only that, they would be no more than a dramatized version of La Bruyère. Each of Molière's comedies, going beyond specific failings and obvious ridiculous ways, transcends manners and characters. Each one is a veritable comedy of passion, just as tragedy in Racine is said to be tragedy of passion. The ridiculousness of Molière's characters is not merely an accidental outgrowth of human nature: it is that nature. *Dom Juan* and *Le Misanthrope* prove that the soul is not definable in terms of free will and understanding, modified—disastrously but only on occasion—by the vices of the time; it is essentially vice, accompanied by an illusion of freedom. Molière (along with Racine) is the gravedigger of Descartes.

But the comedy of Molière is not exhausted in that almost Jansenist statement. On the human level Molière clearly desired earthly happiness, an attitude incompatible with Jansenism and related rather to a certain Gassendist naturalism that no one has yet managed to define satisfactorily. The union of Philinte and Éliante, in *Le Misanthrope*, is one of Molière's dreams, a dream that came from his generosity, his love for man—but what a pitiful embodiment! In this realm there is a kind of optimism, but it is a despondent optimism.

Although despondent as a man (that is, the man Molière considered from the perspective of his works, for we hae no right to speak of any other), Molière was not despondent as a playwright. By means of the theater, that higher game, he achieved a state of joy. Comedy is probably the only solution for pessimists, for without denying the horror of the human condition, comedy absorbs it to provoke laughter about an illusion that is frankly an illusion. Boileau made his friends laugh by imitating Molière as he snickered during the last scene of Act II of *Le Misanthrope*. In other words, Molière, who had written the part for himself, re-established the superiority of the illusory miracle of theater at the last second: a striking contradiction between his vision of the world as a dead end and a gratuitousness which, despite man's despair as a prisoner, reaffirmed, no doubt unconsciously, a freedom that Molière found in thedual creative act of the poet and actor.

In all probability, Molière was not a happy man in private life. But through the prisoners he created for the duration of a performance, it is equally probable that he experienced something which the world had forbidden him to believe in: his own freedom. Having, as writer and actor, created a parodic universe, he was both God and the creature.

To our mind, *Dom Juan* and *Le Misanthrope* (however successful they were at the time) are at once masterpieces and experimental plays: master-pieces because experimental. After them, Molière was in complete possession of his acquisitions. He invented no longer; he perfected. With *Les Femmes savantes* he even presented an anthology of his capabilities. The craftsman of the theater, who had achieved his mastership with *L'École des femmes*, now produced a kind of academic exhibition piece, in which he brought together all the fruits of his experience: themes, devices, recognition of his sources. Tartuffe fuses with Mascarille; Orgon, in changing his sex, cleverly absorbs Magdelon: Arsinoé is satisfied to grow younger, whereas Cathos draws near to menopause, Gorgibus takes on the coloring of Dandin, and so on. Trissotin, Philaminte, Armande, Bélise, Chrysale: what a review of what we already know! And what a conscious repetition of the basic design of all family comedy: the young couple, the obstacle to their happiness in the form of one parent's obstinacy, the rival whom that parent inflicts on the girl—all too beautiful, too perfect, to be true. At the age of fifty, with *Les Femmes savantes*, Molière carved out his own official statue for posterity. A fine statue, it commands respect but teaches us nothing we had not already known. If it touches us, the reason for it is indirect: one year before his death, the King's upholsterer was haunted by a concern for the dignity of French craftsmanship.

After the impasse portrayed in *Le Misanthrope*, Molière directed his energy to rediscovering a *possible* form of comedy and to re-establishing, at least fictitiously, the notion of mutual consent. The stroke of genius was to have put Tartuffe on the side of consent in *Les Fourberies de Scapin*. Putting the knave in the service of others was no doubt a return to an old Latin tradition. But that return was due neither to chance nor to the mere coquetry of the theatrical virtuoso. Here we have a manipulation both magical and highly conscious. True, Scapin is the height of farce, the intellectualization, by a mature man, of all he had learned about a certain form of theater. Yet comic illusion also triumphs: evil finally serves good—good being, in an imaginary Naples, one creature's consent to another. In this play the clown's "turn", the romanesque convention, and the crime of knavery are combined (as in *Le Mariage de Figaro*) to impose, by means of the most frankly imagined artifice, the illusory solution to man's condition: good and evil merged in the indisputable joy of consent.

For after the difficult trilogy *Tartuffe–Dom Juan–Le Misanthrope*, Molière's theater was indeed to be concerned primarily with joy, without illusion but not without hope. The lack of illusion can be found in the ambiguous first scene of *L'Avare*. In the very first line Molière affirms that Valère and Élise are lovers, in the modern sense of the word; then the dialogue turns to the convention of chaste and "precious" lovers. But the harm has been done: the romanesque element, which Dullin so well spotted, simply sends both the spectator and the characters back to the tradition of artificial propriety. The characters put on masks to perform a comedy according to the rules, but the masks are necessarily transparent; hence the spectator, who has been made aware of the reality, is obliged to play the game with them, knowing well that it is a game. Brutally, we are told that Valère and Élise had consented to one another as far as consummation and the anguish of infidelity that follows—and once that has been accepted, the entire play takes on its meaning as a *theatrical* solution. After three minutes of dialogue, the playwright revirginizes Élise and restores to the couple a "precious" chastity that fools no one. The concession to convention allows a salutary escape to a more beautiful world where, thanks to the magic spell of scenic poetry, the miserly and love-smitten old man pushes the unreal logic of his nature to the extreme; where he is the ideal obstacle to "honest" loves; where an order is established by the poet despite insoluble or unpleasant realities, leading to a poetic finale which is not a concession to convention but an affirmation. Only the playwright can take the evil of human nature and render it inoffensive.

This theatrical solution seems to be the key to Molière's works at about the time he was finally authorized to perform *Tartuffe*. It takes the forms of the romanesque, breaks out enchantingly in the court plays, underlies the carnival clownery of *Le Bourgeois gentilhomme* or *Le Malade imaginaire*—all plays of consent, but thanks to the intervention of the unreal. Carnival? Yes, for the mask, in its noble form (the extravagant mythological spree of the court plays) or in its popular form (*turqueries* and syringes), is the instrument of salvation and liberation. Hence the comedy of Molière was no longer troubling; except for a few skirmishes, his struggles seemed to be over. There were the unpleasant dealings with the composer Lully, who played some mean tricks on him, but that kind of quarrel did not call into question the very essence of his works.

Yet, for a moralist, Scapin is as much a knave as Tartuffe, Jourdain as dangerously obstinate as Orgon, Harpagon as possessive as Arnolphe (and with ever less generosity), Argan as stupid as Sganarelle, and as devout—in medicine—as Organ is in religion. Moreover, an element of the macabre was added here and there: so many doctors as prophets of death, a few counterfeits of death itself or the death agony (in the case of Harpagon, Scapin, Argan, and in certain respects, in *Psyché*). But, on the other hand, the provocation did cease: the disquieting search was replaced by a peremptory affirmation, that of an art sufficient unto itself which resulted in the free form of *La Comtesse d'Escarbagnas*, in the somewhat cold perfection of *Les Femmes savantes* and above all, in the theatrical entertainments.

It is difficult to imagine a ballet bringing together Alceste and Célimène at the end of *Le Misanthrope*. But it is a ballet that saves Dandin from drowning himself. This kind of *fête* is more than an ultimate escape, a skillful pretense. It is a manifestation of comedy's role. A mechanism to reveal the true by means of the truer than true, comedy is also a lesson. But this didacticism is, as Pascal would have said, "of another order". Indeed, in *Le Malade imaginaire*, it is not actually Béralde who teaches us how to live well. Argan himself—at the moment that he is admitted among the doctors—instructs us by the spectacle of delirium being absorbed into a super-delirium, of nature being beaten at its own game by an act characteristic of man and called a game, or rather a super-game, involving the wonders of reflection and imagination. The spectacle produces joy precisely because it entails the intense satisfaction of being superior and of knowing that one is superior. So conceived, comedy is not an escape; it is an affirmation.

It was while making an affirmation against death that Molière died. Suddenly taken ill during a performance of *Le Malade imaginaire* on February 17, 1673, he was brought home and there he died during the night. That day the actor, who was really ill, had joyously played the part of a man who pretended to be ill. The double deceit of actor and character, meeting head-on the truth of death at the end of a double lie, has caused much ink to flow, and continues to move deeply the glorifiers of Molière. In point of fact, chance served Molière well, and that ideal end transformed his life into a destiny.

We are still touched by that destiny, the notion of which has been kept alive by Madame Dussane and many other theater people. But is it enough to give us an understanding of Molière's works? There is no reason to believe that sentimental biography limits our understanding of them. Yet a mixture of divinization of the man and dull moral interpretations of the works had, in the past, worked to fix a rather boring image of the poet. Twentieth century criticism has, on the whole, proved to be more exciting.

We do not take into account here the historical research which, not very long ago, with its established methods of detection, freed Molière from certain tenacious myths: Michaut's fundamental work was published only in 1922–25. We prefer to dwell on that which has led to a better understanding of Molière's theater as theater, and on the perspectives given us by new methods of criticism. For there we have perhaps the two most original contributions of our times.

Since the beginning of the century, scholars and men of the theater have contributed to the real "retheatricalization" of Molière's works. For the general public the director Louis Jouvet has been particularly instrumental in this, not only by his celebrated staging of *L'École des femmes*, but also by his lectures, certain words of which still right out in the minds of critics and men of the theater:

Made to please the multitude, Molière's plays have been plucked from their finality by all sorts of exegetists who believed that classicism was their property. The actor was robbed for the benefit of academic storehouses. Having been forsaken by the public and the scholars . . . it is up to the actor to rediscover and recover that heritage; to get at the both simple and complicated dramatic mechanism by which a work of genius was originally set in motion; to rediscover, for everyone's use, its plot, the freshness of its story, everything that charmed the audience and the actors who performed it for the first time. . . . The comedies of Molière must be judged under the stage lights, not in the books of expositors. And although one reads them in the silence of a room, one must realize that he wrote them for the crowd.

Yet, to be fair, we must go back even further: as early as 1901 an article by Gustave Lanson recalled the very sources of Molière's art; at the period of the First World War Jacques Copeau, in his productions and explanations, rediscovered the playwright and the actor of farce by concentrating particularly on *Scapin*, which he brought back into esteem; and although none of the writings of Jacques Arnavon is included here, the "reforms" he suggested did save Molière from a scenic and academic rut—unfortunately, by making use of a naturalism that was salutary at the time but not relevant today. Gustave Lanson, René Bray, and Alfred Simon, on the one hand, and Copeau and Dullin, on the other, represent here the artisans of the retheatricalization of Molière.

The eternal question of the relations between the man and his works has also been stated in new terms. To be sure, certain critics—such as René Jasinski in his very detailed and highly erudite study of *Le Misanthrope*—consider that Molière's works represent, above all, a personal confession, along with the affirmation of a temperate wisdom. But other critics have challenged that kind of interpretation. Many of these (mostly English and American new critics, followers of Will G. Moore) reject almost entirely the "person" Molière; others continue to bring him in, but essentially in terms inseparable from the structure, the dramaturgy, and the problem of poetic creation as such. In any case, a universe of characters will henceforth be dealt with, and if Molière the man happens to be spoken of, it must be less in terms of his relations with his wife, for example, than with his works—including their demands and, if need be, their social and political implications.

Finally, not the least of the twentieth century's contributions, in addition to rediscovering the theatricality of farce (latent in all the works, or frankly asserted, as in Scapin), has been the revival, by our critics and men of the theater, of one of Molière's most ambiguous plays: *Dom Juan*. Once no more than a poor and misunderstood relative, the Dom has recently given rise to a profusion of commentaries, often and necessarily conflicting. By virtue of this, a fair share of this anthology is devoted to him; for whether or not he corresponds to certain "heroes of our times", he has become the center of attraction among all the works. This is perhaps the most striking indication of the fact that Molière of the twentieth century is no longer the mouthpiece of "petit-bourgeois" common sense, but rather the poet of frenzied struggles which the *vis comica* makes every effort to control.

W. G. MOORE

Mime

Perhaps the most obvious thing to say about Molière is just that he was an actor. It was as such that he was first, and chiefly, known to his contemporaries. It was for acting rather than for reading that he composed his plays. It would seem natural therefore to begin the study of Molière's work from this professional angle. Yet such has not so far been the case. The evidence concerning the actual art on the stage of 'le premier farceur de France' has never been assembled or discussed. May it not prove that passages otherwise obscure find a plain and natural explanation in the fact that they conform, not to any abstract code of aesthetics, but to the demands of a repertory company? The present chapter is an attempt to present, and then to evaluate, the evidence. So distinguished an actor as M. Louis Jouvet has complained that the academic theories of Molière scholars are of no use to the actor seeking an interpretation of the main roles, and that, despite two hundred and fifty years of criticism, we are still forced to stand in uncomprehending bewilderment ('désarroi') before his work.

It is interesting that what is possibly the earliest reference to Molière as actor speaks of him also as an undergraduate. The fragment bears no date, and is in the form of a note appended by Tallemant des Réaux to his paragraph on La Béjard. It runs as follows:

From *Molière: A New Criticism.* © 1949 Oxford University Press.

'Un garcon nomme Molière quitta les bancs de Sorbonne pour la suivre; il`en fut longtemps amoureux, donnait des avis à la troupe, et enfin s'en mit et l'epousa. Il a fait des pièces où il y a de l'esprit. Ce n'est pas un merveilleux acteur, si ce n'est pour le ridicule. Il n'y a que sa troupe qui joue ses pièces; elles sont comiques.'

The passage is clearly gossip, like most of Tallemant, albeit faithfully reported. One could hardly imagine so industrious a collector not knowing more about Molière after, shall we say, the success and polemic of the *École des Femmes*, so the information would seem to date from 1662 at the latest. It is in several respects inaccurate. There is no likelihood that Molière did study at the Sorbonne, and he certainly did not marry Madeleine Béjard. But on the matter of his acting, Tallemant would appear to be giving the general opinion. Molière played many tragic parts and was famous in none. Some years after his death the daughter of his fellow actor Du Croisy explained this fact as due to his physique being unsuited for tragic acting. Contemporaries had certainly made fun of it and had provoked sharp rejoinders on Molière's own stage. Mascarille is astonished that the 'Précieuses' ask him to which actors he will give the play he has written. 'Belle demande. Aux grands comediens; il n'y a qu'eux qui soient capables de faire valoir les choses; les autres sont des ignorants qui récitent comme l'on parle; ils ne savent pas faire ronfler les vers et s'arrêter au bel endroit.' Four years later the thrust was repeated, and rammed home by actual mimicry. In *L'Impromptu de Versailles* Molière portrays himself as reproving a young colleague who recites lines from *Nicomède* 'le plus naturellement qu'il lui aurait été possible': 'Comment, vous appelez cela rociter? C'est se railler. Il faut dire les choses avec emphase. Écoutez-moi . . .' and he proceeds to ridicule the 'emphase', and lack of natural diction, of five of his contemporaries at the Hôtel.

The point at issue between Molière and his rivals seems to have been more than one of pique at his failure to score success in tragicparts. His attempt to make tragic diction more 'natural' seems to have been too much for contemporary taste, which wanted tragedy to be almost intoned, or at any rate declined with a solemnity removed from ordinary speech. His irony in referring to them as 'les grands comédiens' was itself ironical since the public, in spite of all that Molière could do or say, continued to think that the acting at the Hôtel was 'proper acting'. Perhaps for such a reason the young Racine removed his *Alexandre* from Molière's theatre. There is certainly evidence to support Molière's defence of a new and natural diction. Tallemant, as we have seen, admits that in funny plays he was very successful. Two of his own actors, paying tribute to him nine years after his death, make much of his skill in 'le jeu naïf du théâtre'. Their description has peculiar authority:

'Il n'était pas seulement inimitable dans la manière dont il soutenait tous les caracteres de ses comédies; mais il leur donnait encore un agrément tout particulier par la justesse qui accompagnait le jeu des acteurs: un coup-d'œil, in pas, un geste, tout y était observé avec une exactitude qui avait été inconnue jusque là sur les théâtres de Paris.'

It would seem that Molière, whether or not he was disappointed at failing to succeed as an actor of tragedy, established for the theatre-going public of mid-seventeenth-century Paris a new style of acting, in which he not only himself excelled but succeeded in training his company. Whereas the dominant tradition of his day insisted on declamation as the mark of good acting, Molière seems from the first to have essayed something not only more ordinary but much nearer mimicry. It is referred to by epithets such as 'naturel', 'nait', 'justesse', 'observé avec exactitude'. Should one not conclude from this that the 'realism' we find in the plays is the outcome not of poetic or satiric intention, or of literary attitude, but of a type of acting which proved successful in practice? That it was successful was due no doubt not merely to Molière's personal talent but to the taste of the public, of that cultivated public which about 1660 seemed to appreciate the 'natural'.

> Maintenant il ne faut pas
> Quitter la nature d'un pas.

So commented La Fontaine, perhaps after he had seen Molière act.

Traces of this taste for, and skill in portraying, the 'natural' can be found in all Molière's plays. He used to the full the comic tradition of ordinary gesture and situation. The physical is everywhere in its own right and very often symbolical of the moral. Sosie's cowardice is conveyed by his stammer, Sganarelle's excitement by a tumble, Harpagon's universal suspicion by his comments on the actual audience in front of him. L'Avare is full of concrete illustrations of moral qualities; nothing is described, everything is shown in and by physical act: Harpagon searches his man's clothes, runs after his money, wears glasses and a ring on his finger, crawls under the table. Are not these but the mummified remains of what was once alive and spontaneous in 'le jeu naïf du théâtre'? Even congealed in the text they are calculated to rejoice the heart of the actor seeking to live a part.

Admitting that Molière was a brilliant exponent of 'le jeu naïf', is it possible to discover whether he invented a method to suit his gifts, or took over a tradition other than that of his tragic rivals? A little research proves that, like other men of genius, Molière was attaching himself to something already established rather than creating a completely new medium. Both the performance and the theme of seventeenth-century French tragedy, for example, go back to a Renaissance revival of the academic productions of medieval students. One medium of seventeenth-century comedy goes back to the same movement; one may think of Corneille, for instance, as writing comedies in a style perfected by Larivey and others on the model revived by Jodelle. Molière has other and more earthy roots. It was not for nothing that he was called a *farceur*. The name was an accurate description not merely of the sort of play he preferred but of his style and tradition of acting. For the tradition of the French farce had never lost its popularity, though it had rarely achieved respectability. It was in this tradition, as M. Lanson showed us forty years ago, that Molière was trained and that his own powers developed. From the indecent *gauloiserie* of the farce to the elegance of *Le Misanthrope* may seem a far cry, yet both are in the same literary tradition. It is clear even to the outsider that Molière discarded much, and grafted entirely new elements on to what he kept. It is the task of scholarship to find out how much was kept, and the vital factor to have in mind when studying his choice is that he was as much, and as instinctively, an actor as he was an author.

Most of the evidence of Molière's early contacts with farce has been lost. We do not know what farces he watched, or played in, or wrote, or adapted, before 1658. He may as a boy have watched the famous Tabarin. It would be strange if a boy of his temperament had not made early acquaintance with Gross René, Gaultier Garguille, Floridor, and Jodelet. On the other hand, we have evidence of his contacts with the farces played by the Italian actors of the *commedia dell'arte*. His enemies reproached him for having been their too servile disciple. The skit of 1670 called *Élomire Hypocondre* contains (in the judgement of M. Michaut) more than a little actual biography. This upstart of the stage presumes to attain perfection in a new art:

> Veut se rendre parfait dans l'art faire rire,
> Que fait-il, le matois, dans ce hardi dessein?
> Chez le grand Scaramouche il va soir et matin,
> Là le miroir en main et ce grand homme en face,
> Il n'est contorsion, posture ni grimace
> Que ce grand écolier du plus grand des bouffons
> Ne fasse et ne refasse en cent et cent façons.
> Tantôt pour exprimer les soucis d'un ménage,
> De mille et mille plis il fronce son visage;
> Puis, joignant la pâleur à ces rides qu'il fait,
> D'un mari malheureux il est le vrai portrait.

The arrow is barbed by a frontispiece, still to be seen in the copy in the Arsenal Library, but said to have been destroyed by Molière's efforts in all the others, showing the Italian master, whip in hand, making gestures, copied by the pupil holding a mirror, and the legend: 'Qualis erit tanto docente magistro?'

This testimony is later confirmed by Tralage, who had no axe to grind, and was probably merely noting what he found to be common knowledge: "Molière estimait fort Scaramouche pour ses manières naturelles; il le voyait fort souvent et il lui a servi pour former les meilleurs acteurs de sa troupe.' (Among the characters in *L'Avare* occurs the name of Brindavoine, another of Scaramouche's favourite pupils.)

The farce and the *commedia dell' arte* clearly had much in common and it is now, I think, possible to determine what Molière owed to each. Both were played in masks. Both relied on the realistic and even gross presentation of a few set types, such as the old man, the pedant, the valet, and the nurse. The *commedia* as played in Paris after 1650 had probably lost many of its original features, such as the partition of roles to suit the various Italian dialects. One suggestion is that it differed from the farce in dealing with imaginative caricature rather than earthy reality. But perhaps the main difference was that it had few or no written parts. Its actors were trained to improvise and embroider a 'canevas' or skeleton of plot, and thus to rely more on mine than on speech. The fact that they played to audiences largely ignorant of their own tongue no doubt enforced this practice. An Italian actor of Molière's own day has left evidence that brings out the extreme importance of this fact:

'Les comédiens italiens n'apprennent rien par coeur; il leur suffit pour jouer une comédie d'en avoir vu le sujet un moment avant que d'entrer sur le théâtre. . . . Qui dit "bon comédien italien" dit un homme qui a du fond, qui joue plus d'imagination que de mémoire, qui marie si bien ses actions à ses paroles, avec celles de son camarade, qu'il entre sur le champ dans tout le jeu et dans tous les mouvements que l'autre lui demande, de manière à faire croire qu'ils s'étaient déjà concertés.

Clearly the Italian practice expected more from the actor and evoked more remarkable power than the native French tradition. Such men as Biancolelli (died 1688) as Arlequin, and Fiorelli (died 1694) as Scaramouche, provided a standard of acting to which no French contemporaries (before Molière) could approach.

This suppleness demanded of the actor seems at first sight to accord ill with the rigidity of character associated with the farce and in particular with the mask, which was the chief mark of the actor, known in advance and intended to be recognized at once. But there is little doubt that here too

Molière conformed to, and learnt much from, the farcical tradition. He was trained to act in a mask, he probably did so in at least one Paris play. The name Mascarille ('little mask') suggests this, an engraving of 1666 also does, and a text of 1663 supplies corroborative evidence: 'Il contrefaisait d'abord les Marquis avec le masque de Mascarille; il n'osait les jouer autrement; mais à la fin il nous a fait voir qu'il avait le visage assez plaisant pour représenter sans masque un personnage ridicule'. Details of roles played in masks support this assertion that Molière did not use it for long. *Les Fourberies de Scapin*, when revived in 1736, had the old men played in masks but not Scapin himself. According to Guy Patin, who had every chance to know and no inducement to lie, the doctors in *L'Amour Médecin* were masked. Lulli the musician performed parts in *Monsieur de Pourceaugnac* and *Le Bourgeois Gentilhomme*, both with the mask. The naive counterpart to the mask seems to have been heavy clown's make-up. Jodelet in the *Précieuses* was thus 'enfariné'. One gathers that the 'flour' was not so much for scenic as for farcical effect. Sauval speaks of an actor who 'ne portait point de masque, mais se couvrait le visage de farine, et menageait cette farine de sorte qu'en remuant seulement un peu les lèvres il blanchissait tout d'un coup ceux qui lui parlaient'.

The mask has some claim to represent the oldest of all European traditions of acting. Gilbert Murray has written that 'it is significant that both in Greek and in Latin the word for mask is also the word for character; and Dramatis Personae means, strictly speaking, "the masks needed in the performance". The cross elderly uncle had one sort of mask, the indulgent elderly uncle another. The Obstinate Man, the Flatterer, the Bragging Soldier and the Modest Soldier were got up in such a way that the audience could recognise each type, whatever his name or adventures might be. But here at all events is Molière's starting-point. The mask performed a double service. It freed the actor and it fixed the character. By making the actor anonymous it allowed him to fool to the top of his bent without fear of giving offence. In the sixteenth century it was said that 'nous voyons les Comediens italiens masquer leur Pantalon et leur Zani de Jehan Cornet à fin de plus hardiment jouer, et se moquer, car le masque ne rougit point'. But even more important than this liberty of the actor was the fixity of his role, ensuring that all his efforts were bent to fulfil a clear conception, a definite character. And it seems that Molière the dramatist started from, and indeed in essentials kept close to, this conception of character as fixed. 'Molière a conçu d'abord le caractère sous la forme du masque italien que les farceurs français s'étaient approprié. . . . Arnolphe, Harpagon, Tartuffe, Alceste ont ce trait du masque italien de porter à travers toutes les situations de la pièce la fixité invariable de leur caractère . . . la permanence de leur type est éclatante et inaltérable.'

Such are the words of M. Lanson's famous article, confirmed by much recent investigation and easily verifiable. One can hardly fail to notice that in Molière's dramas there are, as one scholar puts it, no conversions. The great characters may be sobered by misfortune, but they leave the play very much as they entered it, unaltered in essentials. This has been welcomed as proof that Molière, as we say, remains true to life. But English students must beware here. The cliché is deceptive. These impressive figures may give us the illusion of life, but variety and individuality are not the keynotes of his drama. The keyword is rather clarity. It is French drama.

Consideration of the mask as symbol would lead us to the animating principle of comedy as Molière evolved it, and the discussion goes beyond the framework of a chapter on Molière as actor. But it is interesting to notice his fondness for a quite different type of situation, in which he could drop the mask and appear, on the stage, in his own character and with his own name. The attraction of that delightful green-room scene, *L'Impromptu de Versailles*, lies in the appearance of a company of actors as they really were, in everyday costume and occupation, Molière playing the harassed role of actor-manager that needed no rehearsing. The same trick—is it not an actor's fancy?—opened the performance of the *Fâcheux* in 1661 and is thus described in the Preface:

'D'abord que la toile fut levée, un des acteurs, comme vous pourriez dire moi, parut sur le théâtre en habit de ville, et s'adressant au roi avec le visage d'un homme surpris, fit des excuses en désordre sur ce qu'il se trouvoit là seul, et manquoit de temps et d'acteurs pour donner à Sa Majesté le divertissement qu'elle sembloit attendre. En même temps au milieu de vingt jets d'eau naturels, s'ouvrit cette coquille que tout le monde a vue; et l'agréable naïade qui parut dedans s'avança au bord du théâtre, et d'un air héroïque prononça les vers que M. Pellisson avoit faits et qui servent de prologue.'

This charming note gives a glimpse of the informality and co-operative effort that preceded the 'divertissements' for which Molière became famous. A third and quite distinct example of the actor bringing himself into the play is the discussion in *Le Malade Imaginaire*. That Argan, played by Molière, should shake with rage over 'that fellow Molière' and prophesy his end was in itself a brilliant dramatic effect, which was heightened only by the fact that Molière did actually meet his end as he played the part.

These experiments with dramatic illusion are, I think, a sign of this actor's constant preoccupation with the actor's chief problem, that of communication across the footlights. Molière seems to have been anxious to come out of the play to meet the audience, and in one noteworthy case he has brought the audience into the play, a significant return to medieval practice. Harpagon, seeking for the thief, determines to scrutinize everyone he meets and realizes that there is a mass of people in front of him

> 'Que de gens assemblés. Je ne jette mes regards sur personne qui ne me donne des soupçons, et tout me semble mon voleur. Eh, de quoi est-ce qu'on parle là? De celui qui m'a dérobé? Quel bruit fait-on là-haut? Est-ce mon voleur qui y est? De grâce, si l'on sait des nouvelles de mon voleur, je supplie que l'on m'en dise. N'est-il point caché là parmi vous? Ils me regardent tous et se mettent â rire.'

It is hard to recollect another case in modern drama where the audience is not only given a part but where their emotional reaction is mentioned, and reckoned upon, in the text. Such realism needs the great actor to give it full scope. Here is Charles Dullin's picture of what happens: 'Il s'arrête en voyant tous les yeux des spectateurs fixés sur lui . . . il s'avance jusqu'à la rampe, il s'adresse à la dernière galerie . . . il s'agenouille et supplie. A ce moment on rit de lui. Il se relève et crie ses menaces; la passion lui ôte toute mesure.

    This actor was an actor-manager. His plays had to be compounded of such acting material as lay to his hand. The condition of repertory is the limited number of actors available. Is it any wonder that he suited the parts to what they could play, that he used even their physical characteristics in his (always hasty) dramatic composition? He gave Harpagon his own cough and mentioned La Flèche's limp. The chief ladies' roles were written no doubt with his talented young wife in mind; they have her artless grace and ease and charm. As an actress has said: 'En déshabillant les coquettes de Molière, nous retrouvons toujours la même Armande.' They acted together. In the *Impromptu* he says to her with a rudeness that must in a seventeenth-century theatre have seemed refreshingly natural: 'Taisez-vous, ma femme, vous êtes une bête.'

    Were his more serious speeches addressed to her likewise? We here touch upon the sorest point in Molière criticism. There is evidence that they did not get on, gossip was busy with her affairs, and for a time they lived separately. When, therefore, Alceste (the man who can never conceal his feelings) cries out: 'C'est pour mes péchés que je vous aime', is it not Molière who speaks through him? To what extent this was so, no one will ever know. There is, however, all the difference between using a role for personal confession and using an actual situation as starting-point for a role. Molière's only public reference to his private affairs amounts to no more than a request that his enemies should leave them alone. Anything in the nature of subjective romantic confession is quite unthinkable from such a man, working in such a milieu, at such a trade.

Provided that we do not commit the anachronism that Musset's description of Molière suggests, we are free to think that such a play as *L'Éole des femmes*, for example, owes something to the circumstances of Molière's company in 1661. It was his first full-length Paris, comedy, his first attempt to fuse elegant comedy with the farce in which he felt at home; it turned out to be an unexpected success and a turning-point in his career. Having to find a role for himself and the young wife whom he had just married, can we not imagine him reading Scarron's story of 'La Précaution Inutile' and thinking that the two of them might 'make something of that situation'? As he was considerably older than Armande, why not adapt the traditional comic role of the elderly husband? It is surely legitimate to assume that, encouraged by the success of 1662, he should write for himself and Armande such twin roles as Orgon and Elmire, and Alceste and Célimène. If his writing were subjective these pairs of characters would not differ greatly. But Orgon is as different from Alceste as he is from Arnolphe. The one common feature is the opposition of a middle-aged (choleric?) man and a pretty 'ingénue'.

As a final piece of evidence for the influence of the actor in Molière's comedy we should perhaps note the number of his characters who are themselves made to act. This is a feature of his playmaking, and will as such be considered in its place, but this inventor of parts was inventing them even within the plays and scenes that he had invented. Apparently not satisfied with a man playing a part, Molière's dramatic instinct (or acting mania, some would say) makes that man pretend to be even other than what he is as an actor pretending to be. This is what one scholar has aptly termed 'le démon du théâtre. It may well be one facet of that itch for drama, for play-acting, that accounts for the extraordinary animation of all Molière's scenes. This implies, as his dramas show, an acute sense of the reverse, of the process of unmasking, of causing the mask to fall. Nor is this to be thought an idiosyncrasy of the poet Molière; it is a thread that runs through the society that was all round him and that supported his plays. Could he put any better mirror up to that society than that of the mask? Were they not all compelled by etiquette to assume the mask, to act a part, to keep up their social role? Does not all society imply the mask in its constraint upon natural impulse? Can one ever, to other people, speak one's full mind? What is politeness but a cloak, a mask, thrown over self-interest? All this was tirelessly driven home by Molière's great contemporary, La Rochefoucauld, for whom 'le monde n'est composé que de mines'. It may be no accident that in a whole group of his *Maximes* the Duke refers expressly to actors as presenting a type and figure of all social behaviour.

But here we come upon the difference between Molière and his dramatic teachers. In their hands the mask is fixed, so that the character affixed to the player may be recognized. For Molière, impressed as he was with the affixed character, it is only affixed, and to a living organism. The point of interest for him, and for us, is the point when the mask slips or falls, when the underlying man appears. This distinction is never absent from Molière's plays. All his situations gravitate to that moment when the mask is removed; he steers them towards this abandonment of the mask and consequent emergence of the natural. We must now inquire how far this is a principle on which his plays are actually built.

MICHAEL S. KOPPISCH

Dom Juan's Equal Opportunity Rivalry

Dom Juan is a figure of mythic proportions whom Molière appropriates and, in a very real sense, domesticates. Dom Juan's occasional heroic gestures, however, are undercut by the character's knavery. Like the vulgar bourgeois of other Molière plays, Dom Juan is self centered and obsessive; he fails to understand that what he really desires is a sign from others that he is who he wants to be. Only the submission of others to his will can convince Dom Juan of this. Each victory remains but an evanescent sign of his power and must swiftly be followed by yet another conquest.

To validate his own identity, the Don must compete with other characters in the play. The stake is high, the struggle to win fierce. Dom Juan is not the only one for whom the losses can be considerable. Elvire, Charlotte, and Mathurine, for example, all stand to win—or lose—their man. Sganarelle's freedom and money are on the line. Monsieur Dimanche thinks only of hard cash, but Francisque believes that his eternal salvation is threatened. Far from being intimidated by the odds against him, Dom Juan eagerly confronts them, sabotaging all order as he fights a diverse array of battles.

No more high-minded than Tartuffe, the Don does have a distinct set of beliefs that he unhesitatingly articulates. *Dom Juan* is a continuation of *Tartuffe*—Georges Couton calls it a "placet"—in which the protagonist

From *Papers on French Seventeenth Century Literature* 27, no. 53 (2000). © 2000 Gunter Narr Verlag Tübingen.

reflects upon what motivates him and speaks explicitly about the beliefs that underlie his behavior. Dom Juan's hypocrisy is more than just a means to an end. It becomes a creed. In what the Don says and in what he does there is a schematic element that has the effect of making the goals of his behavior and its results more immediately apparent. Tartuffe's presence infects Orgon's household with a contagion that causes Damis to sound very much like Tartuffe. Dom Juan incorporates that same leveling of differences between rivals into his credo and, with Monsieur Dimanche, goes so far as to explain it to his victim. A disease spreads when Tartuffe becomes part of Orgon's family. Dom Juan knowingly engages in biological warfare, attacking his rivals with the germ that Tartuffe carried.

Dom Juan is a despicable character. He lies, he cheats, he coldheartedly plays off one of his victims against another. He has even committed murder. Despite his malevolence, the Don has a certain engaging charm. Quick-witted and at times honorable, he often seems winningly spontaneous. Until, that is, he embraces hypocrisy. Although this is far from being Dom Juan's most heinous crime, it is the misdeed that turns the tide against him. Molière saves his protagonist's espousal of hypocrisy for the last act of the play, as if all the rest of Dom Juan's reprehensible behavior culminates in his cynical announcement that he will henceforth be a hypocrite. The Don's hypocrisy further emphasizes his direct lineage from Tartuffe.

Both Tartuffe and Dom Juan are motivated by their will to supremacy over others. As Lionel Gossman has shown, Dom Juan's histrionic displays of independence and freedom from all social and moral constraints hide his inability to do anything without first thinking of others with whom he must compete to prove to himself and to them that he stands above the law, above society's legitimate expectations, and ultimately, above even the will of God.

His pursuit of absolute superiority does not allow Dom Juan to distinguish among his rivals. This explains the curious combination of characters who cross the Don's path and the disjointed plot that their often unexpected appearances create. From Dom Juan's perspective, everyone is a rival to be subdued, and like Pascal's hunter, he loses all interest in his quarry once it has been bagged. Dom Juan's encounters with others are not only the occasion for him to demonstrate his superiority over them. They also represent a real danger that he will not appear in the eyes of others as all that he claims to be. What Dom Juan parades before his audience is a contradictory nature in which swaggering self-assuredness and a vulnerability born of deep-seated feelings of weakness come together.

Pierre Force has compared Molière's characters to patients on a psychoanalyst's couch, who, without realizing it, reveal their innermost truths to an attentive audience. Nowhere does this occur more vividly than in the famous speech in which Dom Juan defends his promiscuity. The speech builds in brassiness as the Don, with great bravado, wishes for other worlds where he might extend his sexual prowess: "je me sens un cœur à aimer toute la terre; et comme Alexandre, je souhaiterais qu'il y eût d'autres mondes, pour y pouvoir ètendre mes conquêtes amoureuses". For the bellicose lover, love is a battle to be won by courageous soldiers. Having won the battle, a newly energized Dom Juan, goes out in search of new conquests. The Don portrays himself here as a heroic figure, valorous in battle and never content to rest on past laurels.

Alongside the bombast in this speech runs a current of fecklessness that betrays a character quite different from the public Dom Juan. His language emphasizes his incapacity for personal commitment: "J'ai beau être engagé, l'amour que j'ai pour une belle n'engage point mon âme à faire injustice aux autres". Dom Juan is not just an unusually aggressive suitor. He cannot prevent himself from being attracted to all women: "je ne puis refuser mon cœur à tout ce que je vois d'aimable". His is a paradoxical form of impotence in which desire burns hotly but is always beyond his control: "Il n'est rien qui puisse arrêter l'impétuosité de mes désirs". So vehement is his desire that it leaves no time for Dom Juan to consummate a love affair. Rather than alluring Dom Juan, beauty overcomes him, and he surrenders to it: "la beauté me ravit partout où je la trouve, et je céde facilement à cette douce violence dont elle nous entraîne". This would-be Alexander shows himself to be exceedingly weak-willed.

Dom Juan does not distinguish among the women he tries to seduce: "Toutes les belles", he says, have the right "de nous charmer", and they all have "justes prétentions . . . sur nos cœurs". The right, though, is theirs, not his. The Don draws no distinctions among the relative merits of his potential partners, nor can he: "je conserve des yeux pour voir le mérite de toutes, et rends à chacune les hommages et les tributs où la nature nous oblige". What is normally a lover's free choice becomes for Dom Juan an obligation imposed by nature itself. Love invigorates Charlotte, Mathurine, and Elvire. It enervates Dom Juan.

Dom Juan's *divertissements*, to use Pascal's word, rely heavily for their success upon the cooperation of others, all of whom are, or quickly become, the Don's rivals. Of the play's twenty-seven scenes, Dom Juan appears in twenty-five, never alone. His servant, Sganarelle, is always at his side. The servant's role is to validate his master's superiority by telling him that it is real. If Sganarelle does not do this or if Dom Juan does not perceive that he is doing it, the servant, like everyone else, becomes a rival in the eyes of his master. When this happens, Dom Juan uses against Sganarelle the same tactic that he employs against others.

Dom Juan opens with one of the play's most perplexing scenes. Sganarelle proposes that by exchanging tobacco, everyone, presumably even a servant like himself, becomes an honnête homme. Desire, which normally promotes rivalry and the delineation of differences, is reduced, for "l'on court au-devant du souhait des gens" to offer others tobacco before it occurs to them to want it. In Sganazrelle's utopian vision, everyone is happy not because desire is fulfilled, but because everyone is the same. Dom Juan functions in precisely the same way as tobacco, except that while tobacco elevates its users, his pursuit of women lowers all his victims to the same level. As Sganarelle tells Gusman, who has come to urge Dom Juan to return to Elvire, "Dame, damoiselle, bourgeoise, paysanne, il ne trouve rien de trop chaud ni de trop froid pour lui".

Despite his pride in displaying how well he understands his master, Sganarelle is more than once subjected to Dom Juan's method of defeating his rivals: When called upon by Dom Juan to explain why, abandoning Elvire, "je suis parti", the fearful servant speaks of "notre départ" thereby identifying himself with the malicious behavior of his master. Later, as he seduces Charlotte, the Don again brings Sganarelle into the action by demanding that he confirm the girl's physical beauty and his master's honorable intentions. Dom Juan thus limits Sganarelle's individuality and independence of spirit by drawing him into the libertine's sphere and minimizing the differences that separate them.

Dom Juan often compels Sganarelle to act on his behalf or to accompany him on a perilous mission. It is Sganarelle who is commissioned to invite the statue to dinner, and he must stay in the room when the Commandeur comes to dine. That Dom Juan has earlier had his servant sit down at table with him alone indicates that more is at stake in these episodes than the Don's display for Sganarelle of fearlessness, courage, and superiority. Social mores dictate that master and servant not eat at the same table. By breaking this convention, Dom Juan de-emphasizes the difference between his servant and himself. When, in order to flee twelve horsemen pursuing him, Dom Juan suggests that Sganarelle disguise himself as the master, it appears that the two will, by exchanging roles, momentarily become identical. Sganarelle wisely declines the honor of dying for his master. In his subservience to another master, money—"Mes gages, mes gages, mes gages!" he cries out at play's end—Sganarelle manages to retain his identity against Dom Juan's relentless efforts to force his servant's thoughts and actions to coincide with his own.

Others are not nearly so fortunate. Having rid himself of Charlotte's fiancé, Pierrot, Dom Juan is about to conclude his successful seduction of her when her rival, Mathurine, appears. So schematically drawn are Dom Juan's tactics, the defeat of the two female rivals, and Sganarelle's intervention at the end of the scene, that the audience understands precisely how rivalry unfolds and undoes its victims. Charlotte and Mathurine have both been promised by Dom Juan that he will marry them, and both insist that he confirm his commitment in the presence of the other. He replies to each, sotto voce, that she is right and her rival wrong; he says the same thing to Charlotte that he says to Mathurine, treating them identically. To Mathurine, he declares, "Je gage qu'elle va vous dire que je lui ai promis de l'épouser" and to Charlotte, "Gageons qu'elle vous soutiendra que je lui ai donné parole de la prendre pour femme". The two young women, each in opposition to the other, sound more and more alike as they appeal to their "fiancé" to end the confusion:

> CHARLOTTE. Oui, Mathurine, je veux que Monsieur vous montre
>   votre bec jaune.
> MATHURINE. Oui, Charlotte, je veux que Monsieur vour rende
>   un peu camuse.
> CHARLOTTE. Monsieur, vuidez la querelle, s'il vous plaît.
> MATHURINE. Mettez-nous d'accord, Monsieur.
> CHARLOTTE, à Mathurine. Vous allez voir.
> MATHURINE, à Charlotte. Vous allez voir vous-même.
> CHARLOTTE, à Dom Juan. Dites.
> MATHURINE, à Dom Juan. Parlez.

Having undermined their capacity for certainty, Dom Juan extricates himself from the dilemma by telling both women that they must rely upon what they themselves know and believe: "Est-ce que chacune de vous ne sait pas ce qui en est, sans qu'il soit nécessaire que je m'explique davantage?" The nature of rivalry in Molière's theater is to destabilize the rivals' sense of who they are. Dom Juan's behavior in this scene demonstrates how that happens, and Sganarelle underscores the point, making it impossible for the women to trust language. He tells Charlotte and Mathurine that "Mon maître est un fourbe; [. . .] c'est l'épouseur du genre humain", but spying Dom Juan, who might overhear him, then says exactly the opposite: "Mon maître n'est point l'épouseur du genre humain, il n'est point fourbe". What are Charlotte and Mathurine to believe? Which of Sganarell's contradictory statements is true? Words no longer speak a reality on which the characters can rely.

Dom Juan reneges on his financial obligations in much the same way that he turns aside the appeals of women he has lured. Instead of refusing to receive his creditor, Monsieur Dimanche, the Don treats the rich bourgeois as a social equal. Having settled him into an armchair, to which only a noble would be entitled, Dom Juan makes no secret of the tactic employed to dispense with the troublesome creditor: "je ne veux point qu'on mette de différence entre nous deux", he tells Monsieur Dimanche. It is a small, if not altogether logical, step from the contention that Dom Juan and Monsieur Dimanche are socially equal to the conclusion that between creditor and debtor there is no difference and, therefore, no debt to be repaid.

Even when Dom Juan chooses to observe the social code of the nobility, he represents a danger to the well-being of his class. Dom Juan poses as the protector and friend of Dom Carlos. At the same time, he is Carlos's bitter enemy, the very man whom Elvire's brothers are hunting down to avenge their sister's disgrace. Friend and enemy, "grand seigneur" and "méchant homme", Dom Juan cannot but sow discord within the ranks of the nobility. Dom Alonse and his brother disagree over whether retribution should be exacted from Dom Juan on the spot or later. Their dispute goes to the core of what it means to be noble, and Dom Juan stands by quietly as the brothers quarrel about whether honor or life itself is more important. Once again, he has pitted his rivals against each other and shown the underlying fragility of the social order. That order will be hardpressed to survive the obliteration of distinctions so essential to it.

Dom Louis holds firmly to his belief in an aristocratic order and castigates his son for not living up to its values. Dom Juan's corruption so degrades the nobility that his father would prefer the "fils d'un crocheteur qui serait honnête homme" to a monarch's son "qui vivrait-comme vous [Dom Juan]". By this statement, Dom Louis tacitly admits that nobility has no essence separating it from the people and is, therefore, vulnerable to the attacks of those like his son. Dom Juan knows perfectly well how to neutralize the old man; he treats his noble father exactly as he has treated Monsieur Dimanche: "Monsieur", he says to Dom Louis, "si vous étiez assis, vous en seriez mieux pour parler". A meddlesome father with whom he shares social rank and a pushy bourgeois creditor present a similar problem for Dom Juan, and he dispenses with them in the same way.

When, along his path, the Don meets the hermit Francisque, a representative of his ultimate rival, God, his behavior remains perfectly consistent. He refuses to acknowledge the superiority of his rival and does what he can to shrink the immense difference between himself and God. Francisque is a poor hermit who offers advice to travelers and begs for alms to maintain his meager existence. Understanding that his charity will not bring the hermit over from God's camp, Dom Juan insists that Francisque swear in order to receive a gold coin. The poor man refuses, and Dom Juan disdainfully tosses him the coin, with the famous line, "je te le donne pour l'amour de l'humanitè". These words deny the implied precedence of a good act performed for the love of God over a gesture in the name of humankind alone. The Don's verbal adroitness carries the day, but his success is short-lived.

Whatever nobility of spirit Dom Juan might have gained from his boldness in the face of death disappears. When, at the end of the play, he assumes the mask of the hypocrite, he falls into the same trap he has all along set for his rivals: he loses his own personal distinction, becoming just another clone of the likes of Tartuffe. The Don reveals to Sganarelle that now the master no longer differs from anyone else; all wear the very same mask; "Il y en a tant d'autres comme moi, qui se mêlent de ce métier, et qui se servent de même masque pour abuser le monde".

Sganarelle disapproves of his master's behavior, but, from this point on, there will be none of the reversals of judgment that so often followed the servant's earlier outbursts of indignation. He rebukes the Don for claiming that "la voix du Ciel" prevents his returning to Elvire and entreats his master to repent once the Spectre appears. All of a sudden, Dom Juan's most effective strategy for nullifying his rivals has lost its potency. In becoming like all those he has decided to imitate, he subjects himself to the same punishment that will, in the end, be theirs. There is, once again, a right and a wrong, a true and a false. Dom Juan is on the wrong side of these re-instituted norms and will suffer the consequences.

For a moment, the order that Dom Juan has shattered is restored. United against him, "tout le monde est content"—except Sganarelle. He alone is still miserable, for the wages his master owes him remain unpaid. As Dom Juan confronts his rivals, one after the other, he, like Tartuffe, tries to break down their individual identities. He does not always succeed. Pierrot never really relents in his opposition to Dom Juan. Francisque does not abandon his faith. Elvire finally gives up the hope of having Dom Juan and, for altruistic reasons, counsels repentance. Sganarelle is now firm in his indignation. The rapid movement from episode to episode overshadows Dom Juan's repeated failures. As the curtain falls, Sganarelle's complaint—"Mes gages, mes gages, mes gages!"—bears witness to the impossibility of Dom Juan's realizing his project of absolute superiority over others. Sganarelle's real master is money, not Dom Juan. The Don's attempt to control his servant in order to identify himself through the eyes of others fails for a flimsy reason—hard cash. Similar and equally unsuccessful attempts will find their way into later plays by Molière.

ROBERT MCBRIDE

Dom Juan

The second play which Molière wrote during what I have termed the
Tartuffe period was *Dom Juan ou Le Festin de Pierre*. Although it seems at first
sight to treat a subject less complex than that of *Tartuffe*, it has proved
nonetheless to be even more enigmatic: the nineteenth-century critic Jules
Lemaître aptly described it as 'étrange . . . bizarre . . . hybride . . . obscure en
diable'. It was immediately attacked on its appearance at the Palais-Royal by
the *dévots* who had reacted so violently to the satire of religious hypocrites in
Tartuffe. Rochemont and the Prince de Conti in particular accused Molière
of committing an outrage against decency and piety. It was also defended by
the well-meaning but ineffectual *Réponse aux Observations Touchant Le Festin
de Pierre* . . . and the more stringently argued *Lettre sur les Observations d'une
Comédie du Sieur Molière intitulée Le Festin de Pierre*, the author of which was
certainly one of the Molière's intimate friends, if not the playwright himself.
This initial division of opinion about the intention of the play persists today;
it has either been regarded as not essentially subversive in design, or as
thoroughly impious in intention.

If Molière's intentions have been seen as obscure, his reasons for
writing the play in the first place would appear to be vague and ill-defined.
Most *Moliéristes* have tended to accept the traditional account of why Molière
should have been attracted to the legend. According to this account, *Dom*

From *The Sceptical Vision of Molière*. © 1977 Robert McBride.

Juan was hastily improvised as an *oeuvre d'occasion* after the unexpected interdiction of *Tartuffe*: in addition, Molière did not choose to treat the theme himself, but was persuaded by the members of his own troupe to write a play on the theme of the legend, in order to benefit from its current popularity in Paris. At first sight this may appear acceptable, since the original theme of Tirso de Molina's *El Burlador de Sevilla* had been used by Dorimond in his *Le Festin de Pierre ou Le Fils Criminel* (performed in Paris in 1661, but published in 1659) and by Villiers in a play of the same title (performed in Paris in 1659 and published the following year). It was left to G. Michaut to point out the weakness of this assumption. He argued that when Molière wrote his own version of the legend, four and six years after other Parisian theatres had first performed the contemporary French versions, the theme of Don Juan could scarcely be said to be still in vogue. It is highly improbable, to say the least, that Molière was unaware of this fact, or that he should have needed to rely on the suggestions of others for the choice of a play to succeed *Tartuffe*. As the successful *directeur* of a troupe of actors, he must have known that he needed a play in reserve to meet the contingency of the controversial *Tartuffe* being banned. The source of this traditional account was La Serre, writing not in 1665 but in 1734, in his *Mémoires Sur la Vie et les Ouvrages* de Molière. In fact, it is clear that he attributed the manner of origin of Villiers play to Molière, for the former recounts in his preface how his actors encouraged him to write a French version of the legend, when they saw the popularity enjoyed by the current Italian scenarios of the *commedia dell'arte*.

The reason why Molière chose to treat the legend of Don Juan at this particular time seems to me to be found elsewhere, and is bound up with the experience to *Tartuffe*. It is of the utmost importance to remember the context in which the play was written. *Dom Juan* was first performed in February 1665, and was most likely finished if not conceived during the period from September 1664 to January 1665, that is after the interdiction of the first *Tartuffe* and the *Premier Placet* to the King in August 1664. In other words, the play was cast in its final form, and performed, at a time when its author was profoundly and personally committed to his unrelenting struggle against the *dévots* who had secured the interdiction of *Tartuffe*, thereby threatening to ruin his theatrical career. To remember this is neither to read into the play an extraneous autobiographical meaning, nor to add a false dimension to a work of art, but merely to remember that whichever subject Molière turned to at this time would be treated by a man ruled by genuine indignation and bitter disappointment. One might of course deny this connexion between art and life: 'art is art . . . because it is not life.' But in the case of *Dom Juan*, the contemporaries of Molière were fully aware of the connexion between his experiences after *Tartuffe* and the present play. There is a suggestive passage in the anonymous reply to Rochemont's strictures of *Dom Juan* which underlines the continuity of inspiration which they saw between the two plays: 'A quoi songiez-vous, Molière, quand vous fites dessein de jouer les tartufles? Si vous n'aviez jamais eu cette pensée, votre *Festin de Pierre* ne seroit pas si criminel.' The experience of *Tartuffe* is at the origin of *Dom Juan*, shaping Molière's treatment of the legend's structure, and recasting it in its own terms. The continuity with *Tartuffe* accounts for the original manner in which Molière handles the theme of Don Juan, and in order to determine this more clearly, it will be necessary to consider very briefly the use made of the legend by the dramatists before Molière.

The dramatic theme of Don Juan originated with Tirso de Molina's play *El Burlador de Sevilla* (1630), and was quickly taken up by both the *commedia sostenuta* and the *commedia dell'arte* in Italy, as is shown by Cicognini's *Il Convitato de pietra* (before 1650), and an extant scenario, *L'Ateista fulminato*, probably written about the same times as Tirso's play. It has been convincingly established, however, that Molière's version of the theme owes nothing to these plays, but rather draws for the material details of plot and character on the plays of Dorimond and Villiers. These two authors used a common source—another Italian version of the legend by Giliberto, *Il Convitato de pietra*, written around 1652, but unfortunately not extant.

The plays by Dorimond and Villiers are very similar in structure and in plot, and differ only occasionally with regard to the order and length of scenes. It will be helpful to give a concise summary of their versions.

Act I   Dom Juan overhears Amarille expressing her love to Dom Philippe and immediately plans to supplant him by force. Before executing his plan, both dramatists give a lengthy discussion between the Dom's valet (in Dorimond he is called Briguelle, in Villiers Philipin) and his father about Dom Juan's *libertin* behaviour. The concluding scene of Act I consists of a confrontation between father and son. In both plays, Dom Juan behaves callously towards his father: in Dorimond he insults him, and in Villiers he strikes him.

Act II   Dom Juan attempts to seduce Amarille, is discovered, and kills her father before escaping. Amarille's long lament is followed by Dom Philippe's resolve to avenge himself on his rival. The archers begin to search for Dom Pierre's murderer.

Act III   This opens with a long soliloquy by a Pèlerin on the tranquility
           of solitude. Dom Juan and his valet appear, each disguised in the
           other's clothes. The valet tells Dom Juan that he has been the
           cause of his father's death from grief. Dorimond's Dom Juan
           shows genuine remorse at this news, whereas Villiers' hero is
           content to reproach destiny which persecutes him. Dom Juan
           offers the Pèlerin money in exchange for his habit; when he
           refuses, he forces him to change clothes with him using threats of
           violence. Disguised as a pilgrim, Dom Juan meets his enemy
           Dom Philippe, and under the pretext that heaven forbids the
           wearing of arms in a holy place where they go to pray, he
           persuades Philippe to relinquish his sword and then reveals his
           true identity. In Dorimond, he merely humiliates his rival; in
           Villiers' play he kills him.

Act IV   Master and valet are shipwrecked and rescued by villagers. Dom
           Juan seems to repent sincerely for his past misdeeds and gives
           thanks to providence for having saved him. But at the sight of a
           shepherdess, he promptly yields once again to his natural
           inclinations and seduces her. In Dorimond, after the seduction he
           glimpses a rustic wedding and abducts the bride. Act IV ends with
           Dom Juan and his valet coming to a tombstone, on top of which
           sits the shadow of the murdered Dom Pierre. Dom Juan insults
           the memory of his victim, and to provoke his superstitious valet,
           issues a cavalier invitation to supper which the shadow accepts.

Act V   This begins with the traditional supper scene. The shadow
           arrives, and in Dorimond delivers a lengthy moralizing tirade of
           forty-two lines. Dom Juan insults it, and accepts its invitation to
           supper that evening at the grotto where the Commander (Dom
           Pierre) is buried. In Dorimond there is a scene with Amarille and
           Dom Philippe, in Villiers this is replaced by the wedding scene
           where Dom Juan abducts the bride. The second appearance of
           the shadow follows the traditional pattern of the legend. Dom
           Juan draws his sword in order to kill it, and is struck down by
           divine vengeance.

It will be seen at once that Molière's play adheres to the basic
structure of the legend, at least as it was transmitted to him by the two
contemporary French versions. Apart from traditional features of the legend,
such as the seduction of the fiancée and of the peasant girls, the humiliation
of the poor pilgrim, the murder of Dom Pierre and the intervention of divine

justice, Molière also accepts largely the traits of his hero from Dorimond and Villiers, although he does modify him slightly. The *libertin* of these plays, who nevertheless continues to believe in a supreme monarch of the universe, becomes in Molière's play a cavalier atheist, in the style of many contemporary French noblemen. But the principal difference lies in the manner in which the plays are constructed. Although the two contemporary versions are diffuse and romanesque melodramas, full of excessive action and violence, their authors have endeavoured to make them into *pièces bien écrites* and to provide fairly logical motivation for the sequence of the plot. By comparison, Molière's schema is bare to the point of stark simplicity, with little or no emphasis on actions external to the minds of the protagonists. Dom Juan does not kill the Commander before our eyes; instead of two lengthy scenes at his tomb there is an extremely brief discussion at the tombstone between master and valet; and the intervention of the statue at the end is so rapid that it seems designed to have little or none of the theatrical effect which it is intended to produce in the other two French plays. Such differences in treatment probably account for the standard judgement that the play is incoherent, and that it gives the impression of a series of *tableaux* hastily strung together.

In spite of this undeniable impression of incoherence, there is a recognizable unity in Molière's version of the legend, a unity which is provided not by the traditional and 'set' episodes of the theme as in Dorimond and Villiers, but by the developing relationship between Sganarelle and Dom Juan, who therby acquire a complexity and depth not to be found in the other French versions. This structural and thematic innovation by Molière gives rise to important considerations which arise only with his treatment of the material. Who, for example, is to be taken as Molière's *porte-parole*, Sganarelle or Dom Juan? Or, as Michaut has suggested, does Molière convey his intention through the secondary characters of the play instead? Bound up with this problem is the question of whether Dom Juan is a comic figure or immune from comedy. The basic contention of this chapter will be that *Dom Juan* has an organic and thematic unity not to be found in the other versions, a unity which resides in the comic principle underlying the relationship of man and master, which at once sheds light on the questions raised above and roots the play firmly in the philosophic preoccupations of *Tartuffe*.

In my analysis of the play, I propose to devote as much attention to Sganarelle as to Dom Juan. It is probably true to say that most critics have concentrated largely on the eponym, doubtless because Molière's treatment of the *libertin* was considered to indicate clearly his intention in writing the play, and also because he seems at first sight to enjoy a manifest superiority over the other protagonists. But it is important to note that the role of the valet was played by Molière himself, whereas La Grange played the part of the hero; and in many respects it is the valet who, like Orgon in *Tartuffe*, provides the key to Molière's attitude towards his *libertin*. As A. Simon has remarked perceptively '. . . [Molière] a choisi le meilleur poste pour rester en vue de son héros; pour le voir et être vu de lui.' It is also noteworthy that out of twenty-seven scenes in the play, Sganarelle is on stage for twenty-six of them. This represents the single greatest innovation by Molière in his treatment of the legend; in the other French versions, the valet appears merely as the stock character of farce, whose function is to add set pieces of comedy to the melodrama. At all times he is nothing more than an episodic and subservient type, whereas in Molière's play he has an importance at least equal to that of Dom Juan.

The role of Sganarelle is not only central to the comedy; in his opening speech on the virtues of 'tabac' he illustrates the main theme of the play. It is not just another proof of the play's incoherence, or merely 'un hors d'oeuvre d'actualité,' as Arnavon supposed it to be; the valet's burlesque reasoning exemplifies that subtle transmutation of trivial reality (here *tabac*) into an object worthy of veneration, which illustrates the basic paradox at the heart not only of the most elementary type of comedy but also of the philosophy of *Tartuffe*. Sganarelle has a natural penchant for argumentaion, but what is even more important to note in this scene is the skilful manipulation of appearances and reality, which not only forms the basis of his nature, but also defines his paradoxical relationship with his master. For Sganarelle is simultaneously engaged in the service of Dom Juan *and* in satirizing him to others. After having told Gusman the unpleasant truth about his master, he then adds that 's'il fallait qu'il en vînt quelque chose à ses oreilles, je dirais hautement que tu aurais menti'. Dom Juan is the catalyst who provokes criticism and acquiescence, truthfulness and lying on Sganarelle's part, and the instantaneous conversion of the one into the other. Without having seen his master, we glimpse the element that links his valet to him; this is none other than Sganarelle's nature, which is grounded on the expedient conversion of appearances into reality and vice versa.

Their ambivalent relationship is fully illustrated in their first dialogue in the second scene, when Dom Juan tries to elicit his valet's reaction to the abandonment of Elvire: 'Que t'imagines-tu de cette affaire?' he asks. When Sganarelle expresses his suspicion that some new infatuation has been responsible for the Dom's latest infidelity, he is asked again for his reaction to such a state of affairs: 'Et ne trouves-tu pas que j'ai raison d'en user de la sorte? The truth is that Dom Juan is not at all interested in Sganarelle's answers as such, for his questions are more quizzical than purposive. He certainly does not envisage any possible change of his conduct depending on Sganarelle's response. The valet's answer is equally as paradoxical as his master's question—'Assurément que vous avez raison, si vous le voulez; on ne peut pas aller là contre. Mais si vous ne le vouliez pas, ce serait peut-être une autre affaire'—and is born of his instinctive fear of his master ('la crainte en moi fait l'office du zèle,' he had said to Gusman in the first scene) and of the fundamental characteristic of his own nature, his predilection for argument, which was noted above. Right and wrong depend apparently for him not on any objective principle, but on his master's will. But Dom Juan sees the expediency of such an answer; nothing less than an unambiguous and *truthful* reply from Sganarelle will satisfy him. Thus liberated from his fear of reprisals for being honest, Sganarelle can now express his utter disapproval of the Dom's recent actions. The latter has now achieved what he planned in his initial question: having isolated for a brief moment the true Sganarelle, that is to say the valet too deeply steeped in traditional moral beliefs to share the libertine notions of his master, he can now afford himself his principal pleasure of overthrowing Sganarelle's absolute condemnation of his conduct. He achieves this by a brilliant rationalization of his own *libertinage*, and his argument proceeds in three successive stages: 'Quoi? Tu veux qu'on se lie à demeurer au premier objet qui nous prend . . .' To be faithful to one's fiancée is to cut oneself off from all objects of beauty, to die in one's youth; constancy and fidelity are therefore only the prerogative of fools, who blind themselves to the fact that beauty has the right to charm us wherever we are; it is therefore unjust to refuse to recognize the beauty and merit of others by withholding one's affections.

Dom Juan is not at all concerned with a moral justification of his conduct, but is merely content to demonstrate to his bewildered valet that reasons can be effortlessly adduced against the traditional moral standards of fidelity, honour and chastity, which thereby lose that absolute character with which Sganarelle has invested them. He does not even trouble himself to set these reasons in opposition to those of his valet; they are incidental to his objective of creating doubt in the mind of Sganarelle about the moral code by which people are supposed to live. He is in fact so successful in his reasoning that Sganarelle can only say 'Ma foi, j'ai à dire, et je ne sais que dire; car vous tournez les choses d'une manière, qu'il semble que vous ayez raison; et cependant il est vrai que vous ne l'avez pas. J'avais les plus belles pensées du monde, et vos discours m'ont brouillé tout cela'.

Sganarelle cannot argue with him now on the plane of reason; all he can do is to point to the indubitable fact that his master has *not* succeeded in making the reality of evil evaporate: '. . . je conçois que cela est fort agréable et fort divertissant et je m'en accommoderais assez, moi, s'il n'y avait point de mal'; Dom Juan does not like to be reminded of this unpalatable fact, or of Sganarelle's warning 'que les libertins ne font jamais une bonne fin'. At this point in the play, he would seem to illustrate the principle of the comic, the *disconvenance* which, according to the *Lettre sur la Comédie*, can be seen in contradictory actions proceeding from the same source. It is therefore the dramatist's function to engineer scenes in which such *disconvenance* manifests itself to the spectator. But in the case of Tartuffe, the hypocrite has himself taken over the role of the dramatist as he exploits mischievously the contradictions in language and reason to an extent which threatens to afford him immunity from comedy. Dom Juan is also one of these superior characters whose behaviour is grounded on his ability to manipulate at will the principles by which society coheres. He has triumphantly 'proved' the basis of his morality to Sganarelle, at least in reason and in theory. But how profound is his assurance of the *rationale* of the code which he professes? Does it command complete assent from his will and emotions as well as from his theory of *libertinage*? His reply in this scene to Sganarelle's warning about the disastrous end of *libertins* is highly revelatory in this respect: 'Holà, maître sot, vous savez que je vous ai dit que je n'aime pas les faiseurs de remontrances. This sharp reaction to his valet's homily is certainly proof that his self-assured impunity from traditional moral scruples is purely verbal, and not emotional. It is surely supremely comic that the *libertin* who prides himself on being able to persuade others that black is white and that white is black, should give the impression that he has so succumbed to his own verbal virtuosity as to affect disbelief in the supernatural, of which he seems nonethless to have an emotional conviction! But he is doubly comic in this scene in his remonstrance to his valet; for has he not repeatedly asked Sganarelle to give him his true opinion about his conduct? Now he says that he has previously warned Sganarelle of his dislike of 'les faiseurs de remontrances!' Does he then seek mere approval from his valet? No, because he has just refused the latter's compliant acquiescence. He can only threaten to impose silence on his valet by force, as Sganarelle is used to emphasize the one weakness in the *libertin* credo. Sgnarelle manages however to prolong his satire of Dom Juan's disbelief, by deftly employing the tactic of the *libertin* against him. He does this by reverting to oblique condemnation:

> Je ne parle pas aussi à vous, Dieu m'en garde! Vous savez ce que vous faites, et si vous ne croyez rien, vous avez vos raisons; il y a de certains petits impertinents dans le monde, qui sont libertins sans savoir pourquoi, qui font les esprits forts, parce qu'ils croient que cela leur sied bien; et si j'avais un maître comme cela, je lui

dirais fort nettement, le regardant en face: 'Osez-vous bien ainsi vous jouer du Ciel, et ne tremblez-vous point de vous moquer comme vous faites des choses les plus saintes?'

The *libertin* who delights in providing specious reasoning to justify himself is the victim of Sganarelle's speech, which can always be defended on the grounds that it is concerned with others, and not with Dom Juan. *A bon entendeur salut.*

It is opportune then to raise the question of Molière's attitude to Dom Juan in this scene. It is obviously impossible to identify the author's views solely with one protagonist, since each makes use in turn of the comic principle which is the basis of Molière's comic art. But the fact remains that Dom Juan, in spite of his self-assured appearances, fits into the same comic framework here as does Orgon; the latter is profoundly comic to the extent that he presumes to overstep the bounds of human nature by his overweening desire to know the unknowable. Dom Juan does precisely the same thing in this scene; the basis for his libertine behaviour can only be the absolute denial of divine retribution in an after-life, and it is such a denial which promises to free him from the scruples of traditional morality. Yet Dom Juan can never be absolutely freed from the weakness of human nature (i.e. those emotions and passions which combine to keep such belief in a supernatural after-life alive). If he could be assured in all equanimity of the truth such a denial, it would be unnecessary for him to react so testily to Sganarelle's moralizing. Sganarelle's function in this scene and in the rest of the play is to bear out the impossibility of such a denial by provoking answers from his master which suggest a loss of libertine composure on his part.

Such an interpretation of the thought underlying this scene would seem to be confirmed in an interesting way by La Mothe Le Vayer's similar attitude to *libertins* such as Dom Juan. In discussing *Tartuffe*, I pointed out that both he and the dramatist share common conceptions of reason and humanity which they take as the bases of moral conduct. It is such a reasonable and humane ethic which prompts even the Sceptic to condemn *libertins* such as those described by Sganarelle in this scene, in one of his *Discours ou homilies académiques* (1664). In one homily, *Des Injures*, he writes '. . . y a-t-il rien de plus ordinaire aujourd'hui que les blasphèmes injurieux contre la Divinité, qui véritablement les souffre quelquefois impunément pour les punir en un autre temps avec plus de rigueur, ou plus exemplairement?' This corresponds exactly to the triple *avertissement* given by Sganarelle to his master in this scene about the inevitability of divine retribution for the *libertins*. Whilst it is highly improbable that Le Vayer and Molière believed in a supernatural retribution for the deeds and misdeeds of this life (both in fact seem to have considered the existence of evil as the most cogent argument against the idea of a providence controlling human destiny), their attitude to seventeenth-century *libertins* is to be found *behind* these ironic phrases, in their strong denunciation of such *poseurs*. Both arguments rest on the contradiction perceived between the *libertins'* belief in the superiority of their enlightened attitude and the real motivation for such *libertinage*, which is none other than the vainglorious wish to be distinguished from the common herd: hence Le Vayer's strong condemnation of such unnatural arrogance:

> Mais n'est-ce pas une chose qui doit faire horreur, qu'on affecte de paraître impie, afin de passer pour esprit fort, dans la plus grande faiblesse d'entendement où l'on puisse tomber, qui est celle qui naît de l'irréligion? En effet il se trouve des gens qui n'ont point d'autre motif pour paraître libertins, pour se moquer de ce qu'il y a de plus Saint au-dessus des nues, et pour jeter insolemment des crachats contre le Ciel, qui leur retombent misérablement sur le visage; que cette folle pensée d'être plus hardis et plus clairvoyants que les autres. . . . Certainement c'est être bien aveugle de sa vanité, c'est affecter une liberté bien esclave de sa passion, et ce n'est pas merveille qu'on rogne les ailes à des personnes qui ont le bec si pointu et si offensant, qu'ils ne font pas difficulté de le porter outrageusement contre l'auteur de tout bien, de leur propre Etre, et de toute la Nature.

This passage bears comparison with Sganarelle's bold lesson to the *esprits forts*, part of which was quoted above: 'C'est bien à vous, petit ver de terre, petit myrmidon que vous êtes . . . c'est bien à vous à vouloir vous mêler de tourner en raillerie ce que tous les hommes révèrent. Pensez-vous que pour être de qualité . . . que tout vous soit permis. . . Apprenez . . . que le Ciel punit tôt ou tard les impies. . . .

The second scene of this Act is therefore of great significance, because it is what Sganarelle says and does here which seems to provide the best insight into Molière's attitude towards his *libertin's* actions in the rest of the play. It is the valet, with his apparently weak arguments and innate pusillanimity, who will best expose the libertine pose of Dom Juan. It is, I believe, a basic misunderstanding of the importance of the role of Sganarelle that has largely contributed towards confusion concerning Molière's intentions. We find, for example, that B. A. Sieur de Rochemont anticipates much later ciritcism when he objects that Molière ought to have entrusted the defence of morality and religion to a character equal in argument to Dom

Juan. The author of the *Lettre sur les Observations* answers this charge effectively by saying that had Molière replaced Sganarelle by someone more obviously suited to theological debate, the play would no longer be a comedy but a 'conférence sur le théâtre'. Sganarelle has certainly much in common with his master, notably a remarkable dexterity in juggling with the values of appearances and reality. But to suggest, as recent criticism has done, that he is nothing more than a *coquin* enslaved by Dom Juan, is to confuse his use of the comic principle (the manipulation of appearances and reality which offers both the only way of escape from domination by his master and the triumph of the comic spirit over the *libertin)* with the morality of that principle. In other words, we are surely intended by Molière to enter into complicity with the comic hero (whether he be Sganarelle or Dom Juan), without stopping to consider the morality of his actions. The conclusion of such critics as A. Adam is that since neither protagonist is edifying, the intention of Molière must remain rather dubious. But in fact Molière is merely using the apparent gross inferiority of the valet as a veil beneath which his satire of the *libertin* here is all the more complete and damning. There is no doubt that this satire gains in pointedness by astute deflection rather than by direct application. This is not to say that Sganarelle is the 'âme simple et pure' which J. Arnavon made him out to be, standing against the villainy of his master. He is rather the character in the play who reflects *par excellence* the strength and ultimately the weakness of the *libertin* in the eyes of Molière, and not just 'ce rôle de conscience dérisoire et servile'.

In the following scene Elvire arrives to confront Dom Juan with his act of infidelity towards her. His avowal of surprise at seeing her parallels the moments in *Tartuffe* whenever the mask of 'l'âme de toutes la mieux concertée' involuntarily falls to expose the real face behind it. The *libertin* is disconcerted here because Elvire has penetrated the aristocratic decorum surrounding his infidelity, and he can therefore only ask his valet to present the reasons for his departure to her. Sganarelle's garbled answer 'Madame, les conquérants, Alexandre et les autres mondes sont causes de notre départ' exposes the comic side to the Dom in this scene. The *libertin* who prides himself on the conherence (whether simulated or real) of his actions, is dependent on the incoherence of his valet's inventiveness. Elvire underlines his manifest confusion, by suggesting to him the role he ought to play in such a situation. In order to re-establish in the eyes of others the myth of his coherence, a paradox of the most extreme kind is required to justify his confusion. This is duly supplied when we hear the sinner reply in saintly terms worthy of his great *confrère*, Tartuffe, '. . . que je n'ai point le talent de dissimuler, et que je porte un coeur sincère'. He is correct verbally, for he scrupulously refuses the role of the hypocritical *galant* which Elvire has suggested to him. Instead, he substitutes the higher, more intangible form of deception which consists precisely in telling the truth; the infidelity which Elvire has suspected is perfectly true, but he gives the wrong reasons for it, rationalizing his action by pretexting 'un pur motif de conscience'. He knows that she is not deceived by this stratagem, just as Tartuffe knows that Cléante has not succumbed to his casuistical reasons for appropriating Orgon's *donation*. But both also know that, objectively, their fictitious 'obedience' to the divine will nullifies for the moment the accusation of deceit brought against them. Such an intellectualization of their position gives them the necessary time and freedom to manoeuvre. Elvire, like Cléante, can do nothing against such consummate evasiveness, but as a last resort she imprecates divine retribution for his actions. Apparently the meeting with Elvire has ended in the Dom's victory; yet as she invokes heaven for a second time, Dom Juan can do no other than divert his thoughts from the possibility of punishment to his most recent project of seduction. In reality, however, there is here more than a hint of the loss of composure and self-assurance discernible in the previous scene, on which the comic aspect of the *libertin* is based.

In the scenes with the *paysannes*, we see an illustration of the code elaborated by the Dom in Act I, the 'donjuanism' which he summarized in two points: 'la beauté me ravit partout où je la trouve', and 'je ne puis refuser mon coeur a tout ce que je vois d'aimable'. To follow this instinctive desire to conquer each new beauty is the principle that governs his nature, and in each of his manifestations of passion the Dom is sincere, because he follows the imperious call of that nature. But in order to be sincere to such a credo, he must, by this very nature, be insincere to the individual to whom he spontaneously avows his love, because his sincerity has a purely relative value and is predestined to be transferred continually to someone else. The *paysanne* Charlotte, like Sganarelle in Act I, illustrates the effect of this fundamental ambiguity in his character when she says in answer to his blandishments that '. . . je ne sais comment vous faites quand vous parlez. Ce que vous dites me fait aise, et j'aurais toutes les envies du monde de vous croire . . . je ne sais si vous dites vrai ou non, mais vous faites que l'on vous croit'.

Dom Juan's enslavement to the senses has been seen as providing a comic contrast with his self-confessed awareness of what he is doing. This is in fact yet another facet of the paradox of lucidity and cecity which make up his nature; but whereas the contrast may be said to exist in theory in this scene, in the theatre we have at this point an overwhelming sense of his ability to appear simultaneously as what he is and what he is not. It is this total paradox underlying his nature which is emphasized here, rather than one particular aspect of it. For Dom Juan is so much a prisoner of his paradoxical nature, that he must be sincere and insincere at one and the same time. Sganarelle, in a mocking comment, shows that he does indeed understand perfectly the truth of his master's nature: when the Dom protests that he is different from all the other plausible courtiers of whom the *paysannes* have heard, and that he will certainly marry Charlotte, he unwisely invokes Sganarelle's testimony to him: the valet confirms his affirmations whilst insinuating his discreet contradiction: 'Il se mariera avec vous tant que vous voudrez'. For Charlotte, marriage is the ultimate and unimpeachable proof of a suitor's sincerity; to Sganarelle's practised eye, marriage is but the culmination of the insincerity of a master whom he has described as 'un épouseur à toutes mains'. Sganarelle once again allows us to glimpse momentarily his superiority over his master, as he indirectly exposes for all the see (but not Charlotte!) that true side to the Dom's nature which he is here at pains to hide.

The dialogue between the two *paysannes* and the Dom in Scene 4 provides an excellent example of the way in which the latter manipulates appearances and reality. Called upon to declare unequivocally his love for the one or the other (having promised marriage to both), he extricates himself with a virtuosity which matches perfectly the ballet-like, sequence of *répliques*. He begins his defence with a lie to each *paysanne*. To Mathurine he says that Charlotte wished to marry him, but that he could not because of betrothal to her. He tells the corresponding lie to Charlotte. He follows this with a second lie to each in turn, pretexting that 'no amount of persuasion will convince her that she is wrong'. Having convinced each of the blind obstinacy of the other in maintaining that he promised to marry her, he can now afford to hazard the truth in jest.

He tells each in turn to wager that the other will maintain that he promised to marry her. He has succeeded in diverting attention temporarily from himself, as both now start to quarrel with each other, but the stratagem threatens to rebound on him as both coalesce in pressing him for a definite answer. Dom Juan once again escapes with a masterly *échappatoire*: each, he tells them, has an inner assurance either of the truth or of the error of the claim she makes. It is therefore superfluous for him to try to add to such certainty. He himself inadvertently sums up the principle which has governed the entire dialogue and which he has exemplified so well when he says that 'Tous les discours n'avancent point les choses.' Words, he seems to tell the very people whom he has just deceived by his *belles paroles*, can only possess relative certainty, because their latent and unsuspected meanings can be exploited so easily.

Once again Dom Juan has, to all appearances, secured a resounding triumph of resourcefulness and plausibility. But the last word in the *imbroglio* belongs again to Sganarelle, as he gives a kind of glossary of 'donjuanism' to the *paysannes* at the end of this scene. He profits from his master's momentary absence to tell them the truth about him, a truth which the Dom partially overhears as he comes back to fetch his valet:

> Mon maître est un fourbe; il n'a dessein que de vous abuser, et en a bien abusé d'autres; c'est l'épouseur du genre humain, et . . . [il aperçoit Dom Juan] Cela est faux; et quiconque vous dira cela, vous lui devez dire qu'il en a menti. Mon maître n'est point l'épouseur du genre humain; il n'est point fourbe, n'a pas dessein de vous tromper, et n'en a point abusé d'autres. Ah! tenez, le voilà; demandez-le plutôt à lui-même.

Having instantaneously converted his negative criticism into positive attributes, Sganarelle can now explain carefully to his master that the world is full of calumny, and that the *paysannes* are to disbelieve everything adverse about him. The Dom's own technique of evasion by paradox has again been surreptitiously turned against him and he, like his victims in this scene, has no means of redress against someone who can convert the unpleasant truth into its opposite with such impeccable ease. We admire Sganarelle for his irreproachable *tour de force*, and at the same time share the ironic perspective into which Molière has placed Dom Juan's frustrated attempt at seduction.

The discussion in Act III, Sc. I, between master and valet on medicine and on the existence of heaven, hell and retribution in after-life, has been integrated by Molière into the framework of the legend, and gives the play a philosophical character quite out of keeping with the two French versions. Once again it is the role of the valet which seems to me to provide the key to the significance of this controversial scene. Tradition has viewed the credulity and *naïveté* of the valet as nothing more than a butt for the cynical atheism of his master. Once again it was probably Rochemont who first gave currency to this notion when he described Sganarelle in this scene as 'un extravagant qui raisonne crotesquement [sic] de Dieu, et qui, par une chute affectée, *casse le nez à ses arguments*; un valet infâme, fait au badinage de son maître, dont toute la créance aboutit au Moine bourru . . .'

It is not difficult to see how such a view of the valet's role leads to the conclusion that this scene represents another disquieting triumph for the Dom's scepticism over the well-intentioned but hopelessly inadequate Sganarelle. But such an interpretation tends to overlook the fact that Sganarelle is made to express these naïve views first and foremost for the purpose of comic dialogue; it is important to take into account the extent to which this exigency influences the mode of expression of his ideas, before accepting them literally as a solemn formulation of his own creed. Just as he has previously argued in this scene, in an (unsuccessful) attempt to stimulate a response from his master, that doctors are effective because they manage to kill suffering patients more rapidly than the disease, so he now moves away from medicine to the one subject which he feels can be guaranteed to unloose his master's opinion, religion. Here, therefore, as elsewhere throughout the play, he acts primarily as an ironic and burlesque spectator of his master, both eliciting his opinions and sitting in comic judgement on them. When he has catechized Dom Juan, and has made the not unexpected discovery that the *libertin* professes disbelief in heaven, hell and immortality, (in Act I, Sc 2, 11.114-5 he tells us that 'je sais mon Dom Juan sur le bout du doigt'), he reacts with simulated and pious concern: 'Voilà un homme que j'aurai bien de la peine à convertir. Et dites-moi un peu, le moine bourru, qu'en croyez-vous, eh?'

Of course he does not intend to covert him, any more than he intends to believe in the 'moine bourru'. But since he has exhausted his store of questions on orthodox matters of faith, he resorts to such traditional superstitions to provoke the Dom's exasperated reaction. Eventually he is successful in prompting a sceptical retort from his master: 'Je crois que deux et deux font quatre, Sganarelle, et que quatre et quatre font huit'. This *boutade* has been seen as furnishing one of the articles of Molière's own beliefs; but it is surely impossible either to attribute this to Molière, given the comic context in which it occurs, or to see it as the formalized credo of the *libertin*. Dom Juan is both curiously amused and vaguely irritated by Sganarelle's buffoonery, and he takes the line of least resistance to the importunate questioning which his cavalier riposte offers to him. But hoping to silence the valet by this lapidary remark, he merely provides him with the pretext he has desired so avidly for his discourse on the harmony of man's being, which he takes as proof of his divine origin. The fact that part of his bizarre argument is probably a burlesque version of Pierre Gassendi's treatise on man can scarcely be taken as an indication that Molière shares the philosopher's view about the nature of things. Nevertheless the central part of Sganarelle's argument does seem to indicate the verdict of comedy on the *libertin's* beliefs: 'Il faut avouer qu'il se met d'étranges folies dans la tête des hommes, et que, pour avoir étudié, on est bien moins sage le plus souvent'.

This is no less than a summary of that *folle sagesse* which was, in *Tartuffe*, comedy's conclusion on Orgon's futile attempt to pronounce dogmatically on things which elude the grasp of man. Dom Juan's conduct is based upon such a belief which, although diametrically opposed to that of Orgon, is rooted in the same kind of dogmatism which consists in asserting that a non-empirical proposition is absolutely true or untrue. Rather than dismiss peremptorily the existence of the supernatural, it is better, say Sganarelle and the so-called *raisonneurs*, to be wise within the bounds permitted by our human condition. This will therefore exclude any pretence to absolute knowledge, and will most certainly include a degree of *folie*, which is nothing else than the modest confession of one's own ignorance about such transcendent matters. Sganarelle well illustrates such wisdom, by arguing empirically about the relationship between cause and effect, and then choosing to fall grotesquely on his face just as he reaches the climax of his argument for the harmonious functioning and interaction of the human organs. The burlesque *raisonneur's* self-contradicting 'method' of argument offers an interesting parallel with Le Vayer's *Petit discours chrétien sur l'Immortalité de l'áme* (1637), where he begins by promising, as confidently as Sganarelle, to prove irrefutably the immortal nature of the soul by no less than thirty-three syllogisms of 'apodeictic' value. His conclusion is predictably analogous to that of Molière's scene, namely that 'La grande connaissance fait souvent le même effet que l'extrême ignorance, d'où vient qu'on a toujours remarqué que les plus savants étaient ceux qui avouaient le plus franchement la faiblesse de l'esprit humain. . .'

If Molière and Le Vayer appear to condemn those *libertins* like Dom Juan who fail to recognize this truth of human nature, they also show the absurdity of presuming to demonstrate beyond doubt such an obscure matter as that of the immortality of the soul. Sganarelle's deliberate fall is symbolic not only of his knowledge of what can and cannot be achieved by human wisdom, but also of the futility of trying to prove the improvable. And Le Vayer likewise condemns those Christian apologists (like Silhon, Cotin, Yves de Paris) who maintain the ability of natural reason to prove a belief such as that of the immortality of the soul. 'Au lieu qu'on s'est promis de forcer les plus incrédules à la reconnaissance d'une vérité si importante, par la seule puissance de notre raison, je crois qu'il vaut mieux avouer ingénument sa faiblesse, et la captiver doucement sous l'obéissance de la Foi.'

I do not believe that this scene, or indeed the play as a whole, allows us to say anything of a more specific nature than this about its treatment of religious beliefs. However, a belief such as that outlined above by Le Vayer is consonant with the ideas on religion expressed in *Tartuffe*, and would identify Molière's views in this scene neither solely with Sganarelle, nor with Dom Juan, although Sganarelle's views have more in common with *la docte ignorance* of scepticism than Dom Juan's presumption. This is confirmed by the fact that the valet, although apparently imbued with less intelligence than his free-thinking master, nevertheless glimpses the contradictory essence of man's nature, namely that it is compounded of reason and unreason at the same time. Seen in this light, is it not the *inhuman* Dom Juan who is comic in Molière's eyes in this scene, and not Sganarelle after all?

The following scene, in which *Un Pauvre* plays a central role, is no less ambiguous than the previous one. Although the equivalent scene exists in Dorimond and Villiers (Dom Juan stops a *Pèlerin*, and forces him to forfeit his religious habit), there is a complete absence of the overtly tendentious features of Molière's scene, where Dom Juan commits sacrilege as he offers the hermit money on condition that he swears an oath. His Dom Juan is here no longer just the *libertin* whose independence of religion incites him to maltreat a religious. More obviously than hitherto in Molière's play, he assumes the role of evil incarnate, a Mephistopheles who issues an unequivocal challenge to the good man to recognize the supremacy of an ethic based on self-indulgence and expediency over self-abnegation and moral principle. The hermit resists Dom Juan's temptation to swear in order to gain the proffered *louis d'or*, acceptance of which would imply dissatisfaction with the impoverished state that providence has allowed him. Does such a result represent the triumph of good over evil? G. Michaut at least thought so when he wrote that 'Le Pauvre reste invaincu, dédaigneux des railleries et des séductions . . .' But the implications of the scene seem more complex than such a straightforward judgement would allow. The essence of the scene is contained in three questions, the first asked by the *Pauvre*, the others by Dom Juan. Having indicated to Sganarelle and his master the path to be taken through the forest the *Pauvre* asks:

	Si vous voulez me secourir, Monsieur, de quelque aumône?
DOM JUAN	Ah! Ah! ton avis est intéressé, à ce que je vois.
LE PAUVRE	Je suis un pauvre homme, Monsieur, retiré tout seul dans ce bois depuis plus de dix ans, et je ne manquerai pas de prier le Ciel qu'il vous donne toute sorte de biens.
DOM JUAN	Eh! prie le Ciel qu'il te donne un habit, sans te mettre en peine des affaires des autres.

Molière here crystallizes dramatically the general problem of the play, and also returns in a more forceful and insistent manner to one of the principal reoccupations of *Tartuffe*; to all appearances innocence, goodness and devoutness suffer on earth, whereas the *libertin* Dom Juan prospers with impunity. It is the questions of the *libertin* to the hermit which are used by Molière to bring this situation into even sharper focus:

DOM JUAN	Quelle est ton occupation parmi ces arbres?
LE PAUVRE	De prier le Ciel tout le jour pour la prospérité des gens de bien qui me donnent quelque chose.

DOM JUAN	Il ne se peut donc pas que tu ne sois bien à ton aise?
LE PAUVRE	Hélas! Monsieur, je suis dans la plus grande nécessité du monde
DOM JUAN	Tu te moques; un homme qui prie le Ciel tout le jour ne peut pas manquer d'être bien dans ses affaires.
LE PAUVRE	Je vous assure, Monsieur, que le plus souvent je n'ai pas un morceau de pain à mettre sous les dents.
DOM JUAN	Voilà qui est étrange, et tu es bien mal reconnu de tes soins . . .

I do not think that Molière's answer to the problem raised in this scene is to be found either in the faithful endurance of the *Pauvre* or the truculent incredulity of Dom Juan, but rather in the philosophical vision which imagines and dramatizes such an encounter. In their opposition, the two characters symbolize the kind of question and answer about providence that has always taken place in the minds of those people who have found it difficult, as the author of *Tartuffe* and *Dom Juan* apparently found it difficult, to accept the proposition that 'Just are the ways of God; and justifiable to Men.' Molière is raising such a question, and leaving it without a categorical answer, for such an answer appears to be unobtainable. This tentativeness on his part does not mean that we cannot discern the general tendency of his thought in the dramatic movement of the scene. It is clear that as the dramatist and spectator see this scene, the *Pauvre* is utterly defeated by the Dom's probing scepticism which points out the manifest discrepancy between his fervent praying and his abject state—he is defeated, that is to say, *objectively* and as far as human logic is concerned. He can only 'justify' this discrepancy between his faith and his penury by trusting blindly in the kind of subjective conviction which Milton's lines express so well:

> All is best, though oft we doubt,
> What th'unsearchable dispose
> Of highest wisdom brings about.

To what extent does Molière use Dom Juan to illustrate the problem behind the creation of the scene? There are sufficient indications throughout the play to show that his *libertin* posture is treated in a comic or an ironic way for us to know that Molière does not entirely approve of his ideas; certainly there is not the slightest sign that Molière approves in any way of his actions towards the *Pauvre*. But Molière has *permitted* Dom Juan to go with impunity to the furthest limits of provocative impiety and odious conduct towards the *Pauvre*, not presumably because he approves of his attitude, but because he wishes to place the more urgently before us the ineluctable fact that all too frequently those who live without due regard for sanctity or piety or humanity do indeed flourish, whereas those whose lives are spent in devotion and selflessness, although infinitely more admirable than the Dom Juans and Tartuffes of this world, are inexplicably exposed to suffer their ridicule.

The sceptical implications of this scene are close to one of Le Vayer's problems which he asks and 'answers' in his *Problèmes Sceptiques* (1666). To his question 'Y a-t-il des Prières désagréables à Dieu?' his first answer is 'Non,' but he qualifies this by saying that one must always be careful not to attribute too much to prayerful intercessions. In his second answer, 'Oui,' he quotes with irony the opinion of those who allege that it is ridiculous to pray to someone who knows what we desire even before we ask. Dom Juan is used by Molière in a similar questioning way, as he, like Le Vayer, implies the objections in the path of a simple belief in the Christian theodicy of the *Pauvre*, whose faith and prayers are left unanswered by heaven. The scene ends with the same ironic implication that is found in a passage of Le Vayer's *De l'Ingratitude* where he points out that the sun shines on the wicked just as on the good: 'Tant s'en faut, que la main du Tout-puissant se raccourcisse sur le sacrilège et sur l'impie, que souvent il leur multiplie ses grâces, afin de donner mieux à connaître l'excellence de sa nature et l'immensité de sa bonté.'

The attempt by Dom Juan to sow the seeds of doubt in the minds of others concerning what they hold as true or false, to provoke hesitation on their part with regard to moral issues, is illustrated still more explicitly in the following scene. There he goes to the rescue of Dom Carlos who has been attacked by thieves. Critics have found difficulty in reconciling the cynical and amoral Dom Juan of the previous scene with the 'aristocratic' hero who spontaneously hazards his life for an unknown person. Once again, the entire conception of this episode is original to Molière's play: the brother of Dom Carlos recognizes the Dom as the seducer of their sister Elvire, and demands immediate vengeance to satisfy their honour; Dom Carlos, who before this revelation of Dom Juan's identity had shown himself by his remarks equally as zealous as his brother Dom Alonse in his pursuit of the *libertin*, is now caught in a moral dilemma. He is torn between his 'reconnaissance de l'obligation' which he owes to the man who has just saved his life, and his legitimate 'ressentiment de l'injure'. His eventual solution to the dilemma is of a temporizing nature; he puts off the opportunity to satisfy his family's honour, and is forced into the paradoxical position of having to defend his erstwhile enemy against his pragmatic brother Dom Alonse.

Once again the moral confusion into which Dom Juan throws others is used by Molière to illustrate dramatically one of the basic tenets of scepticism, which is that ethical codes can merely have a relative and not absolute value, because of the situational contingency to which they are exposed. Before Dom Alonse recognized Dom Juan, his brother was as absolute as he in his determination to apply the rigid aristocratic code to the case of Dom Juan: he could not have envisaged any possible circumstance which would change his mind. The debate which ensues between the brothers is the conflict between the absolute nature of Alonse's conception of the aristocratic code—(circumstances such as one's enemy saving one's life do not change the eternal obligation of avenging one's honour; as honour is infinitely more precious than life, it follows that we owe nothing to an enemy who has saved a life which he has deprived of all honour)—and the willingness of Dom Carlos to take Dom Juan's bravery into account and modify the immediate demands of honour. In the same *opuscule* from which I have just quoted, Le Vayer illustrates the kind of morally ambiguous situations where it is impossible to apply a strict rule elaborated in advance. After having stated the traditional moral doctrine of the scholastics and Aristotle, which decrees the separate natures of *vice* and *vertu*, he advances cases where it is somewhat more difficult to distinguish between them. As 'une autre difficulté de Morale' he evokes the moral dilemma which underlies the scene in Molière's play, namely, 'si une injure postérieure peut tellement effacer le bien-fait précédent, que nous en demeurions quittes sans tomber dans l'Ingratitude.' Like Dom Carlos, he is inclined to attribute a lower degree of moral value to an action based solely on expediency rather than on gratitude for the original service: '. . . vu que l'obligation est la plus ancienne, il y faut satisfaire, et puis on avisera au reste.' This is in fact the compromise which Dom Carlos chooses: he will show his gratitude to the Dom by delaying his pursuit of vengeance, but will nonetheless carry out his duty ardently: he tells Dom Alonse that regarding his recent benefactor and ancient enemy '. . . je lui ai une obligation dont il faut que je m'acquitte avant toute chose. . . . la reconnaissance de l'obligation n'efface point en moi le ressentiment de l'injure'.

In Le Vayer's dialectic on moral paradoxes, as well as in Molière's dramatization of the practical difficulties to which they give rise, the kind of inflexible approach of a Dom Alonse is to be avoided in all situations as he estimates whether the 'bienfait' is greater or not than the loss of honour occasioned by its author. Dom Carlos, on the other hand, eschews such attempts to weigh and compare the respective moral values of actions and pleads above all for '. . . une valeur qui n'ait rein de farouche, et qui se porte aux choses par une pure délibération de notre raison, et non point par le mouvement d'une aveugle colère.' So too does Le Vayer, in terms reminiscent of those used by Molière's character: 'C'est être ingrat et injuste tout ensemble, de vouloir user des compensations en des choses qui ne sont pas de même poids, et dont l'une doit toujours prévaloir sur l'autre, si nous ne donnons beaucoup plus à la passion qu'à ce que nous prescrit le droit usage de la raison.'

Dom Carlos makes a 'right use of reason' in this scene which would certainly be acceptable to the Sceptic. Unlike his brother, he has not prejudged Dom Juan's moral character, and events confirm that no one, not even the *libertin*, is totally incapable of performing a good action. The juxtaposition of the Dom's heroism with his cynical temptation of the *Pauvre* is an extreme paradox which only serves to illustrate and confirm Le Vayer's conviction in his *opuscule De l'Ingratitude*, with which this scene has so much in common: '. . . le divorce du vice et de la vertu n'est pas si formel, que l'un et l'autre ne se puissent jamais rencontrer dans un même sujet.'

In the scene with the *Pauvre* and in the encounter with Elvire's brothers. Dom Juan does not appear in a comic light; in those scenes he is exempt from comic irony within the universe of the play, as Molière uses him to demonstrate firstly the strong objections to a belief in a controlling providence operative in human affairs, and secondly, the indefinable nature of the *libertin*-hero which can elude facile attempts to situate it in a precise moral category. But in Scene 5 of this Act Dom Juan and Sganarelle only are on stage—an indication that the Dom's attitude will once more be put into an ironic perspective by his valet. As they find themselves in front of the tombstone of the *Commandeur* whom the Dom has killed, the statue lowers its head. The naïve valet is nevertheless sufficiently open-minded to admit that he *does* see the *Commandeur* move. It is only the stubborn preconception of the *libertin*, that he *will* not and therefore *cannot* permit the supernatural to have an objective existence, which makes him persist in denying the valet's observation. Above all, he is intent on keeping up the myth of his own superiority over the rest of humanity in Sganarelle's eyes. He is comic here because although he is convinced that he is superior to everybody, he cannot (because he will not) see what even the meanest creature can see plainly. He whose boast is that he lives by his senses will not accept the irrefutable evidence which they offer to him!

In the following scene (Act IV, Sc 1) Sganarelle repeatedly stresses to Dom Juan the manifestation of the supernatural '. . . que nous avons vu des yeux que voilà'. The comic aspect of Dom Juan refusing to assent to such a physical sign of the reality of the supernatural is now underlined in his reaction to Sganarelle's renewed warning about divine retribution. His threat to the valet is certainly the most violent and terse which he has yet uttered: 'Écoute. Si tu m'importunes davantage de tes sottes moralités, si tu me dis encore le moindre mot là-dessus, je vais appeler quelqu'un, demander un nerf de boeuf, te faire tenir par trois ou quatre, et te rouer de mille coups. M'entends-tu bien?' Once more the self-assured free-thinker can only have recourse to physical threats as he seeks to keep up his image in front of Sganarelle—and once more Sganarelle eludes adroitly his attempt to dominate him completely by a *réplique* which barely conceals its irony under its compliance: 'Fort bien, Monsieur, le mieux du monde. Vous vous expliquez clairement; c'est ce qu'il y a de bon en vous, que vous ne m'allez point chercher des tours; vous dites les choses avec une netteté admirable'.

Dom Juan can only momentarily re-establish his former superiority in Scene 3, where he makes the most elementary use of polite appearances to conceal his impecunious state from M. Dimanche. Nevertheless his *tour de force* in making his *bourgeois* creditor wish to be his debtor for the obsequious way he has received him does elicit our admiration. But the juxtaposition of the confident Dom Juan in this scene, and the reflective and disconcerted *libertin* of Scene 1, underlines the brittle nature of his superiority, which now depends less on his ability to explain away the existence of the supernatural than on his mere cleverness in profiting from his aristocratic supremacy in order to dominate others.

Even this superior attribute is about to be removed from him in principle, if not in practice, as his father, Dom Louis, arrives to denounce and disown him. This scene corresponds to the traditional scene in Dorimond and Villiers between Dom Alvaros and the hero in Act I. Nevertheless, there is a critical difference both in content and treatment of the confrontation of father and son in Molière's version. In the two other French plays, the scene is composed of the father's conventional moralizing and Dom Juan's filial recalcitrance, whereas in Molière's play this is reduced to an extended speech by the father on the nature of the difference between true and false nobility.

It is clear throughout the play that the Dom's actions are largely motivated by an overwhelming sense of personal superiority over others, which he believes is conferred on him by his aristocratic caste. The theme of this scene has been curiously prefigured in Act I, Sc. 1: Gusman, Elvire's servant, retains the traditional idea about nobility when he says of Dom Juan's infidelity 'Un homme sa qualité ferait une action si lâche?' Sganarelle's reply is worthy of note: 'Eh! oui, sa qualité! La raison en est belle, et c'est par là qu'il s'empêcherait des choses!' The valet is here drawing attention to the paradoxical position of the *libertin*, which the latter exploits to the full: taking the social benefits belonging to nobility (prestige, esteem, etc.), his *libertinage* provokes him to contradict flagrantly the moral code which Dom Louis ascribes to it. In his lengthy speech on true and false nobility, Dom Louis stresses three basic points: it is not sufficient for a nobleman to lay claim to aristocratic origins if he has no *vertu* to accompany them; we have a right to share in the *noblesse* of our ancestors only if we accept the obligation incumbent upon us to imitate their *vertu*; judged by this criterion, Dom Juan falls lamentably short of the requisite behaviour and has no right whatever to call himself a nobleman.

Once again Molière appears to draw on ideas similar to those of La Mothe Le Vayer for this scene and its underlying thought. In a letter entitled *Des Gentilshommes* (1660), the latter underlines Dom Louis' central preoccupation: any fault or merit is independent of one's social status and is one's personal responsibility: '. . . les belles actions de nos prédécesseurs ne servent guères à notre gloire si nous n'y coopérons. . . .' And Dom Louis dwells pointedly on the same truth when he asks his son '. . . qu'avez-vous fait dans le monde pour être gentilhomme? . . . nous n'avons part à la gloire de nos ancêtres qu'autant que nous nous efforçons de leur ressembler'. But often, continues Le Vayer, the noble actions of one's forefathers only throw into sharp relief the mediocrity of their successors:

> . . . mais il n'arrive pas toujours, que ceux qui ont cette puissante recommendation du sang, possèdent le mérite personnel absolument requis pour se la conserver. Souvent au contraire l'on remarque qu'ils en sont tellement dépourvus, que les vertus de leurs ancêtres ne servent qu'à mieux faire reconnaître les défauts qu'ils ont, et combien ils sont dissemblables à ceux, dont ils se contentent de porter les armes et le nom. . .

Similarly Dom Louis tells his son that the glory and honour of his ancestors only serve to illuminate the infamous nature of his actions. Both Le Vayer and Dom Louis agree that the only sure foundation for true nobility is to be found in virtuous conduct on the part of those at present bearing an ancestral title.

The common idea of *noblesse oblige* might seem to be a banal coincidence in thought between Molière and Le Vayer. That might well be the case, were not the same sceptical conclusion from this idea common to both, making mere coincidence highly improbable. In his *opuscule*, Le Vayer asks a question which relates pertinently to this scene in Molière's play: how does one explain the fact that a renowned hero may engender an infamous son? He answers by placing this problem in the wider context of natural development and also uses it to illustrate one of his perennial theses. Such a tendency towards irrational degeneration in the species is by no means uncommon in nature: 'Comme les meilleures viandes et les plus estimées, font les excréments qui ont le plus d'infection et de puanteur; les personnes les plus héroïques engendrent les plus vicieux et les plus méprisables de leur siècle.' To the Sceptic, such an apparent aberration forms an intrinsic part of the unpredictable and irrational processes of nature, as well as a salutary corrective to man's presumption in trying to interfere with natural laws. Dom Louis has ardently attempted to mould nature into his own pattern: he has importuned heaven to give him an heroic son who would be the pride of his life, and he laments the result: 'Hélas! que nous savons peu ce que nous faisons quand nous ne laissons pas au Ciel le soin des choses qu'il nous donne, quand nous voulons être plus avisés que lui, et que nous venons à l'importuner par nos souhaits aveugles et nos demandes inconsidérées.'

In so doing, he has inadvertently come close to that very *hubris* which impels Dom Juan to flout the laws of nature. J. Doolittle has commented on this point in a penetrating manner: 'He has presumed to tamper with the will of Heaven, to set himself, by means of the formal activity of prayer, above his human lot.' It has been customary to regard Dom Louis as a serious character who expresses Molière's own opinion against Dom Juan's misconduct. It has always seemed natural to identify ourselves and therefore Molière against the filial ingratitude of Dom Juan—and thence it is but one step towards seeing the father as Molière's *porte-parole*. Yet it seems that Molière has insinuated an implicit level of irony into Dom Louis' speech which deprives him of the noble Cornelian status which has sometimes been assigned to him. L. Gossman however has noted that although Dom Louis equates natural virtue with nobility—towards the end of his peroration he says that he would prefer the son of a porter whose conduct was *honnête* to the infamous son of a monarch—he does not nevertheless advance a moral code based on nature but rather 'a conventional social code designed to maintain the superiority of some members of society to other members of society. He lays down, in other words, standard signs by which a nobleman may be known and therefore estimated (imitation of the *gloire* of one's ancestors, etc.), all of which tend to elevate nobility by according to its members the special prerogative and obligation of being virtuous. One will always be able to distinguish a virtuous noble from a virtuous *roturier* by reason of the peculiar and ancestral *éclat* which underlines his excellence.

Molière, like his friend La Mothe Le Vayer, would seem to have been too independent a thinker not to grasp the intrinsic absurdity of such reasoning, which is certainly implicit in the attempt of Dom Louis to justify the separate social identity of the aristocratic class. Besides, his theatre is too full of satire against those who desire either to rise above their social station or to convince others of the intrinsic advantages of nobility for him not to assent to Le Vayer's opinion in *Des Gentilshommes* that there is no such thing as the existence of nobility because '. . . ne sommes-nous pas tous sortis d'un même principe? Y a-t-il vilain qui n'ait son extraction de quelque Patriarche? Ou Prince qui ne vienne d'un Planteur de Vigne?' Dom Juan provides the *raison d'être* of this scene, as he provokes this speech on the nature of nobility from his father; he is therefore the agent used by Molière for the discreet exposure of archaic conventions to which even an essentially sympathetic character like Dom Louis clings, and thus remains true to his function in the play as a catalyst of truth and falsehood, appearances and reality.

From the end of Act IV onwards, the importance of the supernatural elements of the play is much more evident than hitherto: the first appearance of the Commander's statue at supper (Act Iv, Sc. 8) follows closely on the warnings of imminent retribution given by Dom Louis and Elvire in Scenes 4 and 6. The reality of divine retribution becomes increasingly inevitable as the Dom appears more and more successful in inverting and perverting the basic human values of filial affection and fidelity; there is only one more step for him to take before he divests himself completely of every human attribute, and he crosses this when he feigns religious conversion to his father, in Act V, Sc.1. This paradox in his own behaviour is brought about not merely for sacriligious and libertine reasons, but rather because he knows that it corresponds to an objective inversion of moral values which has taken place in the world at large: '. . . l'hypocrisie est un vice privilégié, qui, de sa main, ferme la bouche à tout le monde, et jouit en repos d'une impunité souveraine'. These lines crystallize the more extreme confusion of truth and falsehood within the character and the play; in fact they go beyond mere confusion and point to the more permanent paradox of the fusion of truth and error, symbolized by the deference shown to hypocrisy by those who are at the same time aware that it is grounded in falsehood. Formerly, whilst Dom Juan had been able to invest untruth with the appearance of truth, he had only been able to do it long enough to deceive Elvire, the *paysannes* and Sganarelle for a time: he could not do it permanently, because such a situation would automatically have meant the defeat of the forces of morality and good within the play, and the virtual end of the drama. But at this point of the play, no such conflict of good and evil is possible, according to the words of Dom Juan, because society at its worst is composed of hypocrites and scheming rogues, and at best, of those who acquiesce tacitly in the deceptions practised by the numerous Dom Juans in their midst, as well as of those who, like Dom Louis and Elvire and her brothers, penetrate the mask of deception but cannot ensure that its wearer is brought to justice. It is as though Dom Juan's specious inversion of values had been suddenly extended to embrace everyone, and all the moral values of society, neutralizing the forces of good. La Rochefoucauld might have summed up such a situation by saying that 'le monde n'est composé que de mines'. But although everyone has suffered a morally adverse effect from their encounter with Dom Juan, forcing them to contradict in some degree the moral codes by which they profess to live, such a conclusion would be in direct contradiction with the dramatic situation of the play. Dom Juan has not, at this point, triumphed; he has just been denounced by Dom Louis, by Elvire, and is still being pursued by Dom Carlos and Dom Alonse. If human retributive justice fails, there is still the certainty of a dramatic conflict between the divine representative of goodness and truth, the statue, and Dom Juan, the hyprocite. The suspension of the human drama, so strongly implied in Dom Juan's words and actions here, in turn implies that his creator was himself brought to the point where he saw no real opposition to his *libertin*.

Molière has thus permitted Dom Juan to push his deception to its farthest limit (religious hypocrisy), and the *libertin*, like his predecessor Tartuffe, knows the impunity such hypocrisy affords him from human retribution. He illustrates this as he takes refuge in casuistry in front of Dom Carlos (Scene 3). The paradox of Dom Juan the unassailable *libertin-dévot* must therefore call forth a *dénouement* responsible for a still greater paradox—namely, that of the defeat of the *libertin* who cannot be defeated from within the universe of the play. The supernatural *dénouement* implies the recognition by Molière of the Dom's invincibility (or rather the invincibility of his subterfuge), and is thus necessarily and logically motivated by the evolution of Dom Juan's character. This is confirmed by a comparison between Molière's *dénouement* and those of Dorimond and Villiers; whereas in these versions the *dénouement* retains its traditional character of a spectacular set piece which the audience has come to expect as of right, and which is superimposed without due regard for the evolution of the hero (so much so that one has the impression that the plays have largely been conceived as a corollary to the *denouement*), Molière reverses this conception and the *denouement* becomes both the only possible ending to the play and, in the vision of the playwright, at least the symbol of the re-affirmation of justice over falsehood if not of his actual belief in such a possibility.

The fact that in Molière's play the evolution of the hero and the conception of the *denouement* are essentially independent of the legend (although the general structure is loosely retained), means that Molière's condemnation of his *libertin* is based upon something other than a desire to emulate the traditional ending. That he does finally condemn and disapprove of the Dom's impenitent attitude has never been seriously doubted, except by critics so blinded by prejudice as the Sieur de Rochemont. It is equally clear that Molière does not condemn him for the sake of expediency, in an attempt to dispel some of the doubt that might have subsisted as to his religious orthodoxy after *Tartuffe*; had this been his central aim, he could surely have succeeded in doing it in such an unequivocal way that would have been understood by *dévots* and *honnêtes gens* alike. Henri Gouhier seems to have suggested an answer to this question when he writes that 'La déshumanisation du personnage s'accroît . . . à mesure que l'on approche du souper. Molière takes care to alienate the *libertin* progressively from the ties and responsibilities which bind him to his fellow-men: he has nothing but scorn for those in distress, like the *Pauvre*: he does not pay his debts to his social inferiors; he seduces and marries as he pleases; he abandons Elvire whom he has abducted from a convent; he rejects the natural bonds of filial affection; he puts religion to his own perverse ends. If he sets himself above the values by which his fellow human beings live, he seeks in his Promethean independence to reject their God in order to take his place himself. His refusal to admit God's existence (thereby admitting the existence of someone greater than himself) is a transposition onto the plane of myth of his refusal to consider his fellows as anything other than instruments to do his pleasure. By intensifying the moral flaw of the *libertin* in such a way. Molière has made his final attitude towards Dom Juan perfectly clear. To quote once more from Gouhier's excellent article; 'Le Commandeur a donc attendu que Don Juan soit Tartuffe pour le foudroyer: le Ciel punit ceux qui se moquent de lui. Mais Don Juan se moque du Ciel pour se moquer des hommes. . . Or la déshumanisation de Don Juan pose justement la question d'une religion de Molière fondée sur l'accord de la nature et du christianisme. . .'

Gouhier's conclusion to his article is that in punishing Dom Juan, Molière was probably in agreement with Christian humanism, rather than with secular humanism divorced from Christianity. But whilst it is true that the Christian humanist's code of behaviour will certainly include man's humanity to man, he also shares this belief with the free-thinking humanist, in spite of the spiritual inspiration of the former's belief, and the purely human origin of the latter's. The Sceptic Le Vayer belongs completely in spirit, if not in profession, to the second of these groups, and it is interesting, in view of the deep similarities between his thought and that of Molière's play, to note the importance which he attaches to man's avoidance of ingratitude to his fellows. In *De l'Ingratitude*, which was quoted above, he writes that '. . . l'homme est un animal merveilleusement enclin à l'ingratitude, puisque les mêmes choses qui l'obligent le plus à la reconnaissance, opèrent si diversement sur son esprit, et font des effets si contraires.' This is all the more surprising, says the Sceptic, since gratitude is the one quality so deeply ingrained in humanity that all the diverse systems of ethics have agreed that it is fundamental to the preservation of the human race and of society. He evokes the examples of people like Dom Juan who fly defiantly in the face of this categorical imperative of humanity 'comme si tout le genre humain leur devait quelque hommage, et qu'ils ne fussent obligés a rien.' Such behaviour is condemned by all natural laws, and is, to the *libertin* Le Vayer, certainly the greatest sin against humanity and religion. In *Dom Juan* Molière illustrates that ingratitude to humanity which is the cardinal sin to the *libertin érudit*, by making it so heinous that only a supernatural intervention can provide an adequate retribution. Le Vayer adopts precisely the same mythical form of condemnation for it as Molière has done in his play: 'Mais lorsqu'on afflige sciemment ses Bien-faiteurs, qu'on ruine comme le lierre ce qui a servi d'appui, et qu'on fait périr ceux à qui l'on est redevable de sa conservation c'est a l'heure qu'on encourt la malédiction divine. . .' No condemnation is too extreme for those like Dom Juan who, by their wilful refusal to carry out their most basic obligations to their fellows, weaken the fabric of human society and fly in the face of all human and divine imperatives to duty. Molière thus fuses harmoniously humanist standards which ought to govern man's actions with the requirement of a supernatural *dénouement* demanded by the legend, and so accords it both a highly literal and a mythical significance.

In conclusion, it would seem that *Dom Juan* is a much less impious play than it has frequently been considered to be. Written during the fierce polemics surrounding *Tartuffe*, it has owed its impious reputation as much to the controversial circumstances of that play as to the sceptical aura of the legendary figure of Don Juan. Yet the view of W. G. Moore, on the other hand, to the effect that there is nothing in the conclusion of the play to show that Molière did not agree with Pascal in his condemnation of the *libertin* is arguable if in my view an overstatement. Molière's last word on his subject would appear to be at once more ambiguous and nuanced than either of these views.

Nuanced and ambiguous, because the real hero of the play is Sganarelle and not, after all, Dom Juan, in spite of contrary appearances. It may well be said, as seventeenth-century critics did in fact say, that the opinions of the valet are equally if not more subversive from a religious point of view than those of his master—but this does not take into account the comic principle which underlies and shapes the attitude of the protagonists. All the burlesque and extravagant postures of Sganarelle are only of importance to the extent that they elicit or provoke some kind of response from Dom Juan. Their *raison d'être* is, therefore, dramatic before it is moral. Sganarelle provides Molière with a means of acquiring distance from the *libertin*, in a way that would make identification with what the latter says and does totally impossible. How could the author of the defiant posture which Dom Juan strikes accept them seriously, and without reservation, when they are inevitably satirized almost simultaneously by the unassailable irony of Sganarelle? Even though Molière may conceivably have assented mentally to some of Dom Juan's opinions, how could he ever divorce them from the caustic corrective supplied instantaneously by the comic vision? The converse is also true—if he is detached sufficiently from his *libertin* to view him in Sganarelle's ironic perspective, he is also sufficiently detached from the valet to see him as a character playing a part in a comedy assigned to him by his creator. And as the creator of the play, he sees the individual comedies which they play consciously or unconsciously, as well as the comedy of their mutual relationship. In his creative detachment he perceives the manifest inability of the Dom to disprove or to refute definitively the existence of the supernatural: his every reaction to its intimations betokens a man who would like to dogmatize about it, and who does indeed in a certain limited way, but who lacks that ultimate rational proof to secure his assumption and his existence as a *libertin*. Sganarelle also seeks to ground his existence rationally, attempting to prove the immortality of the soul and the existence of God. The *folie* of the first issues in inhumanity, and he comes to grief. The *folie* of the second issues in extreme humanity in all its ignorance of metaphysical matters, and survives. He does survive because the comic vision springs from the refusal to accept one's strictly finite and creaturely nature, and emphasizes man's need to disabuse himself about the limitations of humanity.

'Il nous faut abestir pour nous assagir' writes Montaigne in his *Apologie*; the survival of the fool and the destruction of the wise man is not only a theatrically spectacular endorsement of his maxim, but also an extremely searching comment upon the significance and resilience of the comic vision.

RONALD W. TOBIN

Rehearsal and Reversal
in Le Bourgeois gentilhomme

In 1670, Suleiman Aga, Mutaferraca, ambassador of Mohammed IV, ruler
of the Turkish empire, began to receive guests, above all ladies, in his Paris
lodgings and to serve them what became known as the "liqueur arabesque,"
that is, coffee. In his desire to please his female friends, he went so far as to
provide sugar to sweeten the bitter brew. Not long after that, offering coffee
at social gatherings became *à la mode*, thus making the change in taste from
when Molière, Racine, Boileau, and others were accustomed to retire to a
caberet to drink wine, to the eighteenth century when Diderot,
Beaumarchais, and Voltaire frequented the cafés to seek stimulation of their
faculties from the "somber, exceedingly cerebral liquor"—coffee.

There is a legend that Louis XIV was offended by the irritation
displayed by Mutaferraca when the French monarch did not rise to accept a
letter from Mohammed IV, and that *Le Bourgeois gentilhomme*, with its spoof
of fancy-dress Turks, was written by Molière to avenge the affront. Whatever
the truth of the matter, Mutaferraca became Mustapha Raca of Molière's
comedy-ballet. However, his contribution to French culture—coffee—does
not appear in the play. What we do have, in a gastronomical way, is the
banquet of act IV, scene I, that forms a microcosm of the peculiar structural
patterns of the drama: what we will look at first is, to borrow the title of Jean-
François Revel's book, *Un Festin en paroles*. The passage, spoken by the
nobleman Dorante, is as follows:

From *Tarte à la crème: Comedy and Gastronomy in Molière's Theater*. © 1990 Ohio State University
Press.

Vous n'avez pas ici un repas fort savant, et vous y trouverez des
incongruitès de bonne chére et des barbarismes de bon goût. Si
Damis s'en était mêlé, tout serait dans les règles; il y aurait
partout de l'élégance et de l'érudition, et il ne manquerait pas de
vous exagérer lui-même toutes les pièces du repas qu'il vous
donnerait, et de vous faire tomber d'accord sur la haute capacité
dans la science des bons morceaux, de vous parler d'un pain de
rive, à biseau doré, relevé de croûte partout, croquant
tendrement sous la dent; d'un vin à sève veloutée, armé d'un vert
qui n'est point trop commandant; d'un carré de mouton
gourmandé de persil; d'une longe de veau de rivière, longue
comme cela, blanche, delicate, et qui sous les dents est une vrai
pâte d'amande; de perdrix relevées d'un fumet surprenant; et
pour son opéra, d'un soupe à bouillon perlé, soutenue d'un jeune
gros dindon cantonné de pigeonneaux, et couronnée d'oignous
blancs, mariés avec la chicorée.

In this learned repast, we find, as Dorante says, "des incongruites"—
elements which are not suitable, one to another, or which are, to use another
term from the text, "des barbarismes." However, if we examine the
constitutive elements of the banquet—the actual dishes themselves—we
discover food for thought in this eminently verbal feast. First: "un pain de
rive, à biseau doré, relevé de croûte partout, croquant tendrement sous la
dent," has to do not only with gastronomy, but with texture ("croquant
tendrement sous la dent")—a literary notion, as well as architectural or
sculptural, for if one can spice (*relever*) a meal, one can also *relever une statue*,
or *relever des ruines on un mur démoli*.

Second, "d'un vin à sève velouté, armé d'un vert qui n'est point trop
commandant" bears clear witness, through "armé" and "commandant," of
the invasion of the kitchen by the military, as does the third, "d'un carré de
mouton gourmandé de persil." since "gourmandé" may well mean here
"pierced with" as in "une galère gourmandée de'arquebuse." In his treatise,
Le Cuisiner françois La Varenne confirms this usage when he describes a side
of mutton as "piqué de persil" In addition, "velouté" continues the emphasis
on texture, and "carré" recalls the architectural image, a "membre quarré"
being something that often, according to Furetière's *Dictionnaire françois*,
"termine quelque partie d'architecture".

The fourth item, "d'une longe de veau de rivière, longue comme
cela, blanche, délicate, et qui sous les dents est une vraie pâte d'amande,"
takes up the metaphors of texture ("sous les dents") and perhaps of
geography ("de rivière") that we encountered in the first item with
"croquant. . . sous la dent" and "de rive."

Five and six insist upon architecture ("de perdrix relevées," and "soutenue d'un jeune gros dindon"), upon the musical arts since the opera was known in France at this time, and finally upon heraldry ("perlé," "couronnée d'oignons blancs" "cantonée de pigeonneaux," and "mariés"). Indeed, since "cantonnée" is also an architectural and military term, we have in this final instance a crowning, a veritable wedding (albeit a mixed marriage) of most of the previous metaphors. This is quite fitting since Molière has suggested from the outset of this particular set piece that eating is akin to artistic endeavor: elegance, erudition, taste, *bienséances*, rules, the "pièces" of a meal, the science of "bons morceaux" must be united to create the perfect object that appeals to the imagination, that faculty which is as crucial to cuisine and art as it is to sex.

The banquet menu is, therefore, a microcosm of a play characterized by the interplay of codes. The practice is repeated several moments later when the directions for the drinking song indicate: "Les Musiciens et la Musicienne prennent des verres, chantent deux chansons à boire, et sont soutenus de toute la symphonie." Dorimène's comment on the whole conception is quite apt: "C'est merveilleusement assaisonner la bonne chère, que d'y mêler la musique, et je me vois ici admirablement régalée." If cooks dance, and musicians, accompanied by an orchestra, sing songs about drinking, and Dorante praises the interdisciplinary nature of *haute cuisine*, we undoubtedly have here a salient example of the interpenetration that will include the layering of images in the verbal feast and culminate in two spectacular fusions, the Mamaouchi scene and the Ballet des Nations. But those crowning scenes are preceded by a series of rehearsals and reversals that lend the often debated structure of *Le Bourgeois gentilhomme* its distinctive character.

To trace this phenomenon from the beginning of the play would be to recall, first of all, that we are dealing with a *comédie-ballet* whose general structure rests on or rather springs from the notion of movement inherent in all forms of dance. In fact, Claude Abraham has demonstrated that stage blocking which does not take into account this fundamental aspect of the play dooms the production to awkwardness and constitutes a betrayal of Molière's genius as a director. In the opening scenes, therefore, we encounter a Maître de Musique and a Maître à Danser; two of the arts, which will eventually harmonize in the major scenes of acts IV and V, are represented at the very outset, and their incarnations speak of their agreement, at least on certain matters:

MAÎTRE À DANSER: Oui, la récompense la plus agréable qu'on puisse recevoir des choses que l'on fait, c'est de les voir connues, de

les voir caressées d'un applaudissement qui vous honore. Il n'y a rien, à
mon avis, qui nous paye mieux que cela de toutes nos fatigues; et ce
sont des douceurs exquisesque des louanges éclairées.
MAÎTRE DE MUSIQUE: J'en demeure d'accord, et je les goûte comme vous.

Beyond the metaphors of commerce ("paye mieux"), pleasure ("douceurs
exquises"), and gastronomy ("je les goûte comme vous") to be found typically
in a Molière play, we should note that dance, and its indispensable
companion, music, are in concert at this point.

The two maîtres extend their discussion of harmony and unity to
cover all of human relations as they endeavor to reassure. M. Jourdain of
their value of society, and specifically to someone who would become a social
lion in the course of just one morning:

> MAÎTRE DE MUSIQUE: La guerre ne vient-elle pas d'un manque
> d'union entre les hommes?
> M. JOURDAIN: Cela est vrai.
> MAÎTRE DE MUSIQUE: Et si tous les hommes apprenaient la musique,
> ne serait-ce pas le moyen de s'accorder ensemble, et de voir
> dans le monde la paix universelle?
> M. JOURDAIN: Vous avez raison.
> MAÎTRE À DANSER: Lorsqu'un homme a commis un manquement
> dans sa conduite, soit aux affaires de sa famille, ou au gouverne-
> ment d'un Etat, ou au commandement d'une armée, ne dit-on pas
> toujours: "Un tel a fait un mauvais pas dans une telle affaire"?
> M. JOURDAIN: Oui, on dit cela.
> MAÎTRE À DANSER: Et faire un mauvais pas peut-il procéder d'autre
> chose que de ne savoir pas danser?
> M. JOURDAIN: Cela est vrai, vous avez raison tous deux.

Clearly, the maîtres are appealing to Jourdain's most fundamental
impulse: to produce a union between himself and the image of a noblemen;
in other words, he will go through a series of rehearsals designed to bridge
the gap between the contrasting modes of existence implied in the play's title.

Yet, soon after these harmonious displays, there arrives the Maître
d'Armes whose role in Jourdain's scheme of things is to transform the roly-
poly bourgeois into a being so agile as to be able to strike without being
struck in return. If the dancing and music masters—so necessary to any noble
education—represent here the praise of the arts and the basic movement
typical of a Molière play, the Maître d'Armes introduces another element
discovered in every Molière play from farce through "High Comedy" to

comédie-ballet, namely, violence. The Maître d'Armes threatens the other two, and the three are about to come to blows when the Maître de Philosophie enters. Not long after giving them all a lesson drawn from Seneca's treatise on wrath (*De Ira*), he flies into a rage and brings the growing discord to the point of explosion, shouting: "Je vous trouve tous trois bien impertinents de parler devant moi avec cette arrogance et de donner impudemment le nom de science à des choses que l'on ne doit pas même honorer du nom d'art, et qui ne peuvent être comprises que sous le nom de métier misérable de gladiateur, de chanteur et de baladin!" The four of them then fall into a neatly choreographed tussle that takes them off stage. So much for harmony—and that seems to be one of the points: after establishing the principles for human solidarity, Molière then turns the theme against itself by ironically displaying the disorder that results when principles are tested in practice.

The Maître de Philosophie then returns in act II, scene iv, to give the famous alphabet lesson to M. Jourdain. After having declined to learn logic, ethics, and physics, Jourdain agrees to study writing in order to compose a love-note for the Marquise: no knowledge for knowledge's sake in Jourdain's bourgeois conception, for everything must have its utility. Knowledge is, however, the key to this part of the play, since the notion of learning is yet another factor inherent in many of Molière's dramas, most prominently, of course, in *L'Ecole des femmes* and *Les Femmes savantes*. The equation that Molière prefers to draw is that knowledge leads—or should lead—to enlightenment, and it does here, in its way, as Jourdain exclaims, "Quoi! quand je dis: 'Nicole, apportez-moi mes pantoufles, et me donnez mon bonnet de nuit,' c'est de la prose?" The Maître replies, "Oui, Monsieur," to which Jourdain can only respond, gratefully, "Par ma foi! il y a plus de quarante ans que je dis de la prose sans que j'en susse rien, et je vous suis le plus obligé du monde de m'avoir appris cela".

The enlightenment is neither profound nor extensive, and we can, therefore, suspect that Molière is at it once again, parodying one of his own favorite devices: the presentation of Jourdain's earning his Ph. D. in phonetics is a mockery of the Molièresque theme of knowledge; indeed, it sets the whole concept of learning on its head.

Perhaps, to be completely fair to Jourdain, and to show one last ramification of "knowledge" at this point of the play, I should point out that, obtuse though he may be, Jourdain does not entirely lack perceptiveness and a certain modicum of self-awareness. When the Maître Tailleur tries to persuade him that his new shoes do not hurt—it is only his imagination— Jourdain riposts: "je me l'imagine, parce que je le sens". Or again, when the tailor admits to having taken some of the material Jourdain purchased in order to make an outfit for himself, Jourdain notes "il ne fallait pas le lever avec le mien". Finally, as the litany of the Garcon Tailleur's flattering terms reaches its zenith, Jourdain exclaims "'Votre Grandeur! Ma foi, s'il va jusqu'à l'altesse il aura toute la bourse." In contrast to the usual blindness of the *monomane* of most previous plays, Jourdain is capable of discernment when it pleases and amuses him. And so, even if his *bonnet de nuit* has two horn-like protuberances on it, he is not Molière's typical *cocu*, if one accepts the etymology of *cocuage*: *cocuage* derives from capuchon—a hood that the cuckold symbolically wears in his unawareness and insensitivity.

Molière had, in fact, dramatized the situation of an "unhooded," perceptive cuckold in an earlier effort at comedy-ballet, *George Dandin ou le mari confondu* of 1668. But this bitter and pessimistic drama, with its rough transitions from the comedy, written by Molière, to the dance parts, choreographed by Robinet, hardly belongs to the same category as the joyous *Bourgeois gentilhomme*. In truth, a lesson to be learned from *George Dandin* is that the *comédieballet* succeeds only when the author has brought harmony to all the various components of the theatrical presentation, including the tone and the dénouement. In this respect, the comedy-ballet that preceded *Le Bourgeois gentilhomme* in Molière's corpus by only one year, *Monsieur de Pourceaugnac*, showed the way to the later play since it is, as Claude Abraham has noted, "a fully integrated spectacle."

M. Jourdain seeks to make a spectacle of himself—whether fully integrated or not—when, at the beginning of the third act, he instructs his lackeys, "Suivez-moi, que j'aille un peu montrer mon habit par la ville; et surtout ayez soin tous deux de marcher immédiatement sur mes pas, afin qu'on voye bien que vous êtes à moi." This is but the latest in a series of acts designed to prepare Jourdain for the life of the nobleman, he thinks; in reality, this becomes one of the steps leading to the Mamamouchi scene, where through the theatrical arts, he is miraculously transformed into a Turkish aristocrat; that is, his numerous *faux pas* will logically make him a *faux noble*. But all of these preparatory gestures and actions fall under the same rubric for Molière: they are pretentious. The theme of *affectation*—attempting to become other than what one is—finds its most natural expression, among all of Molière's plays, in the representation of the "Would-be Gentleman." From this point of view, *Le Bourgeois gentilhomme* is not only typical of Molière, it is virtually archetypal. In fact, we could plausibly argue that Molière's *monomanes* are all "bourgeois gentilhommes" attempting to unite the irrevocably separate worlds of gain and *gloire*. Moreover, the display on which Jourdain constantly insists may well be counterproductive for someone who, on some subconscious level, must be yearning not only to enter the aristocracy but ultimately to destroy it and replace it with his own kind. As Jean Baudrillard points out, commenting on Veblen's theory of vicarious consumption: "Les femmes, les 'gens', la domesticité sont ainsi des exposants de statut. . . . Leur fonction n'est donc, pas plus que celle des objets dans la *kula* ou le *potlatch*, économique, mais celle d'institution ou de préservation d'un ordre hiérarchique des valeurs."

Jourdain's obsession with social elevation becomes a major element of conflict when, later in act III, he refuses his permission to have his daughter marry Cléonte because the latter is not a *gentilhomme*, that is, born of noble blood. Here we encounter one of the oldest schemas of comedy: the symbol of authority as an obstacle to the happiness and the union of young lovers. Certain critics, not perceiving the essentially balletic structure of the play, have complained, although *sotto voce*, that there are two acts of prologue before the drama—that is, the usual plot—begins in the third. Yet, Molière does succeed in integrating his plot line cleanly into the structure so that the Bourgeois's obsession becomes part of those components—his dance, music, fencing, and philosophy lessons, his dress, his entourage—that unite in the fourth act's climactic scene of transformation.

Furthermore, if the plot recalls time-worn tactics to create an obstacle that must be overcome, there is a significant alteration: exceptionally, not only does the central character give his permission, later on, for a marriage, but it is his very mania that is responsible for the betrothal of Lucile and Cléonte. Once Cléonte, disguised as "le fils du Grand Turc," asks for Lucile's hand, Jourdain leaps at the opportunity to legitimize his newfound nobility through an alliance with the highest of eastern potentates—a very particular kind of *mésalliance*. His *affectation* bears good fruit and he participates in the positive results of his actions, something that cannot be said of such predecessors in Molière's canon as Arnolphe, Orgon, and Alceste.

Now, if Molière first plays at reversing his normal schema by having the authority figure *contribute* to the young persons' happiness, he then turns back upon himself once again by making of the mother—normally a supportive character—a final barrier to be lifted, thus opening the way to the unsympathetic mothers of *Les Femmes savantes* and *Le Malade imaginaire*. To Jourdain's outraged exclamation of act V, scene vi, "Quoi? Vous la querellez de ce qu'elle m'obéit?" Madame Jourdain responds, "Oui, elle est à moi aussi bien qu'à vous". It is only when her eyes are opened to the game being played that she can safely state, "Oui, voilà qui est fait, je consens au mariage."

To place this last turnabout into context, let me briefly review what usually happens in those seventeen complete comedies by Molière where there exists the pattern I have described (authority as obstacles to happiness of youth), in contrast to the ten that tell the story of cuckoldry—in a sense, the story of what happens when the authority figure initially gets his way. In the "brighter" comedies, all of which can be seen as following the same pattern as an early sketch probably by Molière entitled *Le Médecin volant*, the Arnolphes and the Orgons attempt to impose their will, only to have fate or the family plot against them. When they are thwarted, they benefit from no vision-changing illumination, for they belong to Molière's seventeenth-century, essentialist view of man which implies no radical metamorphoses, and which underlies the philosophical import of *Le Bourgeois gentilhomme*. What does happen in the case of Arnolphe of *L'École des femmes*, for instance, is that others are disabused and illuminated, when they see, finally, that Arnolphe and M. de la Souche are one and the same. All that Molière allows Arnolphe to do is to exclaim "Ouf!" He is not enlightened, he has not changed, he will be present neither at the banquet nor at the marriage.

In *Le Tartuffe*, Organ may finally see Tartuffe's true colors, but he still cannot distinguish the subtleties of human conduct. As Cléanthe tells him:

> Vous ne gardez an rien les doux témperaments;
> Dans la droite raison jamais n'entre la vôtre.
> Et toujours d'un excès vous vous jetez dans
> l'autre.

If Orgon does not suffer the same exclusionary fate as Arnolphe, there are two reasons that come to mind: first, Molière already had a scapegoat to be sacrificed on the altar of society's well-being in Tartuffe; second, the miraculous, *rex ex machina* ending serves to demonstrate, among other things, the power of reunification that lies in the hands of Louis XIV: his action brings together a family previously disunified by Orgon and Tartuffe.

Nonetheless, the pattern is sufficiently clear to mark its distinction from what transpires in *Le Bourgeois gentilhomme* where, in fact, the principle is *inclusionary* rather than exclusionary: the world joins Jourdain in a folly that benefits every single character.

Two of these characters appear for the first time in act III: the aristocrats Dorante and Dorimène. When Mme Jourdain spies Dorante, she sputters, "il me semble que j'ai dîné quand je le vois," which means the opposite of what we might think, for as Furetière notes in his *Dictionnaire françois*, "On dit quand on voit quelque chose qui déplaît: il me semble que j'ai dîné"; in other words, Mme Jourdain is fed up with him. This insistence on an expression meaning the opposite of what is expected literally (dining usually being a pleasant experience) reveals, once again, Molière amusing himself in dealing with reversal.

The two nobles, of course, have been amusing themselves for some time at Jourdain's expense. Here again, we discover Molière involved in imitating Molière (with a twist), for when he previously portrayed Parisian nobles as in *Les Fâcheux*, they were—understandably, given the social hierarchy of the age—presented in a respectful light. Provincial aristocracy (at least an oxymoron, if not an outright contradiction in terms of the Parisian view often reflected on the stage) fared much less well, as we recall from the caricatures of M. et Mme Sotenville in *George Dandin* or the title character of *M. de Pouceaugmac*.

Yet, in *Le Bourgeois*, Molière offers us two Parisian nobles who are, nonetheless, profiting shamelessly from Jourdain's misplaced largesse. We might be tempted to think that Molière joins Voltaire, who in *Candide*, suggests that when you go to Paris, you inevitably meet "Parasites". However, they are portrayed as both Parisian and charming, despite their little game with Jourdain. Once again, Molière will not permit a note of discord to be sounded in his harmonious composition.

Dorimène, the Marquise (the "giver"—a generous person, as the etymology of her name suggests), is the object of Jourdain's desire and the spectator for whom Jourdain has been practicing the role of gentleman. In preparation for offering himself to the beautiful Marquise, he has paved the way with impressive gifts, as Dorante has noted:

> vos fréquentes sérénades, et vos bouquets continuels, ce superbe
> feu d'artifice qu'elle trouva sur l'eau, le diamant qu'elle a reçu de
> votre part, et le cadeau [i.e., "grand repas"—Furetière] que vous
> lui préparez, tout cela parle bien mieux en faveur de votre amour
> que toutes les paroles que vous auriez pu dire vous-même.

Since it was expected in the seventeenth century that only the nobleman, the *honnête homme*, would be privileged to use discourse well enough to seduce, it is only in the natural order of things that a bourgeois would try to impress by a materialistic display, words being reduced to events—reified—or, as we will see shortly, downgraded to nonsense.

All this show of wealth and luxury is supposed to reinforce Jourdain's claims to the Marquise's favors, which is to say that the theme of infidelity is introduced at this point, but with a difference: unlike the other central male characters of the five-act plays, Jourdain is not the object of unfaithfulness, but rather the would-be perpetrator of an extraconjugal affair. In an early three-act comedy, *Sganarelle* (1660), the title character and his wife fall into a series of misunderstandings that lead each to accuse the other of infidelity. But that is clearly not the same as the situation, unique among Molière's bourgeois characters, of a husband seeking to deceive his wife to the point where the wife can say to her servant, "Ce n'est pas d' aujourd'hui, Nicole,

que j'ai conçu des soupçons de mon mari. Je suis la plus trompée du monde . . ."—
and, if we omit the women seduced and abandoned by the aristocrat Dom
Juan, she is probably right, within the confines of Molière's five-act corpus.

Infidelity is mentioned elsewhere in the same act (the accusation is
made by Cléonte of Lucile), but that is little more than the traditional
badinage in a kind of scene that Molière originated in *comédies* like *Le Dépit
amoureux* and *Le Tartuffe*, the *scène de dépit amoureux*. In fact, the doubling of
the characters who partake in this scene in *Le Bourgeois gentilhomme*—the
principal couple shadowed by their servants—constitutes an exact copy of the
structure of *Le Dépit amoureux*. And so, once again, Molière has returned to
his most faithful source: one of his own plays.

At the beginning of act IV occurs the important banquet scene that
I analyzed at the outset. The centrality of the scene may be judged if we view
it as a kind of *mise-en-abyme* placed right after the play's midpoint—where
such *éléments spéculaires* are usually to be found. It possesses the spectacular
qualities inherent in the genre of the *comédie-ballet*; it involves the
interpenetration of codes typical of the entire text; yet it reveals itself as an
incomplete reflection of the proceedings because it does not take into
account the vision of social, national, even international accord that Molière
lends to his ending. Indeed, it is necessarily imperfect in other ways. We can
tall straightaway that the repast will not suit Jourdain's plans for a sharing of
flesh with the Marquise because it is Dorante who presides at table:
"Songeons à manger"; Allons donc nous mettre à table. . . ."

Moreover, as we have seen in other comedies by Molière, the
promise of bread-breaking normally announces closure and the concomitant
social and moral communion (or a parody thereof in *Dom Juan*). Since in the
instance of *Le Bourgeois gentilhomme* Molière situates the meal relatively early
on—as a sign of what is to come—he also has to disrupt it, for even were the
anticipated repast to be consumed, the obstacles to the realization of comic
triumph would still exist. Consequently, Molière has Mme Jourdain destroy
what would have been the traditional symbolism of the banquet when she
makes the point: "C'est donc pour cette belle affaire-ci, Monsieur mon mari,
que vous avez eu tant d'empressement à m'envoyer dîner chez ma soeur". In
Jourdain's opinion, his wife would clearly have been an intrusive element—
and he was right. The banquet is, then, a significant, even if unfinished,
rehearsal of the two scenes of reunion that Molière will substitute for the
conventional invitation to dine pronounced at the end of many comedies.

If the meal does not satisfy Jourdain's appetites, a much more
gratifying event for him takes place in act IV, scene v, when, as Molière puts
it in the directions, "La cérémonie turque pour ennoblir le Bourgeois se fait
en danse et en musique, et compose le quatrième intermède." This scene

represents the culmination of several developments. Since it is composed of *entrées*, it is a kind of coordinated banquet that aims to please the eye. It is also a play-within-a-play complete with special costumes, exotic dialogue, a large cast of characters, music, dance, *son et lumière*, an introduction, a climax, and a dénouement; that is, we have a full *mise-en-abyme* of a *comédie-ballet* within the *comédie-ballet*. Then, it is a social coronation, a knighting of M. Jourdain into the brotherhood of *chevaliers*, which obliges Jourdain to change religions and which causes us to speculate on Molière's choice of a name for his central figure. When Le Mufti chants the following verses,

> *Mahametta par Giourdina*
> *Mi pregar sera è mattina:*
> *Voler far un Paladina*
> *Dé Giourdina, dé Giourdina*
> *Dar turbanta, é dar scarcina,*
> *Con galera é brigantina,*
> *Per deffender Palestina,*
> *Mahametta, etc. . . .*

we learn that this middle-eastern *paladin* has had to take up new citizenship as well, since one of his duties will be to defend Palestine, which is to the east of what was known in the seventeenth century as *Trans-Jordanie*, a former province of the Ottoman empire.

Next, the Turkish celebration furnishes the fourth interlude of the drama, as well as the high point of Bourgeois's personal fantasy: in one moment, a metamorphosis occurs, through the medium of a total theatrical experience that fills the need in Jourdain's life and, at the same time, opens the way for a resolution of the problem of Lucile's having to marry an aristocrat.

This crucial scene has, finally, two additional interesting aspects: the *batonnade* and the "Turkish language". The initiation ceremony includes an orchestral beating of Jourdain—"plusieurs coups de bâton en cadence". The recourse to the *batonnade* as a comic tactic predates *Le Bourgeois gentilhomme* and Molière as well, but here the violence is not a release of energy against a blocking figure; rather, it becomes, with the words, the music, and the dance that accompany it, the means of transforming a thick-skinned bourgeois into another state, so that the rite of initiation also constitutes a right of passage into the only world that could possibly suit Jourdain: the universe of illusion.

As far as the language of the scene goes, there are three comments to be made, and they arise from remarks made by Georges Couton in his edition of Molière's works. At the end of the first speech by the Mufti,

Couton notes; "Le turc dorénavant ne sera plus un galimatias incompréhensible mais n'est pas autre chose que 'la langue franche ou langage franc: jargon qu'on parle sur la mer Méditerrannée, composé du français, italien, espagnol et autres langues, qui s'entend par tous les Matelots et marchands de quelque nation qu'ils soient' (Furetière)" And so, after nonsense, a sensible language is produced. Then, this second language is in interpenetration of several tongues—French, Italian, Spanish, and so forth. Finally, this *lingua franca* is understood by many nations; it can thus be said to bring them together; it is, therefore, a vehicle for harmony.

Act V is linked closely to its predecessor since Mme Jourdain interrupts, at the outset of act V, the "turquerie" scene that closed out IV. The final act is a rather subdued moment before the extraordinary spectacle of the "Ballet des Nations," but it does, however, contain two passages worthy of brief notice. First, Lucile says to her father: "Comment, mon père, comme vous voilà fait! est-ce une comédie que vous nous jouez?"—which elicits the reply, "Non, non, ce n'est pas une comédie, c'est une affaire fort sérieuse." The point is, of course, that we are in fact approaching the end of the *comédie* part of the comedy-ballet, which must be taken seriously by Jourdain for the comedy to have a resolution—even if we are tempted to take the whole business lightly.

Just a minute or two after this exchange, Covielle confides to Mme Jourdain the information that dissolves her objections to the marriage between Lucile and "le fils du Grand Turc": "Il y a une heure, Madame, que nous vous faisons signe. Ne voyez-vous pas bien que tout ceci n'est fait que pour nous ajuster aux visions de votre mari, que nous l'abusons sous ce déguisement, et que c'est Cléonte lui-même qui est le fils du Grand Turc?" This significant moment has caused a great deal of critical ink to flow and it might be worthwhile to review four representative positions which have been adopted over the past fifty years in this respect.

Ramon Fernandez, in *La Vie de Molière* of 1929, promulgated a vast survey of Molière's career that I shall call the Fernandez cycle: at first, there is the ascendancy of the comic spirit, which is then interrupted by a perception of the world's injustice (i.e., in plays such as *Le Tartuffe*, *Dom Juan*, and *Le Misanthrope*). Finally, Molière, sadder and wiser, reverts to comedies in a light vein (such as *Le Bourgeois gentilhomme*) because he had to acknowledge the triumph of society.

In *Le Dernier Molière*, Robert Garapon prefers to see a new direction, an esthetic evolution in Molière's literary production, one that begins around 1668, but that is incomplete at the time of *Le Bourgeois gentilhomme* and does not assume its full dimensions until the two last dramatic seasons of his career, 1671–72 and 1672–73. In these seasons,

Molière succeeded in presenting to his public the result of his experimenting with what Garapon terms "Un Nouvel Art de faire des comédies"; that is, the pursuit of a fullness of comedic art never before attempted.

Harold Knutson's book, *Molière: An Archetypal Approach* appeared at about the same time as Garapon's, but it awards *Le Bourgeois gentilhomme* a more importance place in Molière's corpus. In its methodology that combines Jung, Frye, and Mauron, it illuminates the integration of the father into the New Society. The usual exorcism of what Knutson calls the "Heavy Father" yields to a comic fantasy so powerful that it does not even need sacrificial victims to carry out its mission.

Most recently, in 1989, Gérard Defaux published a controversial, often polemical, but always challenging tome entitled *Molière ou les métamorphoses du comique: de la comédie morale au triomphe de la folie* in which, unlike Fernandez who perceived a circular motion to Molière's career, Defaux traces a linear evolution starting with Molière's early communion with the public, passing afterwards through a stage of crisis, and terminating in Erasmian fashion, in an acceptance of the world's folly.

Our interest in the two latter studies, those of Knutson and Defaux, lies in their distinguishing *Le Bourgeois gentilhomme* as a significant turning point, precisely because the play ends on a universal embrace: no one is excluded, indeed the family is reunited, enlarged, and joins the *monomane* in his entertaining escapism. From the philosophical viewpoint of a Defaux, madness rather than reason has become the rule; from a purely dramatic conception, the world has gone mad, for the intrusive element—the egomaniac preferring delusion to reality, in earlier plays always punished and alienated—is allowed to have his way in a radical move that is at once a reversal (of previous practice) and a new union of elements, both theatrical (dance, music, words, etc.) and philosophical. Indeed the philosophical side is reinforced by the particular fashion in which Molière chooses to end the drama: a triple marriage, a veritable *pot-pourri sociologique*, with Dorante and Dorimène, the nobles, joining the bourgeois Cléonte and Lucile and the peasants Covielle and Nicole in a ceremony that, in parallelism, comes as close as the seventeenth century will allow to symbolizing total accord between all classes. It remains to be demonstrated that such peace is possible on an international scale: the "Ballet des Nations" is about to take place.

The first directions of the "Ballet des Nations" contain precious indications of Molière's intentions: "Un homme vient donner les livres du ballet, qui d'abord est fatigué par une multitude de gens de provinces différentes, qui crient en musique pour en avoir, et par trois Importuns, qu'il trouve toujours sur ses pas." We have diversity which is made one through music, and the notion of "Importuns" recalls Molière's original *comédie-ballet*,

Les Facheux (1661) in which the entire plot was based on the importunate arrivals of a series of bores. And so, the notes of unity through art, and of Molière's harking back to some of his earlier efforts are sounded at the outset. The latter point is taken up again when, during the *Première Entrée*, a Gascon speaks in a provincial jargon as Pierrot had done in *Dom Juan* or, even before him, Mascarille when imitating a Swiss in *L'Etourdi*. Moreover, we should note that the characters in the following "Dialogue des gens" reflect the total social complexus of the seventeenth century as much as the triple marriage did, because there are two "Hommes du Bel Air" (nobles accompained by their wives). "Un Vieux Bourgeois Babillard" (and wife), and then two Gascons and a Swiss, three *campagnards*.

The *Seconde Entrée* consists only of the dance of the "Importuns." The next interesting element occurs in the *Troisième Entrée* where three Spaniards sing and dance. The fourth *Entrée* is for the Italians, to sing, dance, and present a skit in *commedia dell'arte* fashion. The fifth in this hierachical ordering is devoted, naturally enough, to the French. If we recall that the language spoken during the Mamamouchi scene was composed basically of Spanish, Italian, and French, and was created as a primitive Esperanto, a vehicle for uniting nations through communication, it is clear that Molière is here referring us to his other major scene of spectacle and accord, thereby imitating himself within the same play. This intratextuality finds its final expression in the last verses of the ballet where the audience applauds, dances, and sings, "Quels spectacles charmants, quels plaisirs goûtons-nous! / Les Dieux mêmes, les Dieux n'en ont point de plus doux," since, in act I, scene i, the two masters of the arts that form the "Ballet des Nations"—song and dance—had discussed precisely matters of taste and pleasure.

These issues—taste, pleasure, harmony—were a preoccupation of the seventeenth century, but for more than esthetic reasons. *Le Bourgeois gentilhomme* reflects, in the domain of artistic expression, what was being sought in the political. The benevolent "fiat" of the ersatz monarch Mamamouchi Jourdain ends discord and brings new order in a paradise gained, that was the dream of absolute monarchy in France. Even in the world of comedy, the correct values were usually respected: birth and destiny represent the indispensable keys to status and success, and it is the duty of individuals possessing these innate qualities to effect moral and political harmony to the same degree that a *comédia-ballet* (which Molière himself had called "un mélange nouveau des genres") joins the arts on a *Gesamtkunstwerk*.

This goal of unity from diversity, of *e pluribus unum*, brings us back to the staging of the "Ballet des Nations." Until this crowning spectacle, there existed the customary, symbolic wall of exclusion between public and play: we were simply spectators of a theatrical presentation. However, in keeping with his goal of compherensive fusion, Molière expands the limits of his theater with the "Ballet des Nations" so that we join the actors as witnesses of the apotheosis of yet another form of "communion." Molière had prepared us for this role in the banquet scene in which he had Dorante create, in a verbal dimension, what seventeenth-century cooks had been trained to do in matters of cuisine, namely, to produce a *déguisement*. Richelet defines the verb *déguiser* as "Changer. Rendre méconnoissable. . . . Déguiser une viande. Déguiser des oeufs. *Ces derniers sont des Termes de Cuisinier*". Voiture, for example describes a repast thus: "il y eut douze sortes de viandes et de déguisements, dont personne n'a encore jamais ouï parler et dont on ne sait pas encore le nom." Dorante invited Dorimène—and us—to exercise our imagination, to follow his illusion, so that, through the aesthetic means of his discourse, the most basic of realities—food—was disguised as something better, more refined. Furthermore, Jourdain—who had been practicing to become at least the master of ceremonies at his own banquet, the first major step in the seduction of the noblewoman—was upstaged by Dorante, who masqueraded as the host.

The *déguisement*, therefore, translates the fundamental thrust behind Jourdain's undertakings in the play: to convince others that exhibition is capable of changing essence—the impossible dream. Yet Molière succeeds in making us participate, especially in the final moments (in the Ballet des Nations), as guests—*convives*—at the spectacle of total *déguisement*. He makes the world of appearance displace reality to the extent that we are pleased to be in the realm of fantasy. In any other context, we would be intruders, fraudulent participants; yet, *faux témoins* are allowed, indeed welcome in a representation of *faux noblesse*; that is, in an ultimate reversal we all become *bourgeois gentilshommes*.

H. GASTON HALL

Parody in L'Ecole des femmes

First performed in the Palais-Royal theatre 22 December 1662 and published the following February, *L'Ecole des femmes* is Molière's fourth five-act comedy in verse; and it is the five-act play of which the greatest number of performances are recorded in the *Registre* kept by Molière's colleague La Grange during Molière's lifetime (1662–73). In the play, Arnolphe—a Parisian bourgeois aged forty-two has brought up his ward Agnès, aged seventeen, in ignorance of the facts of life. He plans to marry her, as he confidently explains to Chrysalde in the opening scene, in hopes that an ignorant wife would never cuckold him, a fate he fears obsessively. But since Arnolphe is also a status-seeker, he has recently assumed the would-be noble title "de la Souche," a change of name that confuses the youthful Horace, the lover of the play. Shortly before the play opens Horace had arrived in Paris, noticed Agnès during a brief absence on the part of Arnolphe and fallen in love with her, without realizing that she is the ward of Arnolphe, the family connection from whom he accepts money and in whom he confides. Hence scenes in which Agnès in her innocence and Horace under a misapprehension about the identity of M. de la Souche repeatedly inform Arnolphe about the progress of their attachment and plans for elopement, while Arnolphe does his best to feign joy at any signs of progress reported by his rival and distress at any setbacks, which of course delight him.

From *Comedy in Context: Essays on Molière.* © 1984 University Press of Mississippi.

The role of Arnolphe, written by Molière for himself as an actor, is a virtuoso role which dominates the play, featuring in almost every scene. It is a role which appears to have developed out of Molière's own roles as Sganarelle in *Sganarelle, ou le cocu imaginaire* and in *L'Ecole des maris*. Since there is abundant scope for comic mime and grimace in *L'Ecole des femmes*, the continuity of his acting in these related roles seems especially pertinent. It is clear from the contemporary evidence emanating from the "querelle de *L'Ecole des femmes*" that Molière did indeed exploit the opportunities for comic acting everywhere written into the role. In *La Critique de l'Ecole des femmes*, Dorante (a sympathetic spokesman) commends the comic and theatrical use of narrative in the scenes in which Horace unwittingly makes his rival a party to his plans. Those *récits* or reports, argues Dorante, are an integral part of the action,

> d'autant qu'ils sont faits innocemment, ces récits, à la personne intéressée, qui par là entre, à tout coup, dans une confusion à réjouir les spectateurs, et prend, à chaque nouvelle, toutes les mesures qu'il peut pour se parer due malheur qu'il craint.

On Molière's stage the narrative parts of the play were almost more important for what they allow Arnolphe as listener to mime than they are for the verbal content which so dominates the printed page. Yet these *récits*—the scenes with *récits*—also focus major themes of the play: the theme of the lover as blunderer whose blunders confirm his sincerity, which runs from the early comedy *L'Etourdi* through Cléonte of *Le Bourgeois Gentilhomme* to Clitandre of *Les Femmes savantes*; and the theme of useless precaution, which Molière carries forward from his sources in Scarron's tale *La Précaution inutile* and Dorimond's one-act scenario, *L'Ecole des cocus, ou la précaution inutile*, a theme which the inadvertence of Horace underscores far more wittily than any of the sources. The *récit* scenes also represent a convergence of techniques related to the structure of the comedy. They make possible much of the comic irony and some of the *équivoques*, the *revirements* or reversals which heighten suspense in relation to the progress of the lovers, and above all the scope for comic mime.

It may be that *L'Ecole des femmes*, as W. D. Howarth suggests in his excellent edition, is among the more straightforward examples of Molière's theatre. But as the late Raymond Picard observes, readers have not been lacking for whom Arnolphe is a figure of pathos if not of tragedy. This perception of the play takes particular note of the final reversal by which Arnolphe, who had reared Agnès as an object for his own convenience and in abhorrence of cuckoldry, falls in love with her and offers (if only she will marry him and let him love her as he would) to allow her to behave in any way she will:

> Sans cesse nuit et jour je te caresserai,
> Je te bouchonnerai, baiserai, mangerai.
> Tout comme tu voudras tu pourras te conduire;
> Je ne m'explique point, et cela c'est tout dire.
> (*A part*)
> Jusqu'où la passion peut-elle faire aller?
> Enfin à mon amour rien ne peut s'égaler.
> Quelle preuve veux-tu que je t'en donne, ingrate?
> Me veux-tu voir pleurer? veux-tu que je me batte?
> Veux-tu que je m'arrache un côté de cheveux?
> Veux-tu que je me tue? Oui, dis si tu le veux:
> Je suis prêt, cruelle, à te prouver ma flamme.

There is no doubt that at this point Arnolphe's scheme has collapsed; but it is a fundamental misreading to suggest that his world has collapsed, because he is not characterized like that. At this point in the plot the focus is more on Agnès's liberation than on Arnolphe's loss, which the play suggests is in any case necessary and deserved. Evidence from the "querelle de *L'Ecole des femmes*" suggests, moreover, that Arnolphe's declaration as played by Molière himself was farcical. In *La Critique de l'Ecole des femmes*, a hostile spokesman, Lycidas, wonders whether there is not some contradiction in that "ce Monsieur de La Souche..., qu'on nous fait un homme d'esprit, et qui paraît si sérieux en tant d'endroits," makes such a grotesque declaration of love:

> ne descend-il point dans quelque chose de trop comique et de trop outré au cinquième acte, lorsqu'il explique à Agnès la violence de son amour, avec ces roulements d'yeux extravagants, ces soupirs ridicules, et ces larmes niaises qui font rire tout le monde?

Through Lycidas Molière is giving detailed stage directions which really are already written into the lines of *L'Ecole des femmes* in the scene in question, where Arnolphe delivers these lines:

> Ecoute seulement ce soupir amoureux;
> Vois ce regard mourant, contemple ma personne ...

It is fundamental to Molière's characterizations that, as Dorante explains in *La Critique de l'Ecole des femmes*,

> il n'est pas incompatible qu'une personne soit ridicule
> en de certaines choses et honnête homme en d'autres.

But there can be no serious doubt that in his declaration of love Arnolphe as played by Molière was grotesquely comic. To the commentary in *La Critique* to that effect it is hardly necessary to add that, in context, "contemple ma personne" is an old, and very successful comic turn which Molière might have noticed in the role of the braggart soldier Matamore in Corneille's *L'Illusion comique*: "Contemple, mon ami, contemple ce visage". He makes a fool of himself and then calls attention to it. There can be no reasonable doubt that this scene was first acted in the burlesque tradition associated with the role of Sganarelle in *Le Cocu imaginaire*, with Scaramouche and the great Jodelet roles of comedies written for him by Corneille, Scarron and others in the 1640s and 1650s.

Such a scene as this must have had an element of "absolute comedy," or funning for the sake of fun in the burlesque tradition; but Dorante's commentary on it in *La Critique de l'Ecole des femmes* shows that, in the author's mind at least, the acting was also significant as satire of contemporary manners:

> Et quant au transport amoureux du cinquième acte, qu'on accuse
> d'être trop outré et trop comique, je voudrais bien savoir si ce
> n'est pas faire la satire des amants, et si les honnêtes gens même
> et les plus sérieux, en de pareilles occasions, ne font pas des
> choses. . . ?

The word *satire* must suggest some degree of ridicule and scorn for folly if not for vice as manifested in Arnolphe's behavior but Dorante's tone is not fierce; and the passage as a whole would seem to carry also a gentler general implication of humorous enjoyment of social behavior judged to be both odd and yet typical of lovers. More importantly for the present argument, the phrases "trop outré et trop comique" and "satire des amants" confirm that the scene does involve parody, of the comportment of real-life lovers.

The particular forms of parody involved in this scene are often called burlesque, a term which applies to literary as well as to acting styles, convergent in the tradition which leads through Scarron's Jodelet roles and the Sganarelle of *Le Cocu imaginaire* to Arnolphe. However, it is to literary parody, including both low and high burlesque, that I invite attention as a feature of style and as a confirmation of the tone and interpretation of the comedy as a whole, because it can be clearly seen as complementary to the acting style attested by *La Critique de l'Ecole des femmes*.

A good deal of attention has been paid to the development of the burlesque in the mid-seventeenth century in France, for instance by Francis Bar in his thesis, *Le Genre burlesque en France au XVIIe siècle*. The word *burlesque*, according to Gilles Menage (1613–92), was a neologism invented by Jean-Francois Sarasin (1603–54), the satirical poet who secured for the troupe of Molière the reluctant protection of the young Prince de Conti during their wagon days. It tended to replace such synonyms as *grotesque*, *narquois*, *familier*, *goguenard*, *enjoué*, *badin*, and *bouffon*, not all of which convey a dimension of travesty or parody particularly associated with the burlesque especially with low burlesque. One could scarcely improve upon Eugéne Géruzez's definition of low burlesque as

> la transformation des caractères et des sentiments nobles en figures et en passions vulgaires, opérées de telle sorte que la ressemblance subsiste sous le travestissement, et que le rapport soit sensible dans le contraste. . . .

This sort of burlesque is exemplified in such works as Charles d'Assoucy's *L'Ovide en belle humeur* (1650), Charles Beys's *Les Odes d'Horace en vers burlesques* (1652) and especially Scarron's unfinished *Virgile travesti*.

If now we look again at Arnolphe's "transport amoureux," we find that the lines are scripted in literary burlesque in support of the acting style evoked in *La Critique de l'Ecole des femmes*. In line 1595, for instance, "je te *bouchonnerai*" introduces vocabulary typical by its familiarity of the literary low burlesque, but alien to tragedy as written in Molière's time for the Paris stage. Stylistically, *bouchonnerai* intensifies *caresserai* of the line before, while behind the metaphor lurk the main general associations of *bouchonner* with wringing out washing and rubbing down horses. I venture to add that in this context the stem *bouchon* also suggests, improperly, the sort of stopper imagined by Alexander Pope in *The Rape of the Lock:* "And maids turn'd bottles, call aloud for corks." Moreover, Arnolphe's aside, "Jusqu'où la passion peut-elle faire aller?," parodies an intervention by the poet Vergil in his narration of Dido's death in *Aeneid*, "Improbe Amor, quid non mortalia pectora cogis!" Scarron had already put Vergil's apostrophe into the third person in rendering this line in his *Virgile travesti*: "Et jusqu'où fut ta passion!" When allowance is made for the shift from narrative to drama, and from octosyllabic verse to alexandrine in *L'Ecole des femmes*, the lines are as close as it is reasonable to expect any two such lines to be.

With such preparation line 1599 must seem extravagant (as in a similar situation Alceste also does in Act IV, scene 3, of *Le Misanthrope*). "Quelle preuve veux-tu que je t'en donne, ingrate?" seems to use the language of tragedy, but in context can only parody such language, which in any case—and by Arnolphe's design!—must be a foreign language for Agnès. The vocabulary of the following lines fully supports this reading. In French classical tragedies characters weep, and their audiences might weep with them; but in no tragedy to my knowledge does a serious character threaten to weep unless he gets his way with a girl. "Veux-tu que je me batte?" is more evocative of the beatings of farce than of the combat of heroic drama. Characters in great distress in tragedies have been known to pull out some of their hair, or the actors in the role pretend to; but to threaten to do so? This surely is a character who first postures and then climbs down, as the later lines show: like Sganarelle, like Orgon in *Tartuffe*, like Alceste, like Le Bourgeois gentilhomme himself and Chrysale in *Les Femmes savantes*. And so much for the suicide threat:

> Veux-tu que je me tue? Oui, dis si tu le veux:
> Je suis tout prêt, cruelle, à te prouver ma flamme.

Indeed the whole speech has the apparent form of a great tragic outburst: note the anaphora of the repeated questions "Veux-tu. . .?" culminating in its inversion in an insistent, affirmative form: "Oui, dis si tu le veux"; and note the themes of love, tears, and death. In particular the line "Je suis tout prêt, cruelle, à te prouver ma flamme" is flagged with the vocabulary of the *style galant* of contemporary tragedy: *cruelle, flamme*. . . . Such a line might occur in a tragedy. Perhaps this one did and researchers will be able to show where, as for the known sources of other lines in this comedy. In context it is burlesque, like Arnolphe's earlier outburst: "Eloignement fatal! Voyage malheureux!," a parody of tragic lamentation at the beginning of Act II. In Act IV Arnolphe's offer parodies a tragic stance, as Agnès's uncultivated dismissal of such high rhetoric confirms:

> Tenez, tous vos discours ne me touchent point l'âme,
> Horace avec deux mots en ferait plus que vous.

The abruptness of Arnolphe's self-contradiction in response to Agnès's refusal has comic potential of its own if well timed. But the point here is that the posturing which we know from *La Critique de l'Ecole des femmes* formed part of Molière's acting style in the role is scripted with pompous clichés borrowed from heroic drama and grotesquely out of place in such a domestic scene: "Ah! c'est trop me braver, trop pousser mon courroux". That such a line is scripted for parody rather than for pathos is confirmed by the low burlesque vocabulary of the lines which immediately follow, including "bête," "dénicherez," and "cul de couvent," expressions as home in *Le Virgile travesti*, but alien to the great tragic drama of Corneille and Racine.

Arguably this passage combines the techniques of low burlesque—the "transformation des caractères et des sentiments nobles en figures et en passions vulgaires," i.e. in contrast with an ideal tragic "transport amoureux"—with devices of high burlesque or mock heroic, in which the more ordinary events of everyday life are "written up" in heroic language, as in Boileau's *Le Lutrin* and Pope's *Rape of the Lock*. For any reader who remembers his Vergil, the aside "Jusqu'où la passion peut-elle faire aller?" represents low burlesque. But if the model burlesqued in the aside were unknown it could be read as high burlesque, because it introduces some of the rhetoric of heroic poetry into a domestic scene. Unless Molière is taking off some scene of a once familiar and now forgotten tragedy, there would appear to be in the passage more elements of high burlesque than of low burlesque. But both forms of the literary burlesque converge in lines scripted for acting in a low burlesque stage style which contemporaries contrasted with other moments of the role. Elements of parody everywhere written into the lines were scripted for the parody on stage of a "transport amoureux."

The burlesque stagecraft argued for Act V, scene 4, is neither isolated nor untypical of comically heightened scenes in *L'Ecole des femmes*. It is no secret that at the end of Act II Arnolphe orders Agnès to go inside (to exit) with lines borrowed *verbatim* from Corneille's tragedy *Sertorius*, which Molière's troupe had produced in 1662 some months before *L'Ecole des femmes*: "C'est assez. / Je suis maître, je parle; allez, obéissez." Few I think would doubt that at this moment Molière derives comedy from the parody of a tragic stance, and doubtless it is no accident that the final line is a perfect syllogism, with a major premise ("je suis maître"), a minor premise ("je parle"), and the conclusion which follows ("allez, obéissez"). The authoritarian attitude which such a line expresses through its form as well as through its content becomes in Arnolphe's mouth a masquerade, a parody of the masterful and heroic to which the counterpoint is the groveling, permissive, but still possessive "transport amoureux" of Act V.

In Act I, scene 3, Arnolphe's soliloquy is a parody of the challenges of heroic drama:

> Héroïnes du temps, Mesdames les savantes,
> Pousseuses de tendresse et de beaux sentiments,
> Je défie à la fois tous vos vers, vos romans,
> Vos lettres, billets doux, toute votre science,
> De valoir cette honnête et pudique ignorance.

The apostrophe is a great trope of tragedy, and I can point to no specific source for this parody which introduces a theme of Molière's playwriting from *Les Précieuses ridicules* to *Les Femmes savantes*. But there can be little doubt that the form parodied is that of Rodrigue's challenge to absent warriors in Corneille's *Le Cid*:

> Est-il quelque ennemic qu'à présent je ne dompte?
> Paraissez, Navarrais, Mores, et Castillans,
> Et tout ce que l'Espagne a nourri de vaillants,
> Unissez-vous ensemble, et faites une armée. . . .

For Don Rodrigue chivalric love is a spur to chivalric valor, and the effect of his soliloquy challenge is heroic. Arnolphe merely uses an heroic form to express rejection of the feminist literature whose emancipatory ideals he challenges but (unlike Don Rodrigue) cannot defeat. There was a social distinction in Molière's time between the sword and the pen.

There is nothing unusual or impractical about a mature bridegroom offering moral guidance to a teenage wife, as Arnolphe does in Act III, scene 2, with "Les Maximes du mariage." In the early 1660s the poet Jean de La Fontaine, for instance, wrote moral advice to his teenage bride. A few years earlier the English diarist John Evelyn, who married in Paris the teenage daughter of the English resident, presented her with an edifying volume to prepare her for her new role as housewife. It is the emphasis and the absoluteness of Arnolphe's stance which make this scene a parody of such experience, flagged by a line reminiscent of Corneille's tragedy *Horace*. It is line 745 which Arnolphe addresses to Agnès in presenting the "Maximes": "Et je veux que ce soit votre unique entretien." In Corneille's tragedy the legendary Roman here utters the lines parodied in an order to his somewhat less heroic sister that "mes trophées / . . . soient dorénavant ton unique entretien". But that is only one element of a complex parody. It has been suggested that because Agnès reads out ten maxims, Molière intends to mock the Decalogue, though of course she begins an eleventh, which is interrupted. That, combined with Arnolphe's impatience with the boredom for him involved in his scheme even when it seems to be going well, implies more than ten "Maximes." I suggest that there is a more obvious parody—through utter contrast—with the once famous "Douze tables des loix d'amour" of Honoré d'Urfé's novel *L'Astrée*. These twelve tables begin "Qui veut estre parfaict amant," with the emphasis firmly on the obligations of the male lover. And so they continue, as in the seventh:

> Que son amour fasse en effet,
> Qu'il juge en elle tout parfait . . . ,

lines which make just as impressive a contrast with the attitudes of Alceste as a lover in *Le Misanthrope* as they do with the possessiveness of Arnolphe, which they closely resemble in content if not in literary style.

A loose parody of the Ten Commandments is not excluded by implied parody of the "Douze tables des loix d'amour," and any such parody may coexist imaginatively with Molière's more direct travesty of the *Instruction to Olympia* by Saint Gregory of Nazianzus, the Church Father who wrote a tragedy of which Christ is the hero. More precisely the scene travesties a translation, the *Préceptes de mariage de Saint Grégoire de Nazianze* which Jean Desmarets, later Sieur de Saint-Sorlin, presented in 1640 to the king, Louis XIII. This translation appears in the *Œuvres poétiques du Sieur Desmarets* (Paris, 1641), partly a collected edition which was (and still is) the most convenient way of owning copies of most of Desmarets' plays, one of which—*Les Visionnaires*—was in Molière's repertory in 1662 and is a known source of features of *L'Ecole des femmes*. But the parody involves a significant distortion by which the original *Préceptes* becomes a pretext for domestic tyranny. The same may be said for the parody in lines 679 ff. of Boccaccio's story of Griselda, the last tale told in the *Decameron*, a tale traditionally interpreted—e.g. in French translations from Petrarch's Latin translation— as an allegory of the marriage of the soul to Christ:

> Je vous épouse, Agnès, et cent fois la journée
> Vous devez bénir l'heur de votre destinée,
> Contempler la bassesse où vous avez éte,
> Et dans le même temps admirer ma bonté
> Qui, de ce vil état de pauvre villageoise,
> Vous fait monter au rang d'honorable bourgeoise.

From poor "villageoise" Griselda had become Marchioness of Saluzzo, etc. Nor is it far-fetched to suggest a parody of the Griselda story here. In the first place the attitude it embodies, like that of the *Instruction to Olympia*, is highly pertinent through the parody to the question concerning marital relationships raised by *L'Ecole des femmes*. In the second place Molière must have known the *Decameron*, which is a source of the plots of *L'Ecole des maris* and *George Dandin*, both deeply concerned with marital values.

Moreover it is well known that the scene as a whole parodies a conventual relationship. At the outset Arnolphe orders:

> Faites la révérence. Ainsi qu'une novice
> Par coeur dans le couvent doit savoir son office,
> Entrant au mariage, il en faut faire autant.

François Chauveau's frontispiece for the 1666 edition shows Angés standing before the seated Arnolphe before the actual reading begins, like a novice standing before her superior in a convent. Arnolphe's *tirade* on the authority of husbands is a complex verbal fantasy, with elements of the Catholic marriage ceremony, moralist implications of the Griselda story, etc. But Molière is also parodying, in the "chaudières bouillantes" a repressive form of religiosity directed particularly toward women.

Not the least comic aspect of *L'Ecole des femmes* is that, as Arnolphe boasts to Chrysalde in the exposition, he chose as his school for wives a "petit couvent, loin de toute pratique," upon leaving which Agnès could still inquire, "Si les enfants qu'on fait se faisaient par l'oreille". In *La Critique de l'Ecole des femmes*, Dorante suggests that these words "ne sont plaisants que par refléxion à Arnolphe," and that they are not intended so much as a joke in themselves, "mais seulement pour une chose qui caractérise l'homme, et peint . . . son extravagance . . ." In context they also characterize Agnès as ignorant, but not stupid. For Agnès's question—the report of which to Chrysalde gives the actor in Arnolphe's role the opportunity to mime "une joie inconcevable" (as I interpret Dorante's commentary on the line)—also discloses the content and the limits of her education and what she has been able logically to make of one aspect of it. For such a novice might have noticed in an account (or painting?) of the Annunciation that the Virgin Mary conceived through the ear. In the lovely "Hymn to the Blessed Virgin Mary," *Queme terra, pontus*, occur the following lines:

> Mirentur ergo saecula,
> quod angelus fert semina,
> quod aure virgo concipit
> et corde credens parturit.

Auricular conception was fairly popular as a theme in baroque devotional poetry. It occurs in Racan's early hymn "O gloriosa Domina," written between 1603 and 1609:

> Ce qu'une femme avoit perdu,
> Une Vierge nous l'a rendu,
> Lors que la foy te fit concevoir par l'oreille.

It is also found in Cardinal Du Perron's "Cantique de la vierge" published in 1622:

> C'est celle dont la foi pour notre sauvement
> Crut à la voix de l'Ange et conçut par l'oreille.

There were doubtless many variations on this theme, of which Rabelais's joke about Gargantua's birth was one. However, Rabelais does not write that Gargantua was "conçu par l'oreille," but simply that he "nasquit en facon bein estrange" and that he "sortit par l'aureille" (*Livre* I, chapter 6). Perhaps Rabelais's joke involves *contaminatio* or blending of the Annunciation with other mythic and miraculous births, such as that of Minerva from Jupiter's forehead. Agnès's question is much more to the point, as it also characterizes an *ingénue*. Like Rabelais, but more directly, Molière parodies a living tradition of piety. But it is apparently one which by 1662 was falling into disrepute. Little girls like Agnès might have noticed in early-seventeenth-century breviaries the phrase "quae per aurem concepisti" in the *Officium parvum*. However, I could not find any such phrase in the *Office de la Vierge Marie*, the first translation into French verse, dedicated to the Queen Regent Anne of Austria in 1645 by Desmarets de Saint-Sorlin. The phrase also appears to have disappeared from my breviary published around 1700, perhaps in the revision authorized by the Holy Office in 1679—though I suspect it was earlier, as further research could show. Molière is unlikely to have imagined that the "petit couvent, loin de toute pratique" chosen for Agnès as a school for wives kept a stock of the most current editions, which may be part of the joke which caused contemporary offense.

For the background of Agnès's question is not one of general *naïveté* only. It is a pointed reference to a type of establishment where what was proper seems not to have been practical and which continued a style of piety wide open to parody by any witty and clear-sighted commentator. In *La Critique de l'Ecole des femmes* the hostile critics are not satisfied with Dorante's explanation that its words "ne sont plaisants que par réflexion à Arnolphe." Climène considers it "d'un goût détestable," because (I suggest) it exemplifies so well Dorante's point when he remarks elsewhere that in a comedy, "vous n'avez rien fait si vous n'y faites reconnaître les gens de votre siècle". The question which produces Arnolphe's infectious laughter in the comedy is also a comment on the education of a certain sort of seventeenth-century "jeune fille rangée."

Here again parody is an important constituent of satire. But not every intertextual reference in the comedy involves parody. In the opening scene, for example, Arnolphe cites Pantagruel's reply to Panurge in Rabelais's tale: "Presse-moi de me joindre à femme autre que sotte. . ." Arnolphe's allusion is self-characterizing. It further confirms a literary continuity, but not through parody. Or to take another example, Arnolphe congratulates himself after the "Maximes du mariage" scene in a quatrain which calls to mind the myth of Pygmalion, the sculptor who assumed he could possess the beautiful Galatea, because he had made her as the statue which came to life and with which he fell in love:

Je ne puis faire mieux que d'en faire ma femme:
Ainsi que je voudrai je tournerai cette âme.
Comme un morceau de cire entre mes mains elle est,
Et je lui puis donner la forme qui me plaît.

The Pygmalion archetype lends depth to Molière's characterization, but these lines in context are ironic, not a parody.

Let one more illustration suffice. In the opening scene Chrysalde criticizes Arnolphe for taking in mid life the new name "de la Souche," recalling:

Je sais un paysan qu'on appellait Gros-Pierre,
Qui, n'ayant pour tout bien qu'un seul quartier de terre,
Y fit tout à l'entour faire un fossé bourbeux,
Et de Monsieur de l'Isle en prit le nom pompeux.

It is commonly assumed that (despite denials of any personal satire voiced in *La Critique de l'Ecole des femmes*) this is a joke at the expense of the playwright Thomas Corneille, who had recently begun to style himself the Sieur de l'Isle. And so it may well be. But it is also a topos, a variant of which Molière might have found in Erasmus's colloquy *La Noblese empruntée*, as it appears in *Les Entretiens familiers d'Erasme*, translated for the first time into French prose by Samuel Chappuzeau and published in Paris in three volumes in 1662, a few months before the opening of *L'Ecole des femmes*: the basis of plays by Chappuzeau familiar to *Molièristes* as sources of *Le Bourgeois Gentilhomme* and *Les Femmes savantes*. In *La Noblesse emprunteé* Harpale has just admitted to his origins in the poorest village in the province. Nestor asks:

. . . Mais ne se trouve-t-il point quelque éminence voisine de
    ce hameau?
Harpale: Il s'en voit une.
Nestor: Et accompagnée sans doute de quelque roche?
Harpale: Vous pouvez ajoûter des plus escarpées.
Nestor: Il faut donc vous faire appeler désormais, *Harpale de*
    Come, Chevalier de la Roche d'or.

In Chrysalde's lines we have a new form of this old joke from a new version of a Renaissance moralist dialogue. Chrysalde's lines are no parody, but (I would argue) an adaptation to a new context. Molière's rephrasing poeticizes, polemicizes and perhaps personalizes Erasmus's ironic exchange. The change within an intertextual continuity yields satire without parody.

Elsewhere in *L'Ecole des femmes*, however, and widely throughout his other plays Molière has written into the lines elements of parody which, in context, constitute a clear guide to the original acting style of major roles, such as the first scene in *Tartuffe* in which Tartuffe courts Elmire and the last scene in *Le Misanthrope* in which Alceste courts Célimène.

JOSEPH I. DONOHUE, JR.

Restructuring a Comic Hero of Molière: Le médecin malgré lui

Turning from what is arguably the greatest comic trilogy ever created for the theater, comprising *Tartuffe* (1664), *Dom Juan* (1665), and *Le misanthrope* (1666), a student might well be tempted to overlook *Le médecin malgré lui*. This diminutive three-act comedy, hardly longer than a farce, presented for the first time some six months after the completion of the trilogy, has frequently been neglected. (The Georges Couton edition of Molière provides only three pages of introductory material for *Le médecin malgré lui* while allotting forty-nine to *Tartuffe*, twenty-eight to *Dom Juan*, and eighteen to *Le misanthrope*.) Following a long tradition, students may be inclined to see in this modest piece nothing more than a moment of respite for Molière after the Herculean labors of the three great comedies. They need to be reminded that *Le médecin malgré lui* also offers a unique opportunity to interrogate a disabused playwright at the height of his powers on the painful lessons learned about truth and justice in society during the protracted controversy over *Tartuffe*.

In the works preceding Molière's great comedies—especially in plays like *Les précieuses ridicules*, *L'école des maris*, and *L'école des femmes*—the hard-edged characterization of comic mania, set in relief by the irrefutable good sense of the *raisonneurs*, speaks to the relative serenity of the playwright's interaction with his public. Generally speaking, they jointly

From *Approaches to Teaching Molière's 'Tartuffe' and Other Plays.* ©1995 The Modern Language Association of America.

embrace a social ideal emanating from the dominant aristocracy and, along with that ideal, a common sense of what by definition constitutes the target of satiric laughter: variance from reasonable, decorous behavior. While success inevitably brought with it scattered criticism, founded for the most part on envy or bigotry, Molière was able to counterattack skillfully with the good-humored thrusts of *La critique de l'école des femmes* and *L'impromptu de Versailles*. Indeed, up to and including the putative three-act version of *Tartuffe* in 1664, Molière apparently continued to dedicate himself to the task inscribed in the motto of the Comédie Francaise, *Castigat ridendo mores* (that is, Comedy corrects public morals through laughter), there being no doubt about the standards to be invoked in the process. The unprecedented attacks on *Tartuffe*, however, coupled with a wavering of royal support, would soon bring about significant changes in the embattled playwright's view of social man as expressed in his theater and in his relationship to his public.

As early as *Dom Juan* and *Le misanthrope*, one notices that the comic identity of the protagonists has become more problematic, even ambiguous. Dom Juan, for example, seems neither all right nor all wrong, nor is it absolutely certain that he is wrong at all! The same has often been said of Alceste, beginning with the famous letter of Jean-Jacques Rousseau. After *Tartuffe*, the norms shared by Molière and the *honnêtes gens* no longer seems adequate to cover the complexity and bitterness of the life experience with which the playwright has begun to fuel his theater. There are moments in *Dom Juan* and *Le misanthrope* when the comic heroes' criticisms of society could be unsettling for the spectator, but Molière, for reasons touching both the psychology of laughter and politics, never allows them to dominate. On the contrary, he acts to sustain the necessary (for the purposes of laughter) inequality of awareness between comic hero and spectator and, at the same time, to distance himself from the audiences's potentially dangerous criticism by highlighting the manic comportment of the protagonist. It has long been observed by critics that Molière never confronted the public by rehabilitating or reconstructing his comic *aliénés* ("madmen"). Robert Nelson in fact applauds Molière's shrewdness in not reforming his monomaniacs. To do so, Nelson tells us, "would take the spectator into affective and moral regions where the satiric purpose— laughter—might be compromised." Nelson also underscores the necessary inequality of awareness that the playwright must maintain to play's end between the spectator and a Dom Juan or an Alceste: "to make them share our superior view of their previous conduct would come dangerously close to identifying us with them in that previous conduct as well". Molière is loath to attribute to spectators the same follies, dissatisfactions, and, on occasion, subversive reactions that his comic heroes demonstrate.

Nevertheless, in *Le médecin malgré lui*, Molière does take the unprecedented step of rehabilitating the comic hero, while projecting sotto voce the image of an amorphous world seemingly devoid of logic and reason. This complexity is concealed, however, not only by the opulent shadow of the trilogy but also by a frothy layer of wonderful nonsense beyond which few readers have had the heart to penetrate.

The play opens with a domestic quarrel between husband and wife, an opportunity for many students to exercise skills acquired during years of watching the soaps. Like most quarrels of its kind, this one is filled with noise and threats and gives little hint of the real issues dividing the antagonists. Sganarelle's opening speech—"Non, je te dis que je n'en veux rien faire, et que c'est à moi de parler et d'être le maître" ("No, I tell you, I'll do nothing of the sort, it's for me to speak up and be the boss")—suggests that a struggle for dominance is going on in the household. Martine's rejoinder— "Et je te dis, moi, que je veux que tu vives à ma fantaisie, et que je ne me suis point mariée avec toi pour souffrir tes fredaines" ("And I'm telling you, I want you to live the way I say, and that I didn't marry you to put up with your nonsense")—confirms that supposition and indicates that the lady has no intention of being the loser.

Given the primacy of the paterfamilias in seventeenth-century society, one wonders initially about the strength and vehemence of Martine's revolt, but the answer is not long in coming. Sganarelle, it turns out, is a man who squanders his time and what little money they have in drunken idleness. He has even gone so far as to subsidize this way of life by selling off the family's worldly goods. Poor Martine! Sganarelle does seem to be rather subhuman, but what, after all, can she do? He is by force of law and custom head of the house. Besides, why marry such a clod in the first place? As for the quarrel, it is certainly not the first, nor does it promise to be the last. If the dispute accomplishes nothing else, one might conclude on a superficial level, at least it provides needed emotional release for the much-abused wife.

A closer reading of this scene, especially for students fluent in the language of the soaps, should bring to light several significant facts and at least one full-scale revelation. We are dealing with a woodcutter who quotes Aristotle, has had some Latin, served six years under a famous doctor, and who considers himself to be somewhat déclassé. "Trouve-moi," he challenges his wife, "un faiseur de fagots qui sache, comme moi, raisonner des choses, qui ait servi six ans un fameux médecin, et qui ait su dans son jeune âge, son rudiment par coeur" ("Find me a woodcutter who knows how to reason about things like me, who worked six years under a famous doctor, who learned by heart his basic subjects at a very young age"). Martine, who has heard it all before, is not impressed with her husband's vita. "Peste du fou fieffé!" ("A plague on the arrant fool!") she hurls back, eliciting from Sganarelle "Peste de la carogne!" ("A plague on the old hag!"). (Students, who may one day be faced with the same problem, will, however, be quick to note that in some measure the domestic strife in this peasant household is due to the "underemployment" of the husband.) After this latest exchange of insults, Martine intones a well-known lament for the choice she made of a husband: "Que maudit soit l'heure et le jour où je m'avisai d'aller dire oui!" ("Cursed be the hour and the day when I made up my mind to say yes"). When her husband replies disobligingly with an analogous complaint, Martine is frankly outraged:

> C'est bien à toi, vraiment, à te plaindre de cette affaire. Devrais-tu être un seul moment sans rendre grâce au Ciel m'avoir pour ta femme? et méritais-tu d'épouser une personne comme moi?

> Of course, it's fine for you to complain! Should you let even a single moment pass without thanking God that you're married to me? And did you deserve to marry someone like me?

So certain in Martine of her interpretation of the facts that her question seems almost rhetorical. But Sganarelle, equally certain of his ground—or so it appears—counterattacks ironically without missing a beat: "Il est vrai que tu me fis trop d'honneur, et que j'eus lieu de me louer la première nuit de nos noces!" ("It is true that you did me a great honor, and that I had reason to be pleased with our wedding night!"). The protestations of both characters carry an undeniable accent of veracity, and the spectator has little sense of whom to believe as Sganarelle fires the second barrel of his riposte: "Hé! morbleu! ne me fais point parler là-dessus: je dirais de certaines choses. . ." ("Damnation! Don't get me started on that subject: I'd say certain things. . ."). What things? Martine would like to know, but Sganarelle is curiously reticent about the details: "Baste, laissons là ce chapitre. Il suffit que nous savons ce que nous savons, et que tu fus bien heureuse de me trouver" ("Enough, let's drop the subject. It's sufficient that we know what we know, and that you were extremely lucky to find me"). The discussion soon degenerates into violence. Sganarelle will begin to beat his wife—according, one suspects, to some recurring ritual. He picks up a stick and asks, "Vous en voulez donc?" ("So, you want some?")

    It is clear from these exchanges that all Martine's criticisms are aimed at her husband's impossible way of life. Were he to stop wasting his time and make better use of their meager resources, her complaints might easily disappear. Such a change, however, does not seem likely, given the protests and lamentations emanating from Sganarelle. Who, after all, is the injured party here, and what precisely is it that keeps Sganarelle from changing his irascible ways? The only clue to an answer in the text—and here students may be quicker to the mark than the teacher—is the curious reference, heavy with irony, made by Sganarelle to the first night of their marriage ("Il est vrai que tu me fis trop d'honneur. . .") whose resonance he prolongs with a threat to reveal some terrible secret ("[N]e me fais point parler là-dessus; je dirais de certaines choses. . ."). He concludes with a decisive: "tu fus bien heureuse de me trouver." If, playing with the irony implicit in the structure of Sganarelle's speech, we were to understand him as meaning "Tu me fis *trop de déshonneur*" ("You did me *a great dishonor*"), or, to put it another way, were we to posit that he had discovered on his wedding night that his bride was not the virgin he had supposed she was and that he had therefore become a sort of ex post facto cuckold, then certain details take on new significance. Sganarelle, cousin of the Sganarelle in *L'école des maris* and a true creature of Molière in that respect, would have seen himself as doubly dishonored, since he had both been wronged *and* fooled! What to do? Unfortunately; there is nothing to be done without exponentially increasing his dishonor by making it public. He is thus forced to swallow his shame and impotent anger, while over time making everyone—wife, children, and himself—suffer from his frustration. Now we can understand his reluctance, even in the heated exchange with his wife, to dredge up the awesome truth. We understand as well the reluctance of the wife to pursue the enigmatic utterances of her husband, for a discussion could lend substance to what she might otherwise allow herself to regard as mere suspicion on his part. No need here to emulate the mistake of Racine's Phèdre; some things are decidedly better left in the dark.

Sharing the couple's secret, we can now appreciate as well the implications of M. Robert's intrusion in act 1, scene 1. The beating that he thoughtlessly attempts to interrupt is, after all, part and parcel of the modus vivendi that the couple has evolved to deal with an otherwise unresolvable dilemma: Sganarelle relieves his anger the frustration by beating his wife, and she—although with less enthusiasm—receives the blows in acknowledgment of her guilt. "Et je veux qu'il me batte, moi" (1.2) ("And I want him to beat me"), she tells the astonished neighbor when he attempts to come to her rescue, and both she and her husband turn as one to cudgel the well-meaning intruder. For each has the best of reasons to keep the canonical beating a private family matter.

Although a cuckold quite literally in spite of himself, Sganarelle is obliged by an age-old, culturally induced reflex to view himself as without honor, as something rather less than a man. His way of life reflects and confirms this destructive image of the self: impaired by the loss of all self-regard, he has abandoned himself to the more primitive side of his nature. In spite of his vaunted education and talents, he gathers wood for a living, tyrannizes wife and children, and fills his days with drink and idleness. Should he pause at any point to examine his weakness, he is referred back, with the aid of a nagging wife, to its source, and the unholy cycle begins anew. One day, however, perhaps because of a crisis of frustration, a single blow too many, or too heavy, disturbs the equilibrium of their arrangement, awakening in Martine a heightened sense of injustice, which overrides her accustomed guilt and inspires in her, understandably, a thirst for revenge. For reasons more compelling perhaps than her own ironic explanation—"C'est une punition trop délicate pour mon pendard" ("It's too delicate a punishment for this bum")—she has put aside thoughts of cuckolding her husband and, in moment of inspiration, finds for him a perfectly proportioned punishment that will prove to be the salvation of each and both.

Thanks to a vigorous pounding by the servants of Géronte, administered at the behest of Martine, a bewildered Sganarelle soon agrees that he is indeed a doctor—at which point the play embraces a classic comic situation replete with young lovers (Léandre and Lucinde), a blocking character (Géronte), and the equivalent of the wily servant (Sganarelle), who works against Géronte to ensure the union of the young lovers. In the ensuring action, truth and falsehood, reality and illusion are interwoven to advance the causes of both the lovers and the peasant couple Martine and Sganarelle. Sganarelle, who is no doctor, embarks on the cure of a young woman who is not sick and, with the aid of an apothecary who really isn't one, brings about a complete cure, because he knows as much as any doctor of the period—that is, nothing! In the process, the counterfeit doctor acquires a reputation for healing that proves to be the perfect cure for his lack of self-esteem, the result of a mindless but operative view of cuckoldry.

In the final scene of the play, the individuals most deeply concerned make it clear that Sganarelle has been restored to honor and esteem by the dignity of his new calling. Martine claims—as well she should—her share of the credit for her husband's rehabilitation: "Puisque tu ne seras point pendu, rends-moi grâce d'être médecin; car c'est moi qui t'ai procuré cet honneur" ('Since you won't be hanged, you can thank me that you're a doctor; because it's me who got you that honor"). And Sganarelle is willing to pardon the beating in favor of his newly found importance and a manifestly therapeutic self-esteem: "Je te pardonne ces coups de bâton en faveur de la dignité où tu m'as élevé; mais prépare-toi désormais à vivre dans un grand respect avec un homme de ma conséquence. . ." ("I forgive you the beating in view of the high rank to which you have raised me; but prepare yourself from now on to live in great respect for a man of my importance. . .").

In the ontologically problematic world of the *Le médecin malgré lui*, where the categories of illusion and reality apply only in the most idiosyncratic manner, where rules and logic do not pertain, and where the most serious efforts to cope may appear whimsical, Molière appears to delight in the spectacle of fate repairing its misdeeds in the interest of an authentic human response to adversity: The cruel revelation of his nuptial bed had plunged Sganarelle "understandably" into deep despair, leading him "logically," in his frustration, to abuse his wife who, while "justly" seeking to end her own humiliation, succeeded in reshaping her husband's psyche, the fate of Léandre and Lucinde, and her own fate as well. No *raisonneurs*, no privileged values, no grand moral schemes; rather, simple, bruised humanity expresses itself out of need—instinctively, authentically—and carries the day in a world otherwise emptied of justice and meaning. Here surely is the mark of Molière the champion of instinctual humanity as celebrated by Ramon Fernandez in the pages of his still remarkable biography.

Throughout the three great comedies preceding *Le médecin malgré lui*, in particular after *Tartuffe*, Molière seems intent on lacerating, albeit with a caution dictated by the number and power of his enemies, all misrepresentation, all twisted posturing, all defacement of the truth. The fantasyland of *Le médecin* offered an environment in which he might express his anger and frustration with a reasonable expectation of impunity. Molière did, in fact, take advantage of the opportunity to operate the first reconstruction of one of his comic heroes and in the process confirmed his definitively altered rapport with his audience. The criticism implicit in satiric laughter will henceforth be shared by the monomaniac with the ostensibly normal people who surround him, stand-ins for society at large. Having once established the axis for laughter, Molière will bend it subtly; against the laughers. What is more two major comic protagonists, Jourdain and Argan will receive, in the dizzying final moments of their plays, a kind of rehabilitation that, illusion for illusion, compares well with the fates of their would-be critics and exploiters. Finally, in the slide from certainty to skepticism hinted at in the evolution of his comic protagonists, Molière reaches out to Marivaux, whose Enlightenment comedy, in its effort to modify the views of his audience, will routinely reconstruct its comic heroes.

No painter is totally present in a single painting, but all paintings collaborate in the articulation of their creator's vision, and so it goes with a playwright and his theater. By approaching *Le médecin malgré lui* contextually and by remembering that the genius of its creator expresses itself in each of his works, students may enrich their appreciation of Molière and his dramatic imagination.

PETER H. NURSE

Le Misanthrope: *Philosophical Implications*

*L*e *Misanthrope*, first performed in June, 1666, is commonly bracketed with *Tartuffe* and *Dom Juan* as forming a trilogy of Molière's great "problem-plays", for, like them, it has given rise to continual critical controversy and has often been interpreted as hovering uneasily on the frontier that separates comedy from serious drama. The more overtly farcical and burlesque features of plays such as *L'Ecole des Femmes* are here much less in evidence, confined principally to the short scene that ends Act IV, with the intrusion of the clownish figure of Monsieur Dubois—"plaisamment figuré"—and perhaps the portrayal of the two marquis, Acaste and Clitandre, where the puppet analogy is often marked. Antoine Adam therefore voices the general view when he writes: "Plus que *Tartuffe* . . . , cette comédie tends vers le drame, offre un visage ambigu, impose au spectateur cette gêne de ne pas savoir exactement s'il doit rire ou s'emouvoir, et la crainte de commettre un contresens."

More than in any other play of Molière, this ambiguity arises from the fact that there is here no clear grouping of "sympathetic" and "unsympathetic" characters, with the comic protagonist firmly and obviously placed in the latter category, as was the case in *Tartuffe*. To quote the *Lettre écrite sur la comédie du Misanthrope*, which was published together with the original edition of the play in 1667, and which is generally attributed to Donneau de Visé:

From *Molière and The Comic Spirit*. © 1990 Librarie Droz.

> Le Misanthrope, malgré sa folie, si l'on peut ainsi appeler son
> humeur, a le caractère d'un honnête homme. . . Bien qu'il
> paraisse en quelque façon ridicule, il dit des choses fort justes.

Indeed, many of the things which provoke the misanthrope's indignation are presented to us as objectively reprehensible; so much so, that many a spectator has been tempted to share Alceste's responses and to conclude that Molière was seizing the opportunity to vent his own feelings, at the same time inviting our approval of them. Therefore, as we saw in an earlier chapter, some have gone to the extreme point of labelling *Le Misanthrope* a piece of autobiographical "confession", where Alceste's sense of injustice at the duplicity of Célimène is a thinly veiled transposition of Molière's suffering through the infidelity of his actress wife, Armande, and where the sordid machinations of Alceste's rivals—descending at one point to the infamous accusation that he was responsible for publishing a dangerously subversive political tract (the "livre abominable")—reproduce the unscrupulous tactics of the *cabale* that had mounted the onslaught on *L'Ecole des Femmes* and succeeded in bringing about the ban on *Tartuffe* and *Dom Juan*. Even Antoine Adam, who rejects as "indecent" the idea that Molière should ever have publicly evoked his domestic troubles, is ready to affirm that Alceste is the author's spokesman in attacking such aspects of contemporary usage and taste as the "effusion de politesse" with which Philinte has embraced a stranger in the street, or "la mode des poésies galantes", exemplified by Oronte's sonnet.

Significant evidence in favour of seeing *Le Misanthrope* primarily as a *comédie de moeurs*, in which the satirical indictment of contemporary society is made possible by using the protagonist as spokesman, is contained in the *Lettre* where de Visé speaks of Molière's intention in writing the play:

> Il n'a point voulu faire une comédie pleine d'incidents, mais une
> pièce seulement où il pût parler contre les mœurs du siècle. C'est
> ce qui lui a fait prendre pour son héros un misanthrope, et
> comme misanthrope veut dire ennemi des hommes, on doit
> demeurer d'accord qu'il ne pouvait choisir un personnage qui
> vraisemblablement pût mieux parler contre les hommes que leur
> ennemi.

De Visé goes on to explain the rôle of Célimène as essentially performing the same function, for the "humeur satirique" of this witty *médisante* is equally well chosen to serve the author's purpose:

L'on doit admirer que, dans une pièce où Molière veut parler contre les mœurs du siècle et n'épargner personne, il nous fait voir une médisante avec un ennemi des hommes. Je vous laisse à penser si ces deux personnes ne peuvent pas naturellement parler contre toute la terre, puis-que l'un hait les hommes, et que l'autre se plaît à en dire tout le mal qu'elle en sait.

It is true that de Visé speaks of Alceste as being "en quelque façon ridicule", contrasting him unfavorably with the wise Philinte ("si raisonnable, que toute le monde devrait l'imiter"), but the inescapable suggestion is that Molière nevertheless identifies himself with the substance of Alceste's moral crusade, his determination to "n'épargner personne" coinciding with Alceste's "Et je vais n'épargner personne". For de Visé, Alceste's only real fault, it would seem, lies in the *manner* rather than *matter* of his diatribes:

Il est vrai qu'il semble trop exiger, mais il faut demander beaucoup pour obtenir quelque chose; et pour obliger les hommes à se corriger un peu de leurs défauts, il est nécessaire de les leur faire paraître bien grands.

Alceste's case is that the society in which he lives is no better than a human jungle, where every sort of corruption reigns:

Je ne trouve partout que lâche flatterie,
Qu'injustice, intérêt, trahison, fourberie.

Even Philinte accepts that this verdict is substantially correct; less systematic than his friend—for he is ready to concede that there are exceptions to the general rule—he will nonetheless support Alceste's principal contention:

Tout marche par cabale et par pur intérêt;
Ce n'est plus que la ruse aujourd'hui qui l'emporte,
Et les hommes devraient être faits d'autre sorte.

It is this analysis which the incidents of the text illustrate and confirm; insincerity and double-dealing are rife: people praise you to your face, but denigrate you once your back is turned; to win your law-suits you need influence with the judges; and to achieve any kind of advancement you must wear a mask and pander to those cliques who control the corridors of power. These aspects of social corruption, focused in the theme of hypocrisy and already closely examined in *Tartuffe* and *Dom Juan* (notably in the great speech by the Don in Act V, scene 2: "L'hypocrisie est un vice à la mode, et tous les vices à la mode passent pour des vertus . . .") are frequently evoked in such episodes as the one where Arsinoé—whom Michelet called a female counterpart to Tartuffe—tries to buy Alceste's favours with the promise of a post at Court:

> On peut, pour vous servir, remuer des machines,
> Et j'ai des gens en main, que j'emploierai pour vous,
> Qui vous feront à tout un chemin assez doux.

What is at issue in the play, therefore, is not so much the substance of Alceste's view of the human scene—even in *L'Ecole des Femmes* there was never any suggestion that Arnolphe was wrong when he saw *cocuage* as the normal fate of man in society—but rather the validity of his particular reaction to it. In other words, does Alceste's own record of behavior sustain his right to sit in judgement on his fellow men and justify his Juvenalian *saeva indignatio*—"ces haines vigoureuses, / Que doit donner le vice aux âmes vertueuses"? And, as a corollary of this question, is the "sincerity" of plain speaking quite as unambiguously objective a virtue as Alceste would claim?

To frame the question in these terms is, moreover, to place *Le Misanthrope* in the perspective adopted by the Humanists in the sixteenth and seventeenth centuries. Whether in the work of the moralists such as Montaigne and Saint-Evremond, or in that of many authors of aulic treatises dealing with manners at Court, such as Bourdonné's *Le Courtisan désabusé* of 1658, or in fiction, such as *L'Astrée* or *La Princesse de Cléves*, there is a consensus of opinion that human nature is basically flawed and that this is particularly apparent in highly organised society, as is the case at Court, where the vices are concentrated.

The rational solution therefore seemed to many that men with uncompromising moral ideals should shun society and choose to live in *le désert*—whether that be the pastoral life portrayed in *L'Astrée*, or simply the solitude of a country-house as in Mme de Lafayette's novel. Montaigne puts the point with his customary firmness in his essay *De la Vanité*:

> Qui a ses mœurs établies en règlement au-dessus de son siècle, ou
> qu'il torde et émousse ses règles, ou, ce que je lui conseille plutôt,
> qu'il se retire à quartier et ne se mêle point de nous.

Saint-Evremond, in turn, expresses the same argument in his essay of 1668, *Les Sentiments d'un honnête et habile Courtisan*, where he addresses the *vertueux* who demands a rigorous moral idealism:

Je sais que l'ingratitude et l'avarice sont de très vilaines qualités; mais puisqu'elles sont si communes dans le monde, ou résolvez-vous de les souffrir, ou sauvez-vous dans la solitude, et portez dans une retraite cette vertu qui aura fait haïr votre personne dans une Cour.

There is clearly a side of Alceste's nature which is aware of the wisdom of this counsel: Molière thus shows him repeatedly attempting to withdraw—either literally, into the *désert*, or symbolically, into himself, as is the case when Oronte arrives at the start of Act I, scene 2; or during the *scène des portraits*; or, again, at the end of Act V, scene 1, where he retreats into his "petit coin sombre". It is as though Alceste recognises that withdrawal from involvement with those of whom he disapproves is the logical counterpart to the kind of detachment of the will from material interests which is the normal guarantee of the critic's objective rational judgement. It is precisely because, in practice, Alceste is constantly drawn back into heated involvement with the *fâcheux* who compose society that his motives are suspect and his "sincerity" questionable.

No one has made this point more clearly that Rousseau. In the *Lettre à M. d'Alembert* of 1758, he argues that the only acceptable moral basis for a misanthrope's denunciation of vice is that he should be radically immune from that self-interest which is the root of vice in others:

Cette contemplation continuelle des désordres de la société le détache de lui-même pour fixer toute son attention sur le genre humain. Cette habitude élève, agrandit ses idées, détruit en lui les inclinations basses qui nourrissent et concentrent l'amour-propre.

The mark of a genuinely idealistic indignation is therefore that it detaches the misanthrope from

tout chagrin puéril qui n'a nul fondement raisonnable et de tout intérêt personnel trop vif, dont il ne doit nullement être susceptible. Qu'il s'emporte sur tous les désordres dont il n'est que le témoin, ce sont toujours de nouveaux traits au tableau; mais qu'il soit froid sur celui qui s'adresse directement à lui: car, ayant déclaré la guerre aux méchants, il s'attend bien qu'ils la lui feront à leur tour. S'il n'avait pas prévu le mal que lui fera sa franchise, elle serait étourderie et non pas vertu. . . . Il fallait que le misanthrope fût toujours furieux contre les vices publics et

toujours tranquille sur les méchancetés personnelles dont il était
la victime.

What Molière has done, however, is to undermine right from the
start the validity of Alceste's doctrinaire stance by showing it to be the
product of a naturally choleric temperament, which feeds always on strictly
personal grievances. If Philinte's *complaisance* is attacked in the opening
scene, it is because Alceste sees this as implying a slight upon himself—a
failure to discriminate between his own intrinsic merit and that of a mere
stranger. His declared hatred of his fellow men is the angry reaction of an
ego which can only compensate for its wounded pride by proclaiming
universal corruption. Rousseau recognises that such a reaction is irrational
and comments:

> Il est naturel que cette colère dégénère en emportement et lui
> fasse dire alors plus qu'il ne pense de sang-froid.

But the real significance of the episode is that the "sincerity" of plain-
speaking about others is already branded as no more than a rationalisation of
self-centred passion. The fact that behaviour of this kind is "natural" only
strengthens the case for a philosophical distrust of the notion of sincerity:
Alceste *is* sincere in the sense that his hatred *is* real at that juncture, but its
irrationality is further demonstrated by the fundamental inconsistency which
springs from it: while demanding "discrimination" for himself ("Je veux
qu'on me distingue"), he nevertheless denies it to others, since he is ready to
condemn "tous les pauvres mortels, sans nulle exception".

Similarly, it is because of people's *complaisance* towards *his* personal
legal adversary—"le franc scélérat avec qui j'ai procès"—that they are
pronounced guilty. For Alceste, all issues are ultimately judged in terms of a
conflict of interests, and characteristic of this is his reply to Célimène when
she explains that she cultivates Clitandre to secure his influence in the matter
of her own law-suit:

> Perdez votre procès, madame, avec constance,
> Et ne ménagez point un rival qui m'offense.

If the foregoing view of the opening encounter between Philinte
and Alceste is correct, it suggests a difference conclusion from that of M.
Adam when he spoke of Molière's having used Alceste to express his own
scorn for the "effusions de politesse" that characterized seventeenth-century
polite society: for what was really at issue was not the wrongs and rights of

Philinte's behaviour, but rather the degree to which any moral attitude is purely relative to a given temperament, whether it be the *phlegme* of Philinte or the *bile* of Alceste.

There are similar reasons for disagreeing with M. Adam's view that the "scène du sonnet", in Act 1, and scene 2, is intended as a vehicle for Molière's own impatience with the trivialities of *précieux* poetry. Once again, it would seem that it is not the evaluation of the intrinsic merit of the folk-song as against the sonnet that matters, but the demonstration of the subjective nature of taste.

De Visé, in his *Lettre*, was the first to argue that Oronte's sonnet "n'est point méchant selon la manière d'écrire d'aujourd'hui"; it is no better nor worse than innumerable other light-hearted products of *salon* wit, but the real focus of our attention is the fatuous vanity of its author who obviously sees in it a work of genius. When Oronte boasts that "je n'ai demeuré qu'un quart d'heure à le faire", we are inevitably reminded of Mascarille in *Les Précieuses ridicules* and his claim that "les gens de qualité savent tout sans avoir rien appris".

But while Oronte's estimate of his poem is grossly inflated, Alceste's reaction is no less exaggerated. He too treats his relatively simple folk-song as a masterpiece and dwells on it with humourless over-emphasis; and when he proclaims Oronte to be *pendable* for writing such verse (recalling his use of the same term to describe Philinte's flattery of a stranger), it becomes manifest that his judgement is prompted by very dubious motives. It is significant, of course, that Oronte is a rival of Alceste for Célimène's favours, and there is more than a suggestion that what irritates the misanthrope most of all in the sonnet is the fact that its theme reflects his own frustrations: like the lover in the sonnet, Alceste suffers from his lady's *complaisance*; he, too, is irked by "une attente éternelle [qui] pousse à bout l'ardeur de [son] zèle"; and, finally, the conclusion of the verse closely matches his relationship with Célimène: "On désespère, / Alors qu'on espère toujours."

Similar factors underlie the passionate intensity that Alceste feels for his folk-song, for it gives expression to what we have already called his "Galahad fantasy": the desire to possess the beloved, but this desire "sublimated" by his declared readiness to make heroic sacrifices on her behalf. All this fits perfectly his view of himself as one whose love has never been equalled and whose sole aim is to prove it by an *éclatant sacrifice*.

Once this aspect of Alceste's motivation is made clear, it is possible to see the scene in a new light and to re-assess the nature of his *franchise*. As has often been remarked, Alceste's initial reaction to Oronte is completely at odds with the principles he had so dogmatically stated in the first scene: as part of his more rational instinct to withdraw from entanglement with a *fâcheux*, he makes use of all those polite untruths which Philinte had declared necessary for survival in society, coming out with such phrases as "C'est trop d'honneur que vous me voulez faire" or "J'ai le *défaut* / D'être un peu plus sincère en cela qu'il ne faut". And when he does eventually proffer criticism, it is at first hidden behind the fiction that he is reporting what he had said to some other versifier— a device that is in all essentials the same as that used by Arsinoé and Célimène when they criticise each other in Act III, scene 4. The inescapable conclusion is that it is when Alceste is most rational and self-possessed that he disguises his thoughts in the interest of self-protection, and that it is only when his *sang-froid* is destroyed and his bile aroused that he yields to a slanging match which is dressed up in the guise of objective "sincerity".

Many critics of *Le Misanthrope*, while readily granting that Alceste is a figure of comic contradictions in his relationship with society as a whole, have nevertheless found it impossible to accept a comic interpretation of his relationship with Célimène. They admit that Alceste is guilty of inconsistency in loving a woman who so manifestly stands for all that runs counter to his ideals, but they point to the fact that Alceste himself is aware of the inconsistency, and that the consequent self-recognition, with its accompanying sense of shame, is frequently a source of tragic emotion, closely related to the Racinian pattern.

It is true that Alceste has such moments of lucidity concerning the irrationality of his love for Célimène: when first called to account for it by Philinte in Act I, scene 1, he confesses his "faible" and concedes that "la raison n'est pas ce qui règle l'amour". Again, in the first encounter with Célimène, he speaks of his unavailing efforts to master his passion:

> Je ne le cèle pas, je fais tout mon possible
> A rompre de ce cœur l'attachement terrible;
> Mais mes plus grands efforts n'ont rien fait jusqu'ici . . .

But it is above all in the dramatic climax of Act IV, scene 3, that the echoes of tragic style are the most pronounced: having received tangible evidence of Célimène's duplicity, he nevertheless experiences the complete breakdown of his rational will and acknowledges his radical impotence:

> Ciel, rien de plus cruel peut-il être inventé?
> Et jamais cœur fut-il de la sorte traité?
> Quoi! d'un juste courroux je suis ému contre elle,
> C'est moi qui me viens plaindre, et c'est moi qu'on
> querelle!

> On pousse ma douleur et mes soupçons à bout,
> On me laisse tout croire, on fait gloire de tout;
> Et cependant mon cœur est encore assez lâche
> Pour ne pouvoir briser la chaîne qui l'attache
> Et pour ne pas s'armer d'un généreux mépris
> Contre l'ingrat objet dont il est épris!
> Ah! que vous savez bien ici contre moi-même,
> Perfide, vous servir de ma faiblesse extrême,
> Et ménager pour vous l'excès prodigieux
> De ce fatal amour né de vos traîtres yeux!

Here, certainly, is an outstanding example of the *victime pathétique*, and if Alceste is in many respects so sympathetic a character it is because, to quote René Jasinski, "sa grandeur réside surtout dans son humanité, le drame intérieur qui le déchire".

Yet the real mistake of those who dwell on the tragic implications of such moments in the play is that they isolate them from their context in the overall dramatic structure. From the start, Alceste has played the part of an uncompromising critic of others: true to his name (Alceste is derived from the Greek *alkestés*, signifying "strong man"), he has denied any possibility of mitigating circumstances for human shortcomings and proclaimed himself the sole arbiter of moral truth. It is always in close juxtaposition with such grossly inflated attitudes—with all their doubtful authenticity—that the very infrequent and fleeting moments of self-depreciation have to be judged. For instance, the passage where Alceste speaks of his helpless efforts to "rompre de ce cœur l'attachement terrible" follows hard upon the overbearing censoriousness of his first words of greeting to Célimène, when he threatens to break with her unless she mends her ways:

> Madame, voulez-vous que je vous parle net?
> De vos façons d'agir je suis mal satisfait;
> Contre elles dans mon cœur trop de bile s'assemble,
> Et je sens qu'il faudra que nous rompions ensemble.
> Oui, je vous tromperais de parler autrement:
> Tôt ou tard nous romprons indubitablement,
> Et je vous promettrais mille fois le contraire
> Que je ne serais pas en pouvoir de le faire.

It is only when Célimène calls his bluff, threatening in turn to retract what she has said about favouring him above all other suitors, that his "strong-man" pose collapses. Significantly, it is precisely the same pattern that is re-enacted in the big scene of Act IV. The culminating admission of his "faiblesse extrême" has to be set against the ostentatious self-complacence with which he announces to Eliante his intention to confound the coquette and sever all connection with her:

> Non, non, Madame, non, l'offense est trop mortelle,
> Il n'est point de retour, et je romps avec elle;
> Rien ne saurait changer le dessein que j'en fais,
> Et je me punirais de l'estimer jamais.
> La voici. Moncourroux redouble à cette approche;
> Je vais de sa noirceur lui faire un vif reproche,
> Pleinement la confondre, et vous porter après
> Un cœur tout dégagé de ses trompeurs attraits.

In the ensuing scene there are many other factors which prevent the action from ever really escaping from a comic framework—and all of them are a reminder of the kinship of Alceste with Arnolphe. First of all, the reference in lines 1279-1280 to Alceste's *soupirs* and *sombres regards* recalls those deflating physical antics of Arnolphe "lorsqu'il explique à Agnès la violence de son amour avec ces roulements d'yeux extravagants, ces soupirs ridicules, et ces larmes niaises qui font rire tout le monde". (Molière himself acted both rôles and De Visé's *Lettre* suggests the continuity of the same *pantomine*: "Cette ingénieuse et admirable comédie commence par le Misanthrope, qui, par son action, fait connaître à tout le monde que c'est lui, avant même d'ouvrir la bouche.")

Secondly, Molière uses here another device which was effective in *L'Ecole des Femmes*: as several editors have indicated, some of the phrases spoken by Alceste are uncannily reminiscent of famous speeches in Corneille's *Le Cid* and *Horace*, giving a certain air of mock-heroic parody to the alexandrines.

Most significant of all, however, is the fact that this scene shows Alceste making the same kind of moral turn-about as characterized the protagonist of *L'Ecole des Femmes*. Just as Arnolphe's authoritarian stance collapsed in the face of Agnès's resistance and led to the reversal implied in the line:

> Tout comme tu voudras tu pourras te conduire

so, too, Alceste ends by jettisoning his own high-flown moral scruples as soon as it suits him. The man who had demanded of others an uncompromising sincerity in all their relationships now pleads with his coquette that, if she cannot bring herself to be entirely faithful to him, she should at least simulate such fidelity:

> Efforcez-vous ici de paraître fidèle
> Et je m'efforcerai, moi, de vous croire telle.

In other words, Alceste, like those he had previously condemned with such dogmatic arrogance, illustrates the fact that there are times when every man needs to compromise with his own inner weakness and to disguise reality with a veil of insincerity.

It is this above all which demonstrates the inauthenticity of Alceste's whole code of sincerity: the real basis of the demand that others should speak the unvarnished truth of their feelings was the need to have an explicit confirmation of his own superiority, whether as a friend (vis-à-vis Philinte) or as a lover (vis-à-vis Célimène). In spite of his hostility to those whose relationships are determined by self-interest—"On devrait châtier sans pitié / Ce commerce honteux de semblants d'amitié"—Alceste's love for Célimène presupposes a similar *commerce*: "JE ne l'aimerais pas si je ne croyais l'être". But, like Arnolphe, he always speaks in terms of fashioning Célimène to fit his own requirements and it is she who must sacrifice her own identity by following him into *le désert*—"pour trouver tout en moi".

It is essentially because Célimène senses the threat which male possessiveness presents to her independently identity that she has certain affinities with other *précieuses* in Molière's theatre. The reason why she deliberately cultivates the ambiguities of the language of *préciosite* is that it offers a form of protection from complete assimilation by any one of her admirers. Moreover, these ambiguities explain why critics have been divided as to her real character. Jules Brody describes her as a "chronic liar," while Jacques Guicharnaud goes to the opposite extreme, writing of her total lack of hypocrisy: "Célimène est un personnage sans équivoque . . . Elle coïncide avec son comportement . . . elle ignore tout machiavélisme." This judgement is based on the view that she uses the nuances of *précieux* terminology with utmost precision and that she tells only Alceste, quite unambiguously, that he enjoys "le bonheur de savoir que vous êtes aimé". Molière's main concern, according to Guicharnaud, is to show that is the vanity of her suitors—all of them convinced of their innate superiority to others—which is the source of the confusion, since they all read into her words what their ego wants to believe.

However much one may sympathise with the motives that lie behind Célimène's struggle for independence in a predatory, male-dominated society, it is difficult to accept without reservation Guicharnaud's defense of her authenticity. His interpretation becomes more plausible, however, when he re-phrases it in the following terms: "Sa sincérité consiste à user de mots et de figures de style qui correspondent exactement à ce qu'elle éprouve *au moment où elle le dit*". For this introduces a qualification of radical significance, and which puts the whole question of "sincerity" back into the relativistic mode which we have seen to operate elsewhere in Molière's work. Sincerity, like all the "virtues" questioned by La Rochefoucauld in the *Maximes*, ceases to have any absolute status, simply because the human heart is itself a constantly shifting amalgam of hidden interests and instincts: "Rien de si impétueux que ses désirs, rien de si caché que ses desseins, rien de si habile que ses conduites."

Thus, when Guicharnaud says of Célimène that she has "la sincérité de son humeur du moment", it is in the light of La Rochefoucauld's analysis of "le caprice de notre humeur" that such a verdict should be read. Whichever of her suitors she is with or writing to, at any given moment, that is the one whose favors are most important to her; for, as Alceste reproachfully says to her: "Conserver tout le monde est votre grande étude". The ambiguity of her feelings springs from within herself, and perhaps the true key to her nature is provided by Eliante when Philinte asks if Célimène really does love Alceste or not:

> C'est un point qu'il n'est pas fort aisé de savoir.
> Comment pouvoir juger s'il est vrai qu'elle l'aime?
> Son cœur de ce qu'il sent n'est pas bien sûr lui-même;
> Il aime quelquefois sans qu'il le sache bien,
> Et croit aimer aussi parfois qu'il n'en est rien.

It is this aspect of Célimène about which Lionel Gossman has written with considerable perception:

> Célimène has no being of her own. She is a Sphinx-like creature who acquires her reality from her suitors themselves and whose entire being, like theirs, is contained in her appearance for others . . . Like her suitors, she has no autonomous desire or will, only the desire to find herself reflected as desirable in the eyes of others. Only through the sentiments and reactions toward her that she finds in others can she experience her own self. The enigmatic being that all her suitors pursue behind her masks is perfectly elusive, because it does not exist."

Not the least interesting point made here is that, ultimately, Célimène and Alceste both share certain fundamental characteristics—just as it was argued in an earlier chapter that, for all their apparent dissimilarity, there was a common psychological denominator linking Arnolphe and his declared enemies, the *précieuses*. For them both, love is at once a threat to the self and a weapon for the defence of the self, and when Célimène plays off one suitor against another, speaking each time with "la sincérité de son humeur du moment", she is only reproducing the "sincere" reaction of Alceste when, recoiling from Célimène's "betrayal", he rushes to offer his heart to Eliante:

> Acceptez-le, madame, au lieu de l'infidèle;
> C'est par là que je puis prendre vengeance d'elle,
> Et je la veux punir par les sincères vœux,
> Par le profond amour, les soins respectueux,
> Les devoirs empressés et l'assidu service
> Dont ce cœur va vous faire un ardent sacrifice.

In his fable *La Besace*, La Fontaine takes the Aesop story of Jupiter inviting each member of the animal kingdom to voice its grievances about its physical appearance, and promising to grant any demands for improvement. But what happens it that every animal sees itself as a paragon, and spends all its time finding fault with the other species. The fabulist then draws the following moral conclusion:

> Jupin les renvoya s'étant censurés tous,
> Du reste, contents d'eux. Mais parmi les plus fous,
> Notre espèce excella; car tout ce que nous sommes,
> Lynx envers nos pareils et taupes envers nous,
> Nous nous pardonnons tout, et rien aux autres hommes;
> On se voit d'un autre œil qu'on ne voit son prochain.

It is essentially this same vision of men that is dramatised by Molière in *Le Misanthrope*, and it is perfectly summed up by Célimène when she speaks, of

> Ce grand aveuglement où chacun est pour soi.

Prisoners of self-love, we each claim a monopoly of truth, but all we really do is rationalise our own strictly limited and constantly changing personal viewpoint:

> Madame, on peut, je crois, louer et blâmer tout,
> Et chacun a raison, suivant l'âge ou le goût."

This explains why so much of modern criticism denies or minimises the significance of the question of "la morale de Molière" and prefers to emphasise a purely aesthetic contrasting of moral attitudes. Here is how M. Guicharnaud expresses the idea with respect to *Le Misanthrope*:

> Chacun de nous n'a pour critère du Bien et du Mal que son propre désir ou sa propre souffrance. Nous ne pouvons pas, en toute bonne foi, "juger et condamner". Nous ne pouvons que constater, rire du dilemme, c'est-à-dire écrire les comédies. Tout le reste est présomption ou usurpation . . . Il ne s'agit pas dans Le Misanthrope d'un exposé moral, d'un débat philosophique sur le Bien et le Mal, mais d'un conflit d'attitudes qui sont *toutes* suspectes: l'objectivité elle-même n'est qu'un masque ou une arme de l'amour-propre."

In the preceding pages, while discussing *L'Ecole des Femmes*, I have already outlined my views on this question. For Molière, as for the spectator, the play offers the opportunity to experience dramatically certain basic and incompatible aspects of our nature, for in each of us there is an Alceste and a Philinte—an instinct that kicks agains the limitations of life and another instinct that counsels resignation (something akin to the Freudian opposition of the "pleasure-principle" and the "reality-principle"). And Ramon Fernandez was almost certainly right when he spoke of the cathartic release which Molière derived through characters such as Sganarelle, Arnolphe or Alceste:

> Si la raison de Molière contredit son tempérament, c'est ce tempérament qui fait la vie de son œuvre, et il semble qu'à la faveur d'une intrigue qui condamnait d'avance la raideur et l'absolu de ce tempérament, l'acteur Molière se déchargeait, se purgeait si l'on veut, mais se satisfaisait tout de même par l'expression outreé de ses tendances profondes.

But while, through art, the author and his public enjoy what Edwin Muir called an "irresponsible delight in vigorous events", there is always present in Molière's laughter that ironic element which ultimately deflates the self-centred ego and reconciles us with our true human condition. It is in this respect that his work fits so fully into the philosophical tradition of Scepticism, with its main Renaissance sources in Erasmus and Montaigne, that pervades seventeenth-century thought. The Praise of Folly is perhaps the seminal text for it. Based upon the Pauline paradox that the wisdom of the world is the real foolishness, it argues that real wisdom must take into account and accept the irrationalities of human nature. Thus when Philinte tells Alceste in Act I, scene 2 that "il faut fléchir au temps sans obstination" and that "c'est une folie à nulle autre / De vouloir se mêler de corriger le monde" he is echoing Erasmus's Folly who says:

> Comme il est d'une suprême sottise d'exprimer une vérité intempestive, il est de la dernière maladresse d'être sage à contretemps. Il agit à contretemps celui qui ne sait s'accommoder des choses telles qu'elles sont, qui n'obéit as aux usages, qui oublie cette loi des banquets: "Bois ou va-t-en!" et qui demande que la comédie ne soit pas une comédie. Tu montreras du vrai bon sens, toi qui n'es qu'un homme, en te pliant de bon gré a l'avis de la multitude ou en te trompant complaisamment avec elle . . . Ainsi se joue la comédie de la vie.

When Pascal wrote that "les choses du monde les plus déraisonnables deviennent plus raisonnables à cause du dérèglement des hommes" and pleaded for an ironic "pensée de derrière" in our judgement of life, he was essentially expressing the same Sceptic paradox as is contained in Philinte's reminder to Alceste that "A force de sagesse, on peut être blâmable".

It is in this sense that one might apply Fernandez's phrase: "La vision comique souligne le désaccord entre la raison et la vie." Reason, here, is an abstraction which seeks to substitute for the dynamic complexities of existence an artificial simplification. But "life" constantly resists such artificial pressures and triumphantly reasserts its natural resilience, producing in the process those explosions whereby the natural order is restored to an equilibrium. Bergson compared the process to a jack-in-the-box which is always springing back into position whenever someone tries to force it down, providing a new metaphor for the old idea in Boileau's phrase: "Chassez le naturel: il revient au galop". This explains the frequent use of the term "naturalism" applied to Molière's vision of things, and for the same reason M. Bénichou found it legitimate to refer to the inherent amoralism of a world where it was no longer a question of Right and Wrong, but of the sheer force of empirical fact vis-à-vis abstract theory.

That this was a basic feature of Molière's own attitude is suggested by the way he reacted to the controversy over the so-called rules of drama, — pointing out in *La Critique de l'Ecole des Femmes* that the rules advocated by his neo-Aristotelian critics were unreal abstractions of the over-rationalising intellect, whereas what ultimately counted was what we experience as pleasurable:

> Il y en a beaucoup que le trop d'esprit gâte, qui voient mal les
> choses à force de lumière . . . Laissons-nous aller de bonne foi
> aux choses qui nous prennent par les entrailles, et ne cherchons
> point de raisonnements pour nous empêcher d'avoir du plaisir.

It is the adoption of this empirical criterion of felt pleasure as opposed to pure reason which is increasingly characteristic of the age in which Molière lived and which accounts for the eclipse of the Stoicism so popular in the first half of the century, to be supplanted by an Epicurean current. Already in Erasmus and Montaigne it went hand in hand with their Sceptic sympathies, and it re-emerges powerfully in such later moralists as La Rochefoucauld and Saint-Evremond. La Rochefoucauld is on record as saying that, when it came to ethics, Senecca was a hypocrite and Epicurus a saint. Thus his *Maximes* frequently argue that it is consonant with enlightened self-interest to yield to Folly and consciously to accept illusion,—especially "pour nous épargner la douleur de connaître nos imperfections". And Saint-Evremond, similarly voicing his admiration for Epicurus, concludes that true wisdom lies in the pursuit of happiness and in making the best of the in-built rigours of human existence:

> J'ai toujours admiré la moral d'Epicure . . . La volupté est la
> véritable fin où toutes nos actions se rapportent . . . Il faut faire
> peu de réflexions sur la vie, mais sortir comme souvent hors de
> soi; et parmi les plaisirs que fournissent les choses étrangerès se
> dérober la connaissance de ses propres maux.

Is it not in this same direction that *Le Misanthrope* is pointing? The Alceste of the early stages of the play,—with his eulogy of "cette grande roideur des vertus des vieux âges" and his emphatic assertion of personal will-power and "reason" ("Je veux" is his most characteristic utterance)—is manifestly related to familiar Stoic postures, and it is these which crumble finally leaving him a defeated figure, his idealism having been proved hollow and pointless. That is why many critics have felt that *Le Misanthrope* was a watershed in Molière's theatre, issuing in a new phase in which the playwright abandoned any idea of corrective comedy and opted instead for the Erasmian Folly of Philinte which welcomed illusion, conscious or unconscious, as a remedy to life's ills. It is again Ramon Fernandez who argues this approach most penetratingly and who concludes:

> Quand il avait souhaité de corriger le monde, Molière avait
> rapprochè le théâtre du public, invitant celui-ci à s'intéresser à

l'action comme à une affaire qui se fût passée chez lui. Soit fatigue, soit découragement, soit retour aux lois traditionnelles de la comédie, ses dernierès œuvres témoignent d'un autre esprit. En meme temps qu'il atténue les ressemblances extérieures entre le spectacle et le spectateur, il se désintéresse de la leçon morale de la comédie. Ce n'est plus le monde bourgeois, à la fois intéressé et généreux de ses premières grandes pieces . . . c'est un monde cynique, indifférent au bien et au mal que nous présentent *Amphitryon, Georges Dandin* (sic), *L'Avare.*

DAVID SHAW

Legal Elements in Le Misanthrope

'J'ai pour moi la justice et je perds mon
procès!'

Alceste's surprise at losing his lawsuit is a defining image of his idealism.
Supposing his case to be self-evidently just, he omits to observe judicial
convention and so brings defeat upon himself. He is obsessed with an image
of perfect probity, but lives in a society composed of imperfect individuals.
The gulf between his vision and the moral ambiguity of the world to which
he belongs is the source of both comedy and pathos. It is interesting how
often this gulf is defined by references to the legal world.

According to La Grange, the youthful Molière studied law. 'Au
sortir des écoles de droit, il choisit la profession de comédien. He may even
have qualified as a barrister:

> . . . En quarante quelque peu devant,
> Je sortis du collège et j'en sortis savant,
> Puis venant d'Orléans, où je pris mes licences,
> Je me fis avocat au retour des vacance.
> Je suivis le barreau pendant cinq ou six mois,
> Où j'appris à plein fond l'ordonnance et les lois.
> Mais, quelque temps après, me voyant sans pratique,
> Je quittai là Cujas et je lui fis la nique.

From *Nottingham French Studies* 38, no. 1 (1999 Spring). © 1999 The University of Nottingham.

Molière's law studies may explain the number of references to legal procedure in his plays. Unlike Racine, he never wrote a play specifically about the legal world. But his theatre does presuppose a society based on a legal framework. It contains as many law officers as doctors, although the lawyers seem to have received rather less critical attention. As with Molière's medical satire, the more outspoken attacks on legal practice occur in plays containing a high proportion of fantasy or farce, such as *Monsieur de Pourceaugnac* or *Les Fourberies de Scapin*. In the more naturalistic five-act comedies, the legal world simply provides a framework against which to measure the excesses of the monomaniacs and parasites. In *Tartuffe*, the eponymous religious fraud even attempts to use the law to validate his criminal activities.

In *Le Misanthrope*, if the world of law is not the main focus, it constantly underpins the comedy. There is no 'plot', in the conventional sense. Rather, we have an analysis of a situation, that of a lover wishing to ascertain his mistress's feelings. Each time he comes near to achieving his aim, there is a frustrating interruption. Structurally, *Le Misanthrope* resembled *Les Fâcheux*. In the earlier play, a man wishing to be with his mistress is interrupted by an arbitrary succession of eccentric bores. In the more coherent *Misanthrope*, the interruptions all stem from Oronte's desire for revenge after the argument over the sonnet. Two of these touch upon legal matters and are dramatically introduced at the end of an act.

With an interval occurring at the end of each act, it was a wise precaution to make the final scene of an act contain a cliffhanger: a mystery introduced in the final scene to make the audience keener to settle down at the start of the following act in order to know the outcome. In *Le Misanthrope*, Molière does this systematically. After the spat between Alceste and Oronte in Act I, scene 2, we are left wondering about the seriousness of the 'malheureuse affaire' that Alceste has landed himself with. At the end of Act II, the salon conversation is suddenly interrupted by a summons for Alceste to appear before the *Tribunal des Maréchaux*. Unusually for a play written at this time, the main character is then absent for most of Act III as he answers the summons. At the end of Act IV, we have the splendid intervention of Du Bois, Alceste's forgetful valet. The entry of the servant relieves the tension that has built up over the previous scenes. Through his vagueness, he manages to introduce a double mystery: there have been two callers, but he cannot recall their messages. One of these appears to involve the need to flee. Both seem to be concerned with the law. They lead, in Act V, to Alceste's final great explosion, when he discovers that he has lost his lawsuit and may be facing a criminal charge. His gloomy view of human society is thereby confirmed. When his mistress is then shown to be incorrigibly unfaithful, there is nothing left for him in society and he departs.

So, two of the turning points in the play, artfully arranged to intrigue the audience during an interval, involve the sudden appearance of a strangely dressed messenger bringing dramatic news of legal confrontations. They introduce bathos in the contrast with salon sophistication. At the same time, they bring pathos: if the gentlemanly justice of the military tribunal is conciliatory, the harsh lesson of the lawsuit is that being in the right is not enough. They symbolize, through legal metaphor, that Alceste's idea of a relationship with Célimène, based on mutual love to the exclusion of all else ('. . . Pour trouver touten moi, comme moi tout en vous . . .') is hopeless romanticism. The world will always intrude.

If the legal world is often present in *Le Misanthrope*, it is never the target of the satire. On the contrary, legal procedure is presented as a legitimate feature of society. The butt of the satire is not the law but Alceste himself. His bizarre nature is effectively defined by his attitude towards his legal problems. When he first mentions his lawsuit, we hear that his opponent is a 'franc scélérat', a 'traître', 'ce pied plat', 'fourbe, infame et scélérat maudit'. No justification is given for this abuse. We never learn the subject of the lawsuit, nor the identity of the opponent: there is no indication, at this stage, that Alceste's vitriolic remarks are in any way justified. The implication is that Alceste is furious simply because someone has had the temerity to take him to court. And yet lawsuits among the landed gentry were commonplace. According to Donneau de Visé, '. . . il n'y en a presque point qui n'ait quelque procès . . .'. Alceste's hostility towards his opponent, in the absence of a special reason for such fury, is comically out of place.

In the light of Alceste's claim that his opponent is an evil and well-organized hypocrite, his decision not to observe the judicial conventions of the day particularly irrational. Philinte is surprised that he has no plan to contact the magistrates dealing with his case:

PHILINTE	Mais qui voulez-vous donc qui pour vous sollicite?
ALCESTE	Qui je veux? La raison, mon bon droit, l'équité.
PHILINTE	Aucun juge par vous ne sera visité?
ALCESTE	Non. Est-ce que ma cause est injuste ou douteuse?

This kind of exchange has persuaded some commentators that Alceste's sentiments are admirable, a noble indictment of the corruption of his age. Alceste argues that his case should stand or fall on its merits and that visiting the judge in advance is morally dubious. Detached from their context, these remarks can be made to sound heroically virtuous. In seventeenth-century

France however, they would just have seemed ridiculous. The custom of visiting judges before a hearing was a routine part of the judicial process: on a par, perhaps, with instructing one's barrister today. The litigant, or his friends and relatives, would make sure that the judge was fully acquainted with all the facts of the case in advance in order to expedite matters at a time when the wheels of justice tended to turn exceedingly slow. Or it might simply be a question of meeting the judge so that be would be aware of the personalities involved. For Madame de Sévigné, such a visit could be a pleasant social occasion. It was even legal to give the judge small gifts, usually in the form of food ('épices'), in order to secure his good offices. Some people earned a living, quite legally, as *solliciteurs de procés*, from which term the English word 'solicitor' was derived. The practice would survive as a routine feature of French justice for another hundred years. By condemning such a custom, Alceste is setting himself apart as a ridiculous idealist.

He claims that the loss of his case would have an exemplary value, a ringing indictment of the wickedness of human systems of justice:

> J'aurai la plaisir de perdre mon procés
> . . . Je verrai dans cette plaiderie,
> Si les hommes auront assez d'effronterie,
> Seront assez méchants, scélérats et pervers
> Pour me faire injustice aux yeux de l'univers.

This is just silly. The idea that losing a potentially strong case might have any value is foolish enough. But the suggestion of the universe being interested in Alceste's legal affairs is clearly ludicrous. The characteristic direction of Alceste's reasoning is significant. If he had begun by defining a coherent attitude towards society, and had then cited particular examples, his position would have been intellectually more respectable, if less comic. But he goes in the opposite direction. He moves from an expression of anger at the idea of someone opposing him at law to a blanket condemnation of human justice. From the particular to the general: his condemnation of human justice stems, not from a carefully reasoned philosophical position, but from feelings of pique over having to appear in court.

This is very typical of Alceste. At the start of the play, he has already criticized Philinte over his attitude to friendship. Philinte is accused of greeting Alceste and a stranger with the same show of affection: Alceste naturally finds this difficult to accept. As with the lawsuit, he allows this trivial matter to assume massive significance. His misplaced anger with Philinte builds up into a condemnation of duplicitous mankind:

> [Cette aversion] est générale et je hais tous les hommes.

The discussion over the lawsuit thus confirms a fundamental trait of Alceste's character. His plaintive 'Je veux qu'on me distingue' is exemplified by his petulant attitude in respect of his legal matter: as he cannot tolerate receiving only routine expressions of affection, so he cannot stoop to observe the legal procedures accepted by the rest of society. When, in the following act, Célimène mentions her own lawsuit, his reaction again demonstrates his self-centredness. Far more pragmatic than Alceste, she claims that she is obliged to accept Clitandre's attentions because his influence might improve her prospects of winning her case. Alceste's reaction is at least consistent:

> Perdez votre procès, Madame, avec constance,
> Et ne ménagez point un rival qui m'offense.

Célimène must lose her case, according to Alceste, rather than accept help from a man that he regards as a rival. He can tolerate neither opposition nor rivalry and needs constantly to be singled out for special treatment. But the very fact of going to law, with its uncertainties and balanced arguments, runs contrary to these needs. As Donneau de Visé points out, by giving Alceste a lawsuit, Molière has placed him in a situation perfectly judged to illustrate the comic potential of his misanthropy.

If we are given little information about the lawsuit, Alceste's other brush with the law initially promises to be even more mysterious. The arrival of the curt, elaborately uniformed *Garde* is quite unprepared. If Philinte makes the link with the quarrel over the sonnet, Alceste's incomprehension ('Qui? mai, Monsieur?') is here justified. No one could have anticipated that Oronte would lay the matter before the *Tribunal des Maréchaux*. Under the terms of the edict of 1651, this was a court set up to settle matters of honour between aristocrats, in order to prevent duels. It was a powerful body, composed only of the most senior military men of the day and membership of it conferred the title 'Monseigneur.' At the time of *Le Misanthrope*, it had eight members, including national heroes such as Turenne and the Duc de Gramont. These were names of almost legendary significance and the *Tribunal des Maréchaux* itself would have seemed, to the average spectator, a body of unimaginable grandeur. Given the eminence of its members, it could be convened only to deal with matters of particular importance. The *maréchal doyen* would deal with straightforward cases on his own.

However, in the case opposing Alceste and Oronte, the entire body seems to have been convened:

> 'Non, Messieurs, disait-il, je ne me dédis point.'

The *maréchal doyen* has therefore been unable to resolve the dispute without help. The idea of such an august body being assembled to deal with a quarrel over a sonnet would have seemed very funny:

> . . . jamais différend si bizarre, je pense.
> N'avait de ces Messieurs occupé la prudence.

The disproportion between the cause of the squabble and the illustrious nature of the court underlines the vanity and folly of the two men. The court may make them embrace, but the precarious nature of the settlement is underlined by the fact that Alceste refused to soften his judgement on the sonnet and Oronte subsequently makes two more attempts at revenge. The fact that neither will give way hints at one of the many subtleties of *Le Misanthrope*. Alceste is not comic because he is somehow different to all the other characters. He is comic because he is as egotistical and two-faced as the others while *claiming* to be different.

Just as Molière seems to include real legal satire only in farces, so the only joke in *Le Misanthrope* aimed at the legal profession occurs in the one scene of farce. It is an extremely gentle joke. The fussy, forgetful servant Du Bois, in his scene at the end of Act IV, frustrates Alceste in yet another way: he has two urgent messages to transmit and he manages to transmit neither. The 'homme noir, et d'habit et de mine' is clearly a court bailiff come to communicate the verdict of the lawsuit. But we do not learn what the verdict is because his writing was too bad for Du Bois to make it out. In an age when all testimony had to be written down, poor handwriting was a jibe frequently aimed at the legal profession. The other visitor, apparently a friend, has indicated that Alceste is in danger of being arrested—but Du Bois had forgotten to bring his letter. So the act ends in a rare moment of farce. Not the vulgar, sexual farce of *Le Médecin malgré lui*. Even the fleeting presence of an earthy character such as Sganarelle would have made Alceste's relative vulgarity less easy to appreciate. Du Bois is forgetful, not coarse. He creates a moment of confusion signalling another intrusion by the outside world: and again, because it is dressed in legal robes, it cannot be ignored.

At the start of Act V, we have Alceste's furious reaction to the news that he has lost his lawsuit and might be arrested. His magnificent forty-one line speech, with its seventeen exclamation marks, is a supreme example of the bitter-sweet humour of *Le Misanthrope*. On the one hand, his anger is a potent comic spectacle in itself. Harpagon, like Victor Meldrew, is constantly angry. Such characters have lost control. They are out of kilter with the world which, for them, is an exasperating place that refuses to conform to their prejudices. They may be suffering, but they have brought their suffering upon themselves and so we laugh at them. Thus it is with Alceste's lawsuit. If he is amazed to have lost, we know why this has happened. He has neglected to observe the usual procedure and so, as far as we can tell, he deserves to lose. His defeat is less surprising than his inability to understand why it happened. Not a hint of self-reproach:

> On publie en tous lieux l'équité de ma cause;
> Sur la foi de mon droit mon âme se repose.

But this conviction has evidently cut no ice with the court. The idea of the equity of his case being common knowledge is self-delusion. He has not even taken the elementary precaution of putting his case to the judge in advance. In the face of a well-organized opponent, this is presumably why he has lost. But as Alceste cannot imagine being wrong, he can only have been beaten by wickedness:

> Toute la bonne foi cède à sa trahison!

> Il fait par un arrêt couronner son forfait.

His definition of wickedness is someone who plays the underhand trick of observing judicial convention. One of the functions of the references to law in *Le Misanthrope* is regularly to remind us of Alceste's upside-down view of the world.

If the first half of the speech is richly comic, the second half is rather less so. He is in danger of being arrested because a dangerous pamphlet is circulating and it is rumoured that he is the author. The situation is potentially dangerous because Oronte is seeking to implicate Alceste in the matter of the pamphlet. Here is a further irony. Alceste has always distinguished between human systems of justice, which he considers corrupt, and the higher notion of equity, which he claims to have on his side. His two previous brushes with the judicial system may have been personally humiliating. But, despite his unreasonable conduct, the verdicts have been comparatively light: an order to embrace Oronte and the loss of twenty thousand francs, a trifling amount to someone of Alceste's rank. But now he is being unjustly accused of a serious crime. Under a legal system without a law of libel, to be accused of the authorship of 'un livre à mériter la dernière rigueur' might have spelled disaster. Such works were not uncommon. During the 1660s, several pamphlets were circulated attacking various aspects of government policy. Some of them were both scurrilous and, by the standards of the time, treasonable. In one or two cases, had the author been identified, he might have faced the death penalty. Madame de Sévigné's cousin Bussy-Rabutin was sent to the Bastille and then exiled to his estates for the relatively innocuous *Histoire amoureuse des Gaules*. Oronte's reported behaviour is appalling and, for once, we sympathize with Alceste's incomprehension:

> Il aide à m'accabler d'un crime imaginaire:
> Le voilà devenu mon plus grand adversaire!
>
> Pour n'avoir pas trouvé que son sonnet fût bon!

Oronte's attempts at revenge are growing frenzied. The summons over the sonnet, if ludicrous, was basically harmless. Now he seems to be trying to destroy Alceste. It seems as if Alceste's gloomy assessment of human nature is vindicated. The world really does appear to be conspiring against him. His anger at this moment is an object of pity, rather than ridicule.

But the moment of pathos does not last. As ever, the perspective is restored by Philinte. Alceste has not been arrested and the lawsuit verdict can be appealed against. At the mention of the lawsuit, Alceste again explodes:

> Je me garderai bien de vouloir qu'on le casse:
> ... Et je veux qu'il demeure à la postérité,
> Comme une marque insigne, un fameux témoignage
> De la méchanceté des hommes de notre âge.

Once again, according to Alceste, the case is exemplary: if there is no appeal, posterity, if not the universe, will take due note of his defiance. Alceste the moving victim has again been replaced by Alceste the irrational egotist. We are back in the realm of comedy.

A further 'legal element' in *Le Misanthrope*, is the judicial metaphor which underlies much of the play. Célimène is on trial, with Alceste trying to ascertain her degree of guilt. In this respect, he is again idealistic. Is she, as he claims in the opening scene, just guilty of youthful flightiness, of which he can hope to cure her? Or is her crime more serious? The play essentially consists of Alceste's attempts at interrogating her and his growing conviction, as the evidence mounts, that she is not as innocent as he needs her to be. For Alceste, as we have seen, true innocence is a concept which transcends the dubious procedures of the judicial process. But, as we have also seen, his attempted interrogation is repeatedly punctuated by an ironic counterpoint of interruptions associated with the world of legal reality.

In the opening scene, he says he merely wants to tell Célimène of his love. But his discourse to her is much more interrogation than declaration. In the space of sixty-seven lines, he puts to her no fewer than thirteen questions, all variants of the same one:

> Mais qui m'assurera que, dans le même instant,
> Vous n'en disiez, peut-être, aux autres tout autant?

Despite the insulting tone of such remarks, Célimène remains ironic and evasive, often throwing the question back to Alceste:

> Des amants que je fais me rendez-vous coupable?

Had this been a public interrogation, such replies would have been unsurprising. Célimène's standing in the salon depends on her having no publically admitted favourite. All her suitors must retain some kind of hope. But, in this scene, no one else is present. There is nothing to stop her telling Alceste exactly how she feels. But she remains curiously evasive. Had she been similarly non-commital in her letter to Oronte, Acaste, and Clitandre, she would not have had the uncomfortable time she experiences during her 'trial' at the end of the play. But, for the moment, the instinct to keep her suitors guessing is too strong and so she does not tell the whole truth. She goes no further than to assure Alceste, teasingly, that he has 'Le bonheur de savoir que vous êtes aimé.' When he objects to such vagueness, she retreats behind a mask of irony. For the moment, she is able to brush aside Alceste's insinuations by claiming to be shocked by his directness. He has no proof, his evidence is circumstantial, or based on hearsay. And so, under close questioning, the defendant gives nothing away. In the circumstances, that in itself is a kind of admission of guilt: in this court, there is no right of silence.

The second confrontation between Alceste and Célimène, in Act IV, scene 3, takes the interrogation theme a stage further. Superficially, it is a repetition of the earlier scene: the two lovers alone on stage, Alceste on the attack, Célimène elegantly parrying his thrusts. But, as with the two 'seduction' scenes in *Tartuffe*, there is a progression. This time, Alcesté has evidence against Célimène. The 'preuve fidèle' mysteriously evoked by Arsinoé at the end of Act III is a letter written by Célimène to Oronte. The latter has made it public in yet another act of revenge against Alceste. From Alceste's furious description of a 'un billet qui montre tant de flamme', we understand that it expresses the kind of feelings for Oronte that Alceste was seeking in Act II, scene 1. The evidence is therefore overwhelming and Alceste, pouring scorn on her claim that the letter was written to a woman, senses victory. Anyone but Célimène would have admitted her guilt.

However, she manages to turn the tables. Her interrogator is no detached advocate, but a man in love with the defendant. Célimène has only to express imperious anger at Alceste's rudeness to deflate his aggression. In three lines, she reduces him to asking her to be reasonable. Given Alceste's famously volatile temperament, this is an ironic token of her power over him. But she is not to be deflected. Continuing in a tone of offended pride, she rejects his offer of a truce and pretends to lose her temper completely:

> Non, il est pour Oronte, je veux qu'on le croie;
> Je reçois ses soins avec beaucoup de joie.

This is the long-awaited confession—but delivered in such a way that he cannot be sure that she is telling the truth. Like so much of what Célimène says, it is ambiguous. Alceste is non-plussed and delivers one of the most curious and revealing statements in the play:

> Défendez-vous au moins d'un crime qui m'accable,
> Et cessez d'affecter d'être envers moi coupable:
> Rendez-moi, s`il se peut, ce billet innocent:
> A vous prêter les mains ma tendresse consent;
> Efforcez-vous ici de paraître fidèle,
> Et je m'efforcerai, moi, de vous croire telle.

The irony is huge. We now have a parody of the interrogation that Alceste seemed to be conducting so successfully. The roles are reversed, with the interrogator begging for merciful treatment from the accused. The crime of which he is accusing her is unbearable to him so please will she deny it? When she confesses the truth, he accuses her of affectation and play-acting. The prosecutor invites the accused to commit perjury: the seeker after sincerity in all things invites Célimène to maintain a mere show of fidelity and promises to go along with the pretence. Alceste's attachment to the truth is thus shown to be qualified. Despite what he says in the opening scene, he is not interested in all truth. He is interested only in such truth as he can tolerate. Like everyone else in the play, he has comforting images of reality which he is reluctant to give up: he desperately wants to believe that Célimène is capable of loving only him. Where reality conflicts with his image of the world, he prefers comforting falsehood to uncomfortable reality. The judicial metaphor, when abruptly reversed, underlines the comic duality of Alceste's nature.

The play ends with what is clearly a trial scene. With all members present. Célimène is arraigned before the salon, further evidence against her is formally presented and assessed, the accused pleads guilty and her plea is taken note of before the verdict is delivered. The trail image is underscored by the consistently judicial nature of the language:

> CÉLIMÈNE   Vous en êtes en droit [. . .] J'ai tort, je le confesse
> [. . .] mon crime envers vous [. . .] je dois vous paraître coulpable.
> ALCESTE   Oui, je veux bien, perfide, oublier vos forfaits.

Alceste has passed from the role of interrogator to that of judge. Influenced by his feelings for Célimène, he makes a heroic last attempt at showing mercy. Heroic because, as we have seen, of all her suitors, he is the one that finds such tolerance most difficult. He is prepared to forgive her despite his awareness that she is perfidious. At one level, this is an admirable attempt at coming to terms with his own nature. At the same time it is grotesquely wrong-headed. Every scene has confirmed that Alceste and Célimène are temperamentally incompatible. Célimène's refusal to accept the sentence of exile with Alceste ('Moi, renoncer au monde avant que de vieillir!') therefore saves the play from a conventionally romantic ending. If Alceste is ever to know happiness, it will not be with Célimène. It is in this respect that the denouement of this play can be considered appropriate to a comedy. Alceste's departure is a happy ending in so far as the alternative would have been less happy.

But the way in which he arrives at his decision to leave Célimène is as comic as anything in the play. However judge-like Alceste may appear in this scene, it would have been implausible for him to condemn Célimène with anything approaching judicial objectivity. His final decision is motivated less by her infidelities, for which he can forgive her, than by her refusal to follow him into his social desert, for which he cannot. Again, irrational pique, rather than a lucid appraisal. Circumstances and temperament may have cast Alceste in the role of judge, but it would be difficult to imagine anyone less capable of dispassionate judgement.

Such a trial scene at the end of a seventeenth-century comedy is very unusual. The conventional comic ending was for some intervention or revelation to bring about a happy ending symbolized by a marriage. In real life, Tartuffe would have been undone by laws designed precisely to guard against nefarious activities such as his. Such a naturalistic outcome would have obviated the implausible royal intervention. But a legally realistic ending might have resembled a trial, quite out of keeping with the fairy-tale atmosphere of the comedy denouement. Racine's *Les Plaideurs* had been criticized for the trial scene in its closing act even though the scene actually parodies courtroom procedure. A real trial at the end of *Le Misanthrope* would therefore have been unacceptable.

But a metaphorical trial works well. It is one of many reminiscences in *Le Misanthrope* of the world of classical tragedy. By far the most 'regular' of Molière's plays, it obeys all the 'rules' in an apparently effortless manner that anticipates Racine. There is even an air of ironic inevitability about the outcome. Just as Phèdre talks of the need to die five acts before she does so, so Alceste predicts in the opening scene that he will have to leave Célimène's society. In both plays, it is not a question of whether, but when. Similarly, the frequency of 'trial' scenes in the plays of Corneille has often been remarked upon. In the final act of *Horace*, the eponymous hero stands accused of his sister's murder. In the presence of the king, he is accused and defended by members of his family and exposed to the judgment of the audience. Even leaving aside the fact that Corneille was a magistrate, the trial scene is a logical ending to his form of tragedy. The individual operating, with a degree of moral ambiguity, at the very edge of political orthodoxy is judged in the light of the deeds we have seen him accomplish during the play. If for political orthodoxy one substitutes society etiquette, the ending of *Le Misanthrope* is remarkably similar. As in *Horace*, the verdict is not clear-cut and, as in *Rodogune*, there is an ironic twist as the sentence is carried out on the prosecutor. The trial metaphor provides an artistically satisfying means of bringing the play to an end without resorting to the conventional devices of comedy. As in the best classical tragedies, the conclusion is thus arrived at logically, by means of the chemistry between the characters, rather than through some implausible external factor.

So, in *Le Misanthrope*, the references to the law are curiously sustained and ironic. They provide a funny and moving counterpoint to the theme of Alceste's relationship with Célimène. The legal metaphor, culminating in the bitter-sweet trial scene, gives the play a coherence and depth worthy of classical tragedy. Alceste's attitude towards his legal problems is as quixotic as his judgement of Célimène: in both respect, he is and introverted egotist who attempts to ignore the existence of society. As a high-ranking aristocrat he can ignore most things, but disdain for legal reality brings humiliation. Although he claims that 'J'aurai le plaisir de perdre mon procès,' the loss of his lawsuit is still traumatic. His legal problems mirror both his relationship with Célimène and also his inability to adapt to the complexity of life in general. The legal metaphor exposes the hypocrisy of Célimène's society: but it is Alceste who goes into exile. The evidence presented in the trial scene is devastating for Célimène: but the verdict goes against Alceste. If Célimène will probably soon bounce back, for Alceste the sentence will be longer.

JULES BRODY

Love in Tartuffe, *Tartuffe in Love*

As the curtain goes up on *Tartuffe*, we are offered a first view of "love," in the guise of familial affection and worldly courtesy: These are the feelings communicated in a wordless scenic language by Elmire as she accompanies her mother-in-law to the door. The old lady's reaction, brusque and uncalled for, serves both to lay out the drama's background and to anticipate things to come: "Laissez, ma bru, laissez, ne venez pas plus loin: / Ce sont toutes façons dont je n'ai pas besoin" ("Don't trouble, child; no need to show me out. / It's not your manners I'm concerned about"). The word *façons* subsumes in advance the long indictment by Mme Pernelle of modern-day Parisian manners and social life that monopolizes the opening scene of *Tartuffe*. Her rejection and Elmire's solicitous, affable "manners" targets a conception of human relations in which the pleasures and entertainments of polite society play a central role. Despite her edifying "leçons" ("advice"), her son's home has become the scene of one riotous, endless party. This observation launches a detailed denunciation of the entire household, by order of ascending social rank, from the "saucy" servant girl to the "dunce" of a son and the hypocritical daughter who hides her scandalous lifestyle behind a façade of respectability. Mme Pernelle blames the waywardness of her grandchildren on the poor example of their elders:

From *Approaches to Teaching Molière's 'Tartuffe' and Other Plays.* ©1995 The Modern Language Association of America.

Ma bru, qu'il ne vous en déplaise,
Votre conduite en tout est tout à fait mauvaise;
Vous devriez leur mettre un bon example aux yeux,
Et leur défunte mère en usait beaucoup mieux.
Vous êtes dépensière: et cet état me blesse,
Que vous alliez vêtue ainsi qu'une princesse.
Quiconque à son mari veut plaire seulement,
Ma bru, n'a pas besoin de tant d'ajustement.

And as for you, child, let me add
That your behavior is extremely bad,
And a poor example for these children, too.
Their dear, dead mother did far better than you.
You're much too free with money, and I'm distressed
To see you so elaborately dressed.
When it's one's husband that one aims to please,
One has no need of costly fripperies.

This speech defines at the outset the relative positions and values of those who are assembled under Orgon's roof. We learn, for example, that he is a widower and that Elmire, as his second wife, is closer in age to his late-teenage children than to Orgon himself. (In the original production, her role was played by Molière's daughter.) So the conflict is not merely between two different sets of social and moral values but between two generations and between two distinct lifestyles. The stodgy, old-fashioned mind-set of the age of Louis XIII is pitted against the worldview of the "young court" at Versailles, where *Tartuffe* was first performed in 1664 for the pleasure of the twenty-six-year-old Louis XIV and his mistress.

Mme Pernelle's criticism of Elmire's wardrobe is an example: not only is Elmire "dressed like a princess," but her perceived values—her apparent desire to attract other men—smack of the freewheeling, self-indulgent behavior of the aristocratic upper crust. Nor is costume the only measure of Elmire's social orientation. What with the line of carriages at her front door, the crowds of noisy lackeys always hanging around, and the endless socializing, we have all the trappings of the Parisian yuppie lifestyle of the roaring 1660s. Further, we learn that during the wars of the Fronde, during Louis XIV's minority, Orgon had "served his King", the mark of a politically connected family living close to the highest public function.

In brief, this opening expository scene, which teachers will need to explain in detail to their students, introduces us to one of those great, prosperous, upwardly mobile bourgeois families on which Louis's régime became more and more financially dependent with each passing year. In her dress, her pastimes, her manners, and her social attitudes, Elmire emerges as the very emblem of the elegant, newly established leisure classes of the age of Louis XIV. Mme Pernelle is pictured, in stark contrast, as the champion and the mainstay of the conservative religious right, nostalgic for the frugality, the discipline, and the family values of the "old court" and the good old days of the reign of Louis XIII.

The play's opening scene is also noteworthy in this respect: it contains the first in a series of verbal sketches of the title character. The purpose of these portraits of Tartuffe is to prepare for his late entrance at the beginning of act 3 and, in particular, to situate him socially with respect to the elegant milieu where he is viewed almost universally as an intruder. This distancing is clear from the very first mention of his name by Orgon's son, Damis: "Votre Monsieur Tartuffe est bienheureux sans doute . . ." ("Your man Tartuffe is full of holy speeches"). The title "Monsieur" is a giveaway in a social context where everyone but "Madame Pernelle" goes only by a fine-sounding Grecian first name (Elmire, Damis, Cléante, Orgon), reminiscent of the courtly literary genres of pastoral and tragedy: The first thing we learn about "Monsieur Tartuffe" is that his physical demeanor is the outward expression of his more than questionable origins. Again according to Damis, "ce beau monsieur-là" ("that handsome gentleman") is a "pied plat" ("hayseed"), literally a flat-footed, "pedestrian" clod who shuffles around in low-heeled shoes. A peasant in fact and at heart, Tartuffe, strictly speaking, does not even rate being called Monsieur. At best, he is "Monsieur Tartuffe" in the same way that Dom Juan's money-grubbing tailor is "Monsieur Dimanche."

As this verbal portrait develops, Dorine refers to Tartuffe as a barefooted "inconnu" ("nobody"): ". . . un gueux qui, quand il vint, n'avait pas de souliers / Et dont l'habit entier valait bien six deniers" (". . . this beggar, who, when he first came, / Had not a shoe or shoestring to his name"). That a "Monsieur" Tartuffe of this description should have the run of a household like Orgon's raised the specter of an infiltration and a subversion, from below, of the fabric of upper-class life. The physical and social unseemliness of Tartuffe's presence here had a moral dimension as well. Why, asks Dorine, hasn't he allowed them any visitors of late? "Je crois que de Madame il est, ma foi, jaloux" ("[I]f you ask me, / He's jealous of my mistress' company"). This assessment of Tartuffe's motives, setting the stage for his sexual advances to Elmire in act 3, scene 3, evokes an upside-down world in which rustic beggars can take over upscale bourgeois families and, worse, in which moral austerity and religious piety become tools of sexual conquest.

The subsequent installments in this verbal portrait further illustrate Tartuffe's vulgarity through a series of glimpses of his eating habits: he sits at the head of the table, where he packs in enough for six, grabs all the choice morsels, and belches right out loud. These fleeting references to the crudeness of Tartuffe's appetites will be developed in Dorine's first scene with Orgon:

ORGON.	Et Tartuffe?
DORINE.	Tartuffe? Il se prote à merveille.
	Gros et gras, le teint frais et la bouche
	vermeille.
ORGON.	Ah. And Tartuffe?
DORINE.	Tartuffe? Why he's round and red.
	Bursting with health, and excellently fed.

And why shouldn't he be the picture of health, with what he consumes? The other night, Elmire was too ill to look at food, but that didn't bother Tartuffe:

Il soupa, lui tout seul, devant elle,
Et fort dévotement il mangea deux perdrix,
Avec une moitié de gigot en hachis.

He ate his meal with relish,
And zealously devoured in her presence
A leg of mutton and a brace of pheasants.

After supper, he got into his warm bed, and after a good night's sleep he started off the next day with four big glasses of wine.

Tartuffe's existence is depicted as a masterpiece of comfort, well-being, and sensuality. This man, purportedly of God, is reported to us as a monster of corporality. Whereas Orgon sees in him a disembodied soul, what Molière shows us at work in Tartuffe's behavior is a mouth, a belly, an appetite, and, in a manner of speaking, a penis. In symbolic terms, the triumph of this grasping low-class bumpkin over his elegant antagonists forebodes a metaphysical victory of body over spirit, ugliness over beauty.

In Act 2, Scene 1, Orgon informs his daughter, Mariane, that she must marry Tartuffe. Dorine, as the mouthpiece of good sense and reality, denounces this choice by a man of property of a "gendre gueux" ("beggar son-in-law") as what was called in that day a "mésalliance." Her refrain throughout is, How can a man like you marry a girl like her to a creep like him? In the French text her disbelief is marked by the recurrent word *tel* (such): "une telle alliance" ("such a marriage"), "un tel époux" ("such a spouse"), "un tel mari" ("such a husband"; my trans.). In defense of his decision, Orgon maintains that Tartuffe has a noble lineage: "Et tel que l'on le voit, il est bien gentilhomme" ("Poor though he is, he's a gentleman just the same"). Such as he is, that is, contrary to appearances, he belongs to the landed gentry. But appearances count, Dorine insists:

> Parlons de sa personne, et laissons sa noblesse.
> Ferez-vous possesseur, sans quelque peu d'ennui,
> D'une fille comme elle, un homme comme lui?

> Let's speak, then, of his person, not his rank.
> Doesn't it seem to you a trifle grim
> To give a girl like her to a man like him?

In Dorine's view, Mariane is to Tartuffe as Beauty is to the Beast. And Molière makes Orgon admit as much: "Sans être demoiseau, / Tartuffe est fait de sorte . . ." ("Tartuffe is no young dandy, / But, still, his person . . ."). And Dorine replies ironically: "Oui, c'est un beau museau" ("[Tartuffe] is as sweet as candy"). Tartuffe's reported physique is, at this point, a verbal emblem. Later, once we lay eyes on him, it becomes the scenic vehicle of a number of implicit value judgments—"disgusting," "repugnant," "hateful"— that were earlier conveyed by the description of his gluttony and his table manners.

In the next scene, Dorine puts the finishing touches to her physical and moral sketch of Tartuffe:

> Il est noble chez lui, bien fait de sa personne;
> Il a l'oreille rouge et le teint bien fleuri:
> Vous vivrez trop contente avec un tel mari.

> He's a great noble—in his native town;
> His ears are red, he has a pink complexion,
> And all in all, he'll suit you to perfection.

Here again, the physical and moral aspects of Tartuffe coincide. Echoing her earlier comment on his "rosy skin and red lips," Dorine graces Tartuffe with a "sanguine" constitution, which, according to that era's theory of the humors, denoted a full-blooded temperament, powerfully inclined to the pleasures of the flesh. At this point, we are left with a full, vivid mental picture of the still unseen Tartuffe as a grubby, ruddy, horny social climber who has managed, incredibly, to penetrate the highest reaches of the beau monde.

As final object of this feat of social "penetration," Mariane, Dorine warns her, will end up being "tartuffiée":

> DORINE.   . . .Tartuffe est votre homme, et vous en
>   tàterez.
> MARIANE.   Tu sais qu'à toi toujours je me suis confiée:
>   Fais-moi . . .
> DORINE.   Non, vous serez, ma foi! tartuffiée.
>
> DORINE.   Tartuffe's your cup of tea and you shall
>   drink him.
> MARIANE.   I've always told you everything and relied . . .
> DORINE.   No. You deserve to be tartuffified.

In its most obvious sense, the word *tartuffiée* means "married to Tartuffe." But this bizarre proper name overlies a curious etymological and semantic substratum that deserves to be uncovered. In Italian *tartufo* means "truffle"; in French the word is *truffe*. From the Middle Ages to Molière's day, this exotic tuber carried suggestions of trickery and deception, perhaps also of lechery, since the truffle was legendary as an aphrodisiac. Tartuffe's name is the phonic equivalent of his physical and moral ugliness, evoking as it does the bulbous meat of that luxurious black mushroom—the same color as his somber religious garb—that grows underground and is hunted out with the help of pigs. By its immediate associations and its place in the scale of the unaesthetic, *Tartuffe* as mere word rivals the visually and psychologically displeasing associations of other Molière character names like M. de Pourceaugnac (*pourceau* means "hog"), Dr. Purgon (*purge*, "enema"), and George Dandin (*se dandiner*, "waddle like a duck").

The ultimate impact of the statement "vous serez tartuffiée," however, must be sought in its context, where the words echo and relay the sexually charged sentence "Tartuffe est votre homme, et vous en tâterez." This tactile and gustatory metaphor admits of a number of complementary paraphrases—"You will touch him, feel him, taste him, ingest him"—all of which are semantically equivalent variants of the implicit constant "You will know Tartuffe physically"— "in the flesh," as we say. Mariane will be "tartuffified," first and superficially, by becoming Mme Tartuffe but also, far more grievously, by being filled up with Tartuffe, in the sense of the modern French verb *truffer* ("to stuff," as with truffles): she will be crammed full of Tartuffe in the same way as we fill a turkey or a goose with stuffing. At this high point in Dorine's depiction of the fate to be endured by the future Mme Tartuffe, she is saying, in effect, "If you don't shape up, my dear, you're gonna have a bellyful of this fucker." The equivalent in today's French vernacular would be: "Tu ne vas pas tarder à te le farcir."

The participle *tartuffiée*, with its powerful associations of sexual invasion and possession, is literally the last word in the long and elaborate verbal portrait of Tartuffe that spans the play's first two acts. And it is highly significant that when Molière finally puts Tartuffe onstage it is in his capacity as "lover" or "amateur," in the neutral, crude senses of these terms: someone who loves to feast his eyes on women's bodies, who yearns to fondle and sample female flesh in any shape or form. As Molière, observes in his preface to the play, "On le connaît d'abord aux traits que je lui donne" ("The audience recognizes Tartuffe immediately from my description of him"). It is a simple dramaturgical fact that the two successive actions that initiate Tartuffe's effective presence on the stage are driven by the sexual energy that propels his course through life. Each of these scenic moments is subsumed in a single gesture and a single line. In our first glimpse of Tartuffe, he is ogling Dorine's breasts: "Couvrez ce sein que je ne saurais voir" ("Cover that bosom, girl. The flesh is weak"). In the following scene, he has his hand on Elmire's knee: "Je tâte votre habit: l'étoffe en est moelleuse" (["I am] feeling your gown; what soft, fine-woven stuff!").

Tartuffe's physical presence incarnates the full semantic content of his name and actualizes all the distaste that is inspired by the cumulative revelations of his manners, his ambitions, his sexual aggressiveness, his religious hypocrisy, his usurpations both of noble birth and of Orgon's house and hold. What Molière denounces in Tartuffe's demeanor and behavior is an all-encompassing acquisitive appetite that makes of him the exemplary, hyperbolic enemy of the reigning social order. The royal intervention at the play's denouement is not a dramatic convenience but a moral necessity.

Considering the number of Tartuffe's transgressions, the magnitude of his greed, and the scale of his depredations, it is tempting to see in him the embodiment of a force of nature given over to the extinction of culture, a veritable telluric power devoted to the destruction of the good and the beautiful. Tartuffe is a character conjured up out of a nightmare, a maniacal, demonic presence that threatens the very foundations of civilization. Tartuffe, in a word, is the evil spirit that must be exorcised if justice is ever again to prevail over fraud, equity over brute force, spirit over flesh, love over animality, if a "doux hymen" ("sweet union") is, as Orgon hopes, ever to "couronner en Valère / La flamme d'un amant généreux at sincère" ("give Valère . . . the wedded happiness which is his due").

Tartuffe is reminiscent of the cynical barbarian, knowing no higher law than his own desires, who, in Freud's reconstruction, was the ultimate nemesis of the precivilized male: the all-powerful, invulnerable invader who might one day descend on him, drive him from his home, and seize his goods and his women. Surely, this is the essential meaning of Orgon's incredulous remonstration to Tartuffe: "Comme aux tentations s'abandonne votre âme! / Vous épousiez ma fille, et convoitiez ma femme!" ("How soon you wearied of the saintly life— / Wedding my daughter, and coveting my wife!"). In this updated version of Freud's primal dispossession scene, tyrannical force has been replaced by the intellectual, bourgeois vices of contrivance, fakery, and trickery. At the denouement, the terror of Tartuffe's victims is dispelled, their doom is reversed, and the day is saved by the descent on the scene of a godlike *rex ex machina*, whose Supermanlike X-ray vision pierces, miraculously, to the heart of the matter:

> Un Prince dont les yeux se font jour dans les coeurs,
> Et que ne peut tromper tout l'art des imposteurs.

> A Prince who sees into our inmost hearts
> And can't be fooled by any trickster's arts.

ANDREW CALDER

Le Tartuffe

1. Comedy and topicality

Two of Molière's greatest plays, *Le Tartuffe* (1664) and *Dom Juan* (1665), from the moment of their composition to the present day, have continued to be a focus for controversy. Both tackle religious subjects normally beyond the range of the comic stage, and both reflect a lively interest in some of the most topical, moral and theological issues of the time. There has been much disagreement among literary historians as to the precise focus of Molière's satire in these plays. Modern critics, partly in response to this confusion, tend to play down the religious elements and concentrate instead on dramatic techniques and on the timeless questions of human nature raised.

Those with an interest in Molière as a seventeenth-century playwright, however—and, indeed the many who are puzzled by the structural oddities of these comedies—will feel the need to follow up allusions to contemporary issues as fully as possible. The plays raise many questions. Why, for example, did Molière depart from all the conventions of comedy to end *Le Tartuffe* with the direct intervention of the reigning monarch, an ending which modern directors and theatre-goers find ponderous and contrived? Why does the action of *Le Tartuffe* take place under such a brooding weight of menace that, up to the moment when the King intervenes, the audience fears that the forces of evil may prevail? Such

From *Molière: The Theory and Practice of Comedy*. © 1993 Andrew Calder.

a mood is foreign to the traditions of New Comedy. The case of *Dom Juan* is stranger still. Is it even a proper comedy? No one can be said to be happy in the dénouement; the eponymous hero is not, in any normal meaning of the term, a comic character; its episodic structure can easily seem bitty; characters appear and disappear without obvious reasons; they are sometimes inconsistent—when Elvire comes on stage for the second time, she has undergone a transformation from vengeful, scorned wife to angel of love and mercy; for some, the supernatural elements in the play, especially the burning of Dom Juan in hell-fire, are simply too strange to carry conviction on the comic stage. Such an ending is certainly untypical in Molière's *œuvre*.

The study of theatrical conventions and dramatic techniques does not explain such oddities. We need to find out which aspects of contemporary life Molière was imitating. We cannot expect to follow the internal order of a well-constructed play if we do not know what the play is about.

2. Jansenists, Jesuits and the *Compagnie du Saint-Sacrement*

Of the possible targets for Molière's satire in *Le Tartuffe*, the most frequently named are the Jesuits, the Jansenists and the *Compagnie du Saint-Sacrement*. The case for the Jansenists is weakest; it is argued that Molière is satirizing Jansenist rigorism—perhaps as a riposte to their attacks on the theater as a danger to morals—through his portrait of a household plunged into gloom by the strict control over the family's social life and pleasures exercised by Tartuffe and Orgon. In fact, there is little to suggest that Morliere is mocking rigorism—Tartuffe is leading a most self-indulgent life; what he does hold up to ridicule is the use of false rigorism as a means of controlling the lives of others. It was not a common accusation that the Jansenists used rigorism to cloak self-indulgence and cupidity; Tartuffe simply does not have the characteristics which would make him recognizable as the caricature of a Jansenist.

A stronger case has been made for the *Compagnie du Saint-Sacrement*. Raoul Allier, in *La Cabale des dévots*, has shown how this group of powerful men worked together to defend what they saw as the interests of the Church, placing their members and allies in important posts, and seeking to promote their own policies through existing institutions. He argues that Tartuffe's underhand methods and the clear indication that he belongs to a cabal of like-minded schemers could be allusions to the practices of this *Compagnie*. However, Allier himself draws attention to the weakness in his case: the members of the *Compagnie*, though misguided, were genuine high-born zealots working to promote what they considered to be the true interests of the Church, while Tartuffe, a low-born villain, womanizer and trickster, uses the cover of religion to pursue his own narrowly self-interested ends. Another weakness in Allier's case is that the *Compagnie du Saint-Sacrement* appears to have been successful in keeping out of the public eye; Molière's audiences, who had flocked to see his satirical portraits of such familiar figures as the pedant, the *précieuse*, the *marquis*, jealous husbands and tyrant fathers, would not have known whom they were laughing at. It was unlikely that Morliere, so famous for his telling portraits of well-known groups, should suddenly choose to portray such shadowy, little-known figures.

The strongest case can be made for the Jesuits. Tartuffe is presented as a master of the very latest casuistic techniques, and—particularly following the phenomenal success of Pascal's satire of new casuistry in the *Lettres provinciales*—the use of lax casuistry was associated more with the Jesuits than with any other Order. Among many other signposts which would have been clear to contemporaries, perhaps the clearest was Molière's choice of a name for Tartuffe's close ally, the silver-tongued bailiff who, with ten of his men, takes possession of Orgon's house and announces, with every assurance of Christian zeal, that the family must vacate the premises by the following day: the bailiff is called Monsieur Loyal, after Loyola, the founder of the Society of Jesus.

Tartuffe himself, however, is not presented as a Jesuit: he is planning to marry Orgon's daughter, and Jesuits could not marry. Equally, Jesuits, like Jansenists and members of the *Compagnie du Saint-Sacrement*, did not behave like Tartuffe. There were Jesuits of many kinds: some were outstanding scholars and preachers; many were famous as teachers, missionaries or confessors; they saw themselves as apostles of the Counter-Reformation, determined to promote the authority of Church and Pope; among the Jesuits of Paris, there were many polished men of letters and courtiers. Perhaps there were some out-and-out scoundrels among their number, too; in such a large, successful and rapidly expanding organization it would be surprising if this had not been the case. But the typical Jesuit, even with the help of comic perspective, was not a likely model for the villainous Tartuffe. I suspect it is the contrast between the better-known Jesuits—such distinguished men as Petau, Rapin or Bourdaloue—and the gross, unstylish figure of Tartuffe which has discouraged historians of literature from recognizing *Le Tartuffe* as a specifically anti-Jesuit satire.

However, a Jesuit model for Tartuffe did exist: the figure of the caricatural Jesuit, a creation of polemical literature. In the numerous anti-Jesuit tracts published and circulated in France and all over Europe, the enemies of the Jesuits, jealous of their power, appalled by what they saw as Jesuit ruthlessness in pursuing their own policies and interests, built up a composite picture of the scheming, embezzling, hypocritical, spying Jesuit, ready to go to any lengths to please those whom he found useful, but vindictive and pitiless in ruining those who opposed him or attempted to halt the spreading influence of the Society of Jesus.

To see how Molière, among so many others, came to condemn the activities of the Jesuits in such strong terms, it is necessary to look briefly at some aspects of the history of the Jesuits in France.

3. The Jesuit of polemical caricature

There were a number of characteristics particular to the Society of Jesus which provoked controversy in France and elsewhere. The simple fact of the Society's extraordinarily rapid expansion from its foundation in the early 1530s to the point where, by the end of the sixteenth century, there were Jesuits in most great centres, everywhere in the world, was a major source of friction: they had taken over as the major providers of Roman Catholic schools; become confessors to the powerful; opened new churches; achieved fame for their stirring preaching, their mastery of the theory and practice of rhetoric, the plays performed by their pupils, their theological scholarship and their missionary successes. Though many welcomed this new and exciting movement, others resented the Jesuits' presence and disliked their methods of self-advertisement which, to them, appeared thrusting and ostentatious.

The problem was exacerbated by the equivocal legal relationship between Jesuits and bishops: the Jesuits had a peculiarly status, halfway between monk and priest; as members of an Order, they owned obedience to their own general but also, and especially, to the Pope, to whom all senior Jesuits had sworn a special fourth vow of loyalty; as priests working in the wider community they were—in theory, at least—subject to the jurisdiction of the local bishop; quarrels with local priests and, on occasion, refusal to obey a bishop's orders when these clashed with Jesuits policy often caused serious disruption in the dioceses in which they worked.

In France, the Jesuits met opposition in the *Parlements*, in the University of Paris, from the Huguenots, from many of the clergy and bishops—especially those who wished for some measure of independence from Rome in the Gallican Church—and from the Jansenists, who accused them of teaching heretical doctrines on grace and criticized their scholarship and their lax use of casuistry. In 1594 their enemies in France, who accused the Jesuits of inspiring Chastel's attempt upon the life of Henry IV, persuaded the King to expel them for promulgating casuistic opinions which allegedly encouraged regicide. After the Edict of Rouen (1603), permitting their return on strict conditions, anti-Jesuit polemics in France grew in number and vindictiveness again. Their enemies blamed them for the assassination of Henry IV in 1610. They saw the Jesuits as agents and spies of Spain, France's major political enemy, infiltrating French institutions, usurping the rights and privileges of honest Frenchmen, corrupting their morals through lax casuistry, misappropriating their funds, using their schools as recruiting grounds for the Society and taking children away from their parents. They resented, too, the fact that from 1604 the confessors to Henry IV, and then to Louis XIII and Louis XIV, were all Jesuits with constant close access to the reigning monarch.

Towards the middle of the seventeenth century, both before and after the appearance of Pascal's *Lettres provinciales*, polemical attacks on the Jesuits focused more and more upon their alleged misuse of casuistry. As the leading confessing Order, the Jesuits were of necessity specialists in casuistry—the domain of moral theology concerned with cases of conscience. Earlier attacks on Jesuit casuistry had centered on their views on tyrannicide and regicide. Under the influence of Pascal, in particular, the emphasis changed to a broader attack upon the whole range of casuistic opinions. Pascal argued that their lax casuistry was undermining the traditional teachings of the Church. He accused them of using casuistry to serve political ends, arguing that lax casuistry had become an instrument for pleasing and conciliating the rich and powerful in order to extend the influence and power of the Society. In polemical literature generally, a picture emerges of Jesuits who presented a uniformly pious exterior, who were ruled by ambition and pride in their Order, and who worked together secretly as an international force to promote policies agreed in Rome and Spain; to spread their influence, they became adept at attracting funds; they were compliant in serving their powerful allies, and ruthless in crushing their enemies. As their numbers grew, their enemies in France accused them of invading every corner of French life.

From the evidence of *Le Tartuffe*, Molière shared this hostile view of the Jesuits. This did not place him in an odd and fanatical minority. The clergy of Paris in general, many French bishops, most *parlementaires*, Pascal, Racine, La Fontaine, the doctor Gui Patin, *le grand* Arnauld and the Jansenists, and many other groups and individuals who viewed the Jesuits from a great diversity of standpoints, showed the same hostility. Molière's satire, like Pascal's *Lettres provinciales*, found a huge and eager public.

4. A political satire

The action of *Le Tartuffe*, in a simplified caricatural form, traces what Molière saw as the Jesuit invasion of France. He has translated into a domestic context, suited to the genres of New Comedy and farce, a major national and political drama. The political importance of the play is reflected in the fact that even with the support of the King—to which Molière alludes with gratitude in the *Placets* of 1664 and 1667 and the *Préface* of 1669—it took five years and at least two revisions of the text for him to win the right to have it performed freely and openly. In the same *Placets* and *Préface*, Molière made it clear that 'the famous originals' of his portrait were numerous, powerful and determined; and that in his opinion his career in the theatre would be over if the King allowed these 'tartuffes' to succeed in having the play banned. In *Le Tartuffe*, Molière has briefly restored to comedy the function of Old Comedy, central to the plays of Aristophanes, of presenting on stage matters of importance to the public and the state. By portraying a scheming casuist and hypocrite worming his way into a good, dependable French family, attracting alms with loud demonstrations of piety, flattering the head of the house, usurping his power and wealth, and turning treacherously against him once he has him in his power, Molière added his voice to the many others who condemned Jesuit activities in France.

The extraordinary and monstrous character of Tartuffe is constructed from two apparently incompatible sets of qualities. He is a consummate schemer who easily outwits his victim, implements a clever strategy for taking over his house and his wealth and, at the same time, arms himself with enough of his victim's secrets to have him jailed should he ever need to. The other set of characteristics, his self-indulgence, gluttony and carnality, show Tartuffe as a careless, ill-disciplined rogue whose hypocrisy is transparent to any reasonably clear-sighted person. Each of these sets of qualities is built up from different elements of anti-Jesuit polemics.

Tartuffe the schemer is shown putting into practice the policies of the infamous fictitious Jesuit of one of the most widely disseminated anti-Jesuit tracts, the *Montia Secreta* (1612), usually attributed to Jerome Zaorowski, an expelled Polish Jesuit. Molière could have read one of the many Latin editions of this tract or the French translation, *Advis secrets de la Société de Jésus* (1661), probably published in Paris but giving Paderborne as its town of publication to help protect the printer. In this cleverly conceived and skilfully written little tract, the polemicist presents his text as a set of secret instructions from a very senior Jesuit to be communicated only to other Jesuits of the fourth vow. Only professed Jesuits take the fourth vow and the reader is encouraged to believe, as he reads the instructions, that he is entering into the very heart of the Society and sharing in its most secret counsels. He is to learn the techniques and tactics which—the polemicist alleges—have made it possible for the Jesuits to spread so rapidly in so short a time. The Jesuit is instructed in a strategy for attracting alms and support when spreading to new territories:

> He must go to far-off places where he will receive alms, even the smallest contributions, after having displayed the poverty of our members. These must then be handed to the poor, in order to edify those who do not yet known our Society and to encourage them to be more generous towards us.

This is how Tartuffe first ensnares Orgon; with the new convert's enthusiasm, Organ describes his first encounters with his spiritual mentor to Cléante:

> Having been informed by his boy, who imitated him everything, of his poverty and of what kind of man he was, I offered him gifts but, modestly, he always wanted me to take some of them back. 'It's too much,' he would say to me, 'half as much would do; I don't deserve to inspire such compassion'; and when I refused to take the money back, before my very eyes, he would distribute it among the poor.

In the sixth and seventh chapters of the *Monita*, the fictitious Jesuit instructor explains to his advanced pupils how they should set about gaining control of wealth in private hands. They should, when possible, choose wealthy widows as the objects of their campaign but, the instructor says, his advice on how to approach rich widows holds good for merchants and rich, married *bourgeois*, too. The heart of the Jesuit's strategy must be to teach the widow to turn to him and him alone after for advice on all matters, to persuade her that her Jesuit confessor is 'the sole source of her spiritual advancement'. Dorine tell us that Orgon stands in just such a relationship to Tartuffe: 'He admires him on every occasion, cities him at every turn; his least actions appear to him to be miracles, and all his words are so many oracles to him'. The Jesuit, according to the *Monita*, should also make use of confession to discover the state of the widow's finances and learn all her secrets. Again, Dorine tells us that Tartuffe is 'the unique confidant of all his [Organ's] secrets, and the prudent director of all his actions'. Tartuffe's success in laying his hands on secret incriminating papers belonging to Orgon is a crucial element in his plan to put him in his power.

The Jesuit should, at the same time, isolate his widow or rich *bourgeois* from all contacts with society. We learn in the opening scene that Organ's family is suffering from the pall which has descended over the household since Orgon has been persuaded to put an end to visits from friends. The Jesuit's chosen victim should also be isolated from his own family, the main obstacle to an outsider hoping to gain control of his or her affairs. Orgon's estrangement from his wife, children, brother-in-law and even servant is a central theme of *Le Tartuffe*, it is one of his proudest boasts that Tartuffe has taught him to love no one: 'He detaches my soul from all loving-relationships, and I would see brother, children, mother and wife die without caring that [snapping his fingers] for it'. A childless widow or *bourgeois* is always to be preferred, but if the Jesuit has chosen one with children, he must, if he is to gain control of her or his money, sow hostility between parent and child: 'Mothers must be taught to vex their children with scolding and censure from their earliest youth'. Stirring his family into a rage, as Orgon himself proclaims, is his greatest joy.

Behind this quite savage satire, both in the *Monita secreta* and in *Le Tartuffe*, lies the accusation that the Jesuits have sacrificed Christian principles to political expediency. In the *Monita secreta*, where the polemical message is explicit, the Jesuits are portrayed working to increase the resources and power of their Order. Molière, who does not name the Jesuits, paints a similar state of mind and similar behaviour, detaching the crime from the Society of Jesus and attaching it to his caricature of a hypocrite. His method was to portray a set of follies and vices and leave his audiences to decide who might be guilty of them. If the cap fits, wear it.

5. Jesuit policy and Christian doctrine

Tartuffe uses the language, external appearance and authority of Christianity and the Church, while undermining, by the code of conduct he follows and preaches to others, everything that Christianity stands for. In the most detailed and cogently presented seventeenth-century attack upon the Jesuits, the *Lettres provinciales*, this is the picture Pascal painted of the Society of Jesus. Throughout his letters, Pascal's argument was that the Jesuits had traded the substance of Christian doctrine for the appearance of ecclesiastical success; in order to embrace as many people as possible within the Church, they had reshaped doctrine to soften its demands and accommodate it, whatever necessary, to the foibles and even the vices of men and women. He argued, too, that the Jesuits had confused the glory of God with the glory of the Society of Jesus; they had redefined heresy so that it no longer consisted in holding beliefs contrary to the traditional doctrines of the Church, but in professing views critical of the Jesuits. To express his anger against the Jesuits, Pascal borrowed the words of Capuchin friar, Valeriano Magni, a contemporary who, liked Pascal, found himself the object of Jesuit attacks on his good name; Valeriano's denunciation capture the essence of Pascal's view:

> These kinds of men, who make themselves unbearable to the whole of Christendom, aspire, under the pretext of good works, to the highest honours and to domination, distorting to serve their own ends almost every law—divine, human, positive and natural. They attract, through their doctrine, through fear, or through hope, all the princes of the earth, whose authority they abuse in order to bring success to their detestable intrigues. But their wrongs, although so criminal, are neither punished nor stopped; on the contrary, they are rewarded and they commit them as boldly as if they were rendering service to God. Everyone recognizes them, everyone speaks of them with execration, but how few are capable of standing up against such a powerful tyranny; that is what I have done.

In the person of Tartuffe, Molière has scaled down this awesome power to a comic level, but the same characteristics recur. Tartuffe equates the will of God with his own desires; all his crimes are carried out in the name of God and under the cloak of religion. He aspires to dominate and control the small world of which he has chosen to make a conquest; to achieve this, he wins the head of the house and, as soon as he is sure of him, abuses his authority. He moves the boundaries between good and evil to suit his changing interests and desires at different points in the play: the clearest example is his change of attitude to Orgon; while Orgon believes him to be a saint, no praise is too high for him, but as soon as Orgon sees through his hypocrisy, Tartuffe declares him to be a traitor who must at once be jailed. He is in league with others, all behaving in the same way and working to the same ends: we hear of his servant, Laurent, who imitates all his master's ways and meet the bailiff, Monsieur Loyal, who has come to take possession of Orgon's house.

Perhaps the most striking parallel between Tartuffe's behaviour and the behaviour of the Jesuits as described by Valeriano Magni and Pascal is that its dishonesty is known to all, yet apparently unstoppable; though Tartuffe's scheming is crude and most members of the family see through him instantly, the audience is made to realize that only the last-minute intervention of the King can save the family from him.

6. Tartuffe as casuist

Tartuffe the schemer would be a grim figure, too sinister for the world of comedy, if Molière had not combined with the cold, calculating side of his character an unregulated, sensual nature which makes him succumb readily to any temptation of the flesh. Fat, florid, red-lipped, thirsty, greedy, belching, deep-sleeping and, above all, easily roused by the sight of a woman's flesh, Tartuffe is altogether a man, an epitome of all the base appetites which afflict the genus. His status as a man, and nothing more, is proclaimed with delightful irony by Orgon when, lost for words to describe such a paragon, he can only say: 'He is a man . . . who, . . . ah! a man . . . a man in short'. When Tartuffe appears on stage in Act II, roaring like a braggart-soldier about his hair shirt, his whip and his charitable good works, his real nature is immediately revealed as his eyes fix upon Dorine's low-cut dress and he advances towards her unfolding his handkerchief in order to cover her bosom and protect himself from temptation. This oafish, self-deceiving, over confident and lecherous fat-man is a perfect hero of farce.

This side of his character has obvious comic functions, but it is also part of Molière's anti-Jesuit satire. Through Tartuffe's weaknesses of the flesh, Molière extends the range of his satire to include the whole field of lax moral teaching allegedly spread by the Jesuits' innovations in casuistry. Tartuffe's grossness and sensuality are intended not as an accurate characterization of Jesuit behaviour but as a comic portrayal of all the sins a self-indulgent rogue can commit while remaining innocent in the eyes of an accommodating casuist. Pascal claimed that the only sins which could not be rendered innocent by new casuistry were those committed 'with the formal intention of sinning and with no other purpose than sinning'. In the midst of his earthbound enjoyment of the seven deadly sins, Tartuffe never does anything which cannot be shown by an expert new-casuist to be technically innocent. When he says to Elmire, 'Ah! for being a man of God, I am no less a man', he is not confessing to weakness but making the technical point that he can remain devout without sacrificing any of his animal appetites. Tartuffe was not one of those gloomy ascetic Christians who were blind to a woman's beauty. Pascal quotes a passage from the Jesuit Le Moyne's *Peintures morales* ridiculing such a figure: 'For him a beautiful woman is a ghost; and these imperious and sovereign faces, these agreeable tyrants who, without help of chains, make willing slaves of men have no more power over his eyes than the sun over the eyes of owls'; Tartuffe would claim rather to have, in the words of Le Moyne, the 'honest and natural affections' appropriate to a warm-blooded man.

Opponents of the Jesuits accused them of moving back the frontiers of sin, of making the Christian life accessible to all in order to swell the numbers of their converts and allies. Pascal's claim was that this new casuistry, none of it more than eighty years old, was taking the place of the Scriptures, the Church Fathers and the Councils, undercutting the Church's ancient authority and putting in its place new and debased doctrines. The new figures who have replaced all earlier authorities, according to Pascal's fictitious Jesuit father, are:

> Villalobos, Conink, Llamas, Achokier, Dealkozer, Dellacruz, Veracruz, Ugolin, Tambourin, Fernandez, Martinez, Suarez, Henriquez, Vasquez, Lopez, Gomez, Sanchez, De Vechis, De Grassis, De Grassalis, De Pitigianis, De Graphaeis, Squilanti, Bizozeri, Barcola, De Bobadilla, Simancha, Perez de Lara, Aldretta, Lorca, De Scarcia, Quaranta, Scophra, Pedrezza, Cabrezza, Bisbe, Dias, Declavasio, Villagut, Adam à Mandem, Iribarne, Binsfeld, Volfangi à Vorberg, Vosthery, Strevesdorf.

Pascal records his letter-writer's astonished response:

> 'Oh, my Father,' I said in panic, 'were all those people Christians?' 'What do you mean, Christians?' he replied. 'Wasn't I telling you that these are the only people by whom Christendom is governed these days?'

Pascal concedes quite happily that severe Jesuits expected people who came to them for confession to follow God's law as closely as possible, but unfortunately, he adds ironically, the majority of people required confessors who were more accommodating. As a result, with the laudable aim of keeping everyone within the fold, casuists have sprung up on all sides, compromising, introducing ingenious sophisms and adapting their rulings and recommendations to suit each case. If a sin cannot be overcome, it must be redefined and reclassified. The Jesuits, according to Pascal, practised a dual policy: high standards were set for the truly devout by austere confessors, while ill-disciplined rogues needed less exacting confessors; the latter, however, in order to rise to the challenge of 'purifying' behaviour which was often gross and godless, had to be much more skilled in their handling of the sophisticated techniques of casuistry. Pascal recalls ironically that François Hallier had once said of Bauny, one of the more notorious casuists: 'Here is the man who takes away the sins of the world'.

Tartuffe knows his new casuistry and has no fear of sin. He is pleased, too, to place his skills in this science at the service of his friends. When Elmire fears that adultery might displease God, Tartuffe replies:

I, Madam, can dissipate these ridiculous fears; and I know the art of alleviating scruples. God does truly forbid certain satisfactions: but arrangements can be made with Him. There is (according to our various needs) a science of stretching the limits of our conscience, and of rectifying the evil of an action by the purity of our intention. Those are secrets, Madam, in which we can instruct you: you have merely to let yourself be guided. Satisfy my desire and do not be terrified. I will answer to you for everything and take the evil upon myself.

Tartuffe could have cited in support of these reassuring words a passage from Bauny quoted by Pascal, saying that a confessor 'can and must absolve a woman who has a man in her house with whom she frequently commits sin, if she has no honest way of getting him out of the house, or has some reason for keeping him there'.

Tartuffe could easily provide opinions from specialist casuists to cover all his sins. He eats enough for six, starts the day with four good draughts of wine, eats a couple of partridges and half a leg of mutton at a single sitting, but according to Escobar, quoted by Pascal, he is not guilty of gluttony so long as he does not eat until he vomits.

When Damis tells his father that he had just heard Tartuffe declare that he loves Elmire, Tartuffe deftly employs another casuistic trick to deceive Orgon without telling a lie. If a man, as often happened, wished to conceal a particular sin from his confessor—either to conserve his confessor's esteem, or to avoid having to admit that he has slipped back into the same sins as last time—he had only, according to Escobar and Suarez, 'to make a general confession and to lose this sin among all the others he is accusing himself of in general'. Tartuffe abases himself before Organ, confessing quite truthfully that he is a wicked man, an abject sinner, guilty of many a low crime, but not mentioning the particular sin of having tried to seduce his wife, and Orgon, impressed by such a striking display of humility, takes Tartuffe's side, throws his son out of the house and, for good measure, disinherits him in favour of the hypocrite.

In condoning Orgon's decision to make him sole heir to his fortune, to which he has no right, Tartuffe justifies himself with more casuistic evasion. He accepts Damis's money—not for himself or from any desire to harm Damis, but because he, as a holy man, can put the money to a more godly use; his intentions are pure. Another piece of sophistry is used to explain why it is right for the legitimate son of the house to be expelled while Tartuffe remains in residence: if Tartuffe were to withdraw, people would say that he was acting from political expediency and that his withdrawal was equivalent to an admission of guilt; his reputation could be compromised. The best-known piece of casuistry is the double sophistry performed by Tartuffe and his disciple Orgon together. Orgon is persuaded to hand over incriminating papers to Tartuffe in order that he may be able to deny innocently, by an indirect lie, that he has any such papers in his possession. In fact, the whole suggestion is a trick practised by Tartuffe on Orgon: while pretending to offer him friendly support and subtle moral advice, he is really planning to put Orgon in his power so that, should the need arise, he will be in a position to ruin him.

7. Tartuffe as lover

Tartuffe, overweight, repulsive, low-born and ill-bred, makes an unlikely stage lover. Elmire is an attractive and still quite young second wife to Orgon, of good background, elegant, generous with her stepchildren and patient and loyal with her husband. Much of the comedy of Tartuffe's lecherous pursuit of this paragon of womanhood comes from the fact that he is so obviously unsuited to such a task. The strong satirical suggestion, again, is that only Tartuffe's use of the cloak of religion could enable him to cross the social barriers which would normally prevent him to cross the social barriers which would normally prevent him from gaining access to a woman of Elmire's standing. Dorine points out that he was a penniless nobody until Orgon took him in.

Paradoxically—and comically—it is also Tartuffe's use of a religious mask, and his mastery of Christian rhetoric, which permit him to make his gallant declarations to Elmire with so little groundwork. Dom Juan, a more effective and urbane seducer, proceeds quickly enough in his seduction of Charlotte, but he does so by practising the flattering arts and wiles of the seducer. Tartuffe, with the confidence which comes from knowing that lust and adultery can be made innocent by new casuistry, dispenses with the normal preliminaries of the seducer; he can easily square God and his conscience, but forgets that it is not so easy to persuade an honest woman to accept his attentions. As soon as Elmire appears on stage in the third act, he begins to mingle the language of devotion to God with an expression of his devotion to her: the words 'body', 'desire', 'love', 'grace', 'cherish', 'thrilled', 'sweet', 'attractions', 'zealous transports', 'fervour' and many more combine to evoke an atmosphere which might pass for religious enthusiasm, but is really one of erotic excitement.

There is nothing specially Jesuitical in the use of erotic language to describe religious experience; it is a trait common to most mystical writing.

However, it is not to mystical literature in general that Molière is alluding, Tartuffe is using arguments and rhetoric which can be found in the *Peintures morales* (1640–43) of Le Moyne, the well-know contemporary precious poet and Jesuit. Le Moyne had attracted some of Pascal's severest censure for his *Dévotion aisée*. His *Peintures morales* were also cited by Pascal as a text which made a mockery of sacred things: 'Does not his whole book of the *Peintures morales*, in its prose and its verse, display a spirit full of vanity and the follies of the world?'.

Le Moyne's text is written for the court, especially for the women of the court: its style is precious, arch and florid; its contents are leavened with images and conceits which would ensure that the book could be consulted, discussed and read aloud in *salon, boudoir* or *ruelle* without risk of striking a too solemn note. Read in the context of either theology or moral philosophy, the *Peintures* are easily ridiculed. The second volume is devoted entirely to the subject of love, and the chapter from which Tartuffe could have borrowed his reasoning on love is entitled 'The second rule for the sanctification of love: how to contemplate the beauties of the body with the eyes of the spirit'. Le Moyne's stated aim is to encourage the flighty courtier to find God in the features of the many fine women he is likely to admire in the course of his daily life. He argues that as men and women are made in God's image, it is legitimate to love God in these earthly reflections of His beauty; and, secondly, that just as in admiring the qualities of a work of art we are really praising the hand that made it, we can admire God's handiwork in the human bodies which He created and which so effectively reveal His art. Provided sexual desire does not degenerate into 'amour brutal' ('animal sensuality'), it can enrich the spirit:

> If we have eyes sufficiently purified to recognize the royalty of Jesus Christ in the pleasant and natural sovereignty which is imprinted upon beautiful women, we shall learn by this means to cherish His commandments and to accept with pleasure the yoke of His law upon our hearts and our heads.

Le Moyne dwells upon the beauties of the body: 'the Creator has made the human body as beautiful as we perceive it to be, and has given it so many charms and ornaments, in order that it might provide the beautiful robe or the fine dwelling-place of a still more beautiful soul'. He is pleased with his reasoning, concluding: 'I believe I have done love a considerable good turn by the lesson I have just taught her'.

Tartuffe extends the argument that the beauty of the outer robe is a kind a guarantee of the quality of its contents one stage further. His first compliments are paid to Elmire's dress, which he handles freely, exclaiming: 'Heavens! How wondrous is the detail of this stitching! The work of people these days has something miraculous about it; never, anywhere, have I seen anything finer'. His attention soon moves to the woman wearing the dress. Now, he sees Elmier as the curiously worked artefact who reflects the skill of her Maker: 'The love which binds us to eternal beauties does not smother in us the love of temporal beauties; our senses are easily caught in the spell of the perfect creations which God has shaped'. Faithful to Le Moyne's formulation, Tartuffe finds in Elmire both irresistible evidence of God's creative powers and a reflection of His beauty:

> His reflected charms shine in woman like you; but, in you, He displays His rarest wonders; on your countenance, He has poured beauties in profusion which surprise our eyes and ravish our hearts, and I could not look upon you, perfect creature, without admiring in you the Author of nature and feeling my heart smitten with a burning love for the most beautiful of God's self-portraits.

Tartuffe follows Le Moyne, too, in noting that God's image is likely to be reflected more faithfully in the very beautiful, such as Elmire, than in those who are less so. Le Moyne argues:

> God has imprinted upon us the light of His countenance and has made it a sign which shows in our faces; beautiful women, however, have received more this light than others; and its meaning is clearer and more distinct in them. They are, therefore, among visible things, the most perfect images of God, and the most particular representations of His beauty.

Tartuffe could claim that his disconcerting blend of veneration of God and lust for woman is permitted by Le Moyne, who has taught him

> the means of purifying himself through that which defiles, how to turn an object of pleasure into a subject of virtue, how to light a divine fire from the matter of a sensual fire, and how to make oneself agreable to God through the inclination one feels for His creatures.

Le Moyne teaches, too, that beautiful people deserve 'respect and honour, they command almost religion and worship'.

Certainly, Tartuffe has no hesitation in addressing Elmire in language of prayer, making an offering of his heart, expecting nothing from his own infirmity, but waiting upon her bounty to see if she will bring him peace and bliss. He even commits the ultimate blasphemy of perverting the language of the Mass with his reference to 'l'autel où leur cœur sacrifie' ('the altar where [young lovers] make a sacrifice of their hearts').

8. The importance of secrecy

It is at once clear to Elmire and to the audience that Tartuffe has little to offer as a lover. He is without wealth, position, style and even superficial charm. However, he sets much store by one advantage he has over the loquacious young bloods he sees as his rivals. They are boastful about their conquests, while he, with his reputation to protect, will guarantee absolute discretion:

> People like us burn with a discreet fire; with us, you can be quite sure of secrecy: the care we take of our reputation provides a full guarantee to the loved woman, and with us you will find, if you accept our hearts, love without scandal and pleasure without fear.

He returns to the question again, when he believes that Elmire is to be his, to reassure her that there is no harm in adultery: 'you can rest assured of total secrecy; there is any wrong in it only if it reaches the ears of the public; the stumbling block is the worldly scandal: to sin in silence is not to sin'.

This characteristic of Tartuffe reflects another persistent theme in anti-Jesuit propaganda. The Jesuits were accused by their opponents of caring more about their reputation that about honesty, justice or virtue. Hence, it was argued, they would go to any lengths to protect their reputation and, if one of their number slipped into wrongdoing, would care little for the sin itself so long as it could be kept secret. A contemporary pamphlet, *L'Innocence persécutée*, a long anonymous poem circulated in manuscript form, accusing the Jesuits of collaborating with Colbert to ensure the conviction of Fouquet, made precisely this accusation: 'They place their virtue in the art of concealment; what no one hears about is not called sin.'

According to another polemicist, Jarrige, a Jesuit who left the Order and then attacked it bitterly in *Les Jesuistes mis sur l'eschafaut* (1648), this use of secrecy to protect the Society's good name was widespread among Jesuits. He argued that Ignatius, in his rules on chastity, set such a high standard for Jesuits, requiring that they maintain 'angelic purity', that 'he has thrown them into despair of ever achieving success, and, being unable to show that they are angels, for they are too carnal, they have shown, especially recently, that they are men, and among those most attached to the senses and the flesh'. Allegations of this kind add significance to Tartuffe's delightfully understated remark to Elmire: 'But Madam, after all, I am not an angel'. Jarrige claimed that Jesuits had bowed to expediency, shifting guilt from the act of fornication itself to the fact of being found out: 'all lascivious acts between man and woman which discretion has kept hidden were not sins before God, but simply those which came to the knowledge of men'. Jarrige claimed to have heard a woman saying she preferred Jesuits to other priests, as she found them 'more discreet'.

9. Orgon's credulity

In terms of traditional comedy, Orgon plays the fool to Tartuffe's knave; he is the rich, naïve *bourgeois* who falls readily into the traps laid by the villain. His role of gullible fool has satirical functions, too. Within the microcosm of the family, he represents the figure in authority, who is manipulated by the ruthless hypocritical intruder. He also symbolizes, together with his mother, Madame Pernelle, those French men and women whose desire to defend the Church against heretics and libertines were so strong that they easily fell victim to the tricks of hypocrites who appealed to them in the name of God.

The theme of credulity runs through the play; both Madame Pernelle and Orgon confuse credulity with faith. They imitate Tartuffe, naming God and Heaven at every opportunity, making an ostentatious display of devoutness and claiming always to know the mind and will of God. As a result, they feel they have earned the right to condemn as sinners all those who do not share their noisy and aggressive religiosity. In the famous opening scene of *Le Tartuffe*, in which Madame Pernelle scolds the whole household, except for the absent Orgon, the comedy arises in part from the fact that it is not for their shortcomings that this shrill old woman is condemning them, but for their refusal to share her credulous adulation of Tartuffe. True morality is overturned: from inside her cocoon of credulity, this sour, elderly bigot feels entirely justified in proclaiming that God is on her side and that other members of the family, who have done nothing worse than receive visits from friends, are instruments of Satan.

Orgon uses similar perverted logic to discredit Cléante, Valère, and his own wife and children. His behaviour and reasoning are based on an assumption that his own wishes and the wishes of Tartuffe have divine authority and need no other backing, while the wishes and arguments of those who oppose them are contrary to the will of God and carry no weight. When Cléante tries to persuade Orgon that his trust in Tartuffe has been accorded too easily, Orgon responds by condemning his brother-in-law as a libertine, so damning Cléante and everything he says and relieving himself of the chore of having to find answers to his arguments. Cléante protests in vain that, for the credulous, 'a man's a libertine for having a good pair of eyes, and anyone who fails to adore empty grimaces has neither faith not respect for sacred things'.

Valère receives similar treatment; when Orgon decides, without good reason, to break the promise he has made to Valère and to marry his daughter to Tartuffe instead, he shifts the blame for his change of mind from himself to Valère; it is Orgon who is breaking his promise, but by instantly convicting Valère, without evidence, of libertinism and gambling to justify his decision, the sin is transferred from the offender to the innocent victim.

Later, when Orgon is forced to choose between believing his son Damis and trusting his friend Tartuffe, he is not content merely to convict his son of deliberate lying but, to punish him, sentences him to instant exile from the family home and deprives him of his rightful succession to the family fortune. Orgon, blinded by credulity, turns justice on its head: his punishment would be cruel even if his son had been lying; in fact, Damis is innocent and his father, with all his religious prating, has become a monster of injustice. When his wife, supported by the rest of the family, tries to persuade Orgon that Damis has been telling the truth, all are dismissed as liars; the credit they have earned in Orgon's eyes over years of family life proves worthless when balanced against Orgon's newly adopted faith.

His credulity is almost unshakeable; when Elmire is driven to playing the seductress to expose Tartuffe's hypocrisy and force her husband to abandon his faith in him, still, while Tartuffe prepares to take possession of her just a few feet away from his hiding place, Orgon hesitates. Only when Tartuffe himself states unequivocally that Orgon is a fool, asking to be led by the nose, does he finally emerge from under the table with his sight restored.

Molière's play shows how hypocrisy is fostered by credulity. In both the *Placet* of 1667 and the *Préface* of 1669. he complained bitterly that many genuinely good and devout people had been turned against him and his play by the specious arguments of hypocrites. Such good men, he writes in the *Préface*, 'from the warmth of their devotion to the interests of heaven, readily receive the impressions these poeple wish to give them'. Molière makes it clear that Orgon had been a good man before being blinded and corrupted by the combination of Tartuffe's hypocrisy and his own credulity; he had been a loyal Frenchman who had fought for his King in the troubles of the Fronde; it is partly in gratitude for past services that the King pardons him for having given shelter to a fugitive from justice. Molière surrounds Orgon with a loyal and generous family, too, to suggest that before Tartuffe's arrival he had been an affectionate father and husband.

The satirical implication of the portrait of Orgon, when transferred from the context of the family to the wider context of the state, is that according to Molière many a good Frenchman, seduced by the appeal of the external trappings of religion, had lost his judgement, hardened his heart, turned against his friends and become an instrument of injustice. Orgon is not merely fooled and robbed; he has himself become a danger and a scourge to all those who should be closest to him.

10. Orgon's family

The family of Orgon, including the servant Dorine, represents the considerable number of discerning, level-headed Frenchmen who, Molière suggests, have no difficulty seeing through the machinations of hypocritical cabals, but who, especially if they speak out against them, are likely to suffer from their vindictive calumnies. Cléante and Valère, when they are accused of being libertines, are suffering the same fate as other opponents of the Jesuits, including Pascal and Molière. Pascal lists among the names given to him by Jesuit polemicists: 'ungodly, buffoon, ignoramus, joker, impostor, calumniator, knave and heretic . . .' Molière complained to the King that he had been called 'a devil clothed in flesh and dressed as a man, a libertine, a godless man deserving of exemplary torture'.

The family's failure to counter Tartuffe's moves reflects what Molière, Pascal, Valeriano Magni and many others saw as the helplessness of honest people attempting to oppose the advance of the Jesuits. The family's failure is all the more striking for the fact that Tartuffe's dishonesty is so transparent. Molière appears to suggests that the ordinary weapons of honest men and women are powerless against the ruthless methods of even quite clumsy impostors, when they choose to present themselves as envoys specially elect of God. At every turn, the family underestimates the effecitveness of Tartuffe's preplanned series of manoeuvres. While they are still convinced that they have only to undeceive Orgon to put matters right, Tartuffe has already armed himself with enough material to blackmail Orgon, has procured legal ownership of the house and, under the cover of crooked casuistry, is attempting to seduce his wife. Molière creates the impression that this attractive French family, symbol of the wider family of all true Frenchmen, is attacked on every side, unable to foresee or forestall the numerous hidden traps and pitfalls prepared for it by an enemy deploying the full range of Jesuitical skills and stratagems.

11. The perspective of the *honnête homme*

Cléante is a crucial figure in this society undermined by sophistry and credulity: he illustrates, through both the soundness of his arguments and the modesty of his behavior, how a good and honest man should behave. In the words of the author of the *Lettre sur la comédie de l'Imposteur*, Cléante recognizes 'the middle way, in which alone justice, reason and truth are to be found'. Cléante claims nothing more than to be able to distinguish between the true and the false but, as Cicero says, this is precisely the purpose of good dialectic, the art of 'sound discussion and of distinguishing the true from the false'.

Cléante's sound dialectic is deployed most fully in the scene where he first discusses Tartuffe with Orgon. His argument is an expression of the commonplace view of anti-Jesuit writers that Jesuits displayed excessive vindictiveness in their treatment of opponents. He dwells on the difference between the truly devout and the hypocritical. Of the devout, he says:

> These are no braggarts of virtue; you will not find in them this unbearable display of pomp and ceremony, and their devotion is human and approachable; they do not censure our every action: they find too much arrogance in such corrections; and leaving proud words to others, it is through their deeds alone that they reprove our behaviour.

He also shows to what extent Orgon, under Tartuffe's influence, has lost touch with both the theory and practice of Christianity: he has ceased to love and respect his family and friends; he has become arrogantly censorious of others, and unhealthily obsessed with the external signs and gestures of religion. He has replaced Christian humility and love with vindictive religiosity.

Cléante is 'the truly good man' whom Molière introduced into the play, as he says in the *Préface*, to provide a contrast with the hypocrite. Some critics have observed that Cléante is not an ardent apologist for Christianity, and cite his reticence as evidence that Molière, in whom they see a covert libertine, was indifferent or even hostile to the Christian faith. This argument does not stand up to close examination. The authority of the Church and its dogma are not under attack in *Le Tartuffe*, so why should Molière appoint someone to defend them? It is appropriate for a satirist and comic poet to satirize hypocrisy, but it would have been considered most inappropriate for him to defend Christian doctrine on stage. More importantly, we have seen that Cléante argues that it is the Christian's deeds, not his words, which speak most clearly. Molière illustrates this point by portraying Cléante not as a man who talks about Christianity but as a man who does his best to behave in a Christian way.

It is part of the satirical thrust of the play that those who never stop talking about God and Heaven are often the very people who practice their faith least. The writer of the *Lettre sur la comédie de l'Imposteur* argues that Cléante is introduced early in the play so that the audience may see an example of 'true devotion' before seeing the hypocrite; the antidote to the poison of hypocrisy, he suggests, is taken before the spectator can be exposed to risk from the poison itself. Cléante's behaviour is seen to be open, honest, tolerant and modest. He confronts the hostility, folly, dishonesty and treachery he meets in this play with neither anger nor complacent self-righteousness. He argues with Orgon and Tartuffe firmly but with control. When he rebuts Tartuffe's sophistry at the beginning of Act IV, his straight, pellucid and common-sense dialectic shows up the crookedness of Tartuffe's reasoning, but he avoids attacking Tartuffe himself. Tartuffe soon has recourse to the trick used by Pascal's Jesuit Father when arguments run dry: he recollects suddenly that he has urgent business elsewhere.

Cléante's patience with Orgon, though severely tested by the latter's absurd errors of judgement, never deserts him. When Tartuffe's hypocrisy is exposed, Cléante does not yield, as Dorine does, to the temptation of reminding Orgon what a fool he has made of himself. He restrains Orgon when, shocked by Tartuffe's wickedness, he swears undying hatred for all men of God. At this point, Molière gives Cléante a long speech in which he commends moderation and underlines again that it is vital to distinguish between impostors and true men of God; to push his point home, he suggests that if Orgon cannot avoid straying from the mean, he should rather fall into the extreme of trusting the occasional hypocrite than into the opposite extreme of turning against all devout men. Again, as Tartuffe is led off to jail and Orgon prepares to speed him on his way with a curse, Cléante intervenes to urge Orgon to hope rather that Tartuffe might mend his ways. The writer of the *Lettre sur la comédie de l'Imposteur* underlines the symbolic importance of Cléante's forgiving attitude: forgiveness of one's enemies, he aruges, 'the most sublime of evangelic virtues', is the perfect note on which to end the play, which is nothing else but 'a most Christian instruction on the nature of true devotion'.

12. The King's intervention

The same anonymous writer expressed his enthusiasm for the whole dénouement of *Le Tartuffe*; according to him, this feature of the play, the most puzzling to modern directors and theatre-goers, was the best part of the whole comedy:

> It seems to me that, if in the rest of the play the author has equalled all the ancients and surpassed all the moderns, one can say that in this dénouement he has surpassed himself, as nothing could be greater, more magnificient and more wonderful, and yet more natural, more happy and more appropriate . . .

Some of the anonymous author's admiration for the dénouement might be attributed to his wish to please the King by endorsing Molière's portrait of him as the most just and clear-sighted of monarchs; justice and lucidity, this writer argues, are the very qualities which best characterize Louis XIV. In stressing the appropriateness of the ending, however, the author is making the point that the action of the play and the dénouement are well matched. It is a most unconventional dénouement—even fictitious kings did not appear on stage in New Comedy and farce. To present an officer of a reigning monarch who, with full authority from his master, intervenes directly to change the course of events and ensure a happy ending, is an extraordinary procedure. It is unlikely that Molière made use of the King's name without first seeking his permission. If, however, Le Tartuffe is a political play translated into a domestic context, an unconventional ending involving a political solution is appropriate. The ending is a reminder to the audience of the wider meaning of the play.

There is evidence that Louis XIV did support Le Tartuffe from its inception, encouraging and applauding the play when first performed, in its earliest three-act version, before him and the court at Versailles in 1664, and that even when yielding to pressure to ban further public performances, he did not withdraw his personal support from Molière or the play. Brossette, writing more than thirty years later, reports that, according to Boileau, Molière read the first three acts of Le Tartuffe to the King before the first performance. A more immediate and reliable source of evidence is Molière's own Placets and Préface to the play. In his first Placet, addressed to the King in August 1664, Molière expressed his gratitude to Louis XIV for the trouble he had taken to explain why he had thought it appropriate to ban a comedy in which he, personally, could find nothing to censure. Molière added, in the same Placet, that his play had also enjoyed the approval of the papal legate, Cardinal Chigi, and of most of the bishops of France. In the following year, 1665, Louis displayed his support for Molière and his players in a most public manner by naming them La Troupe du Roi and increasing their royal pension. When the play was banned again, in 1667, while the King was with his army in Flanders, Molière wrote his second *Placet* to the King; in it, he makes it clear that this modified version of his satire, renamed *L'Imposteur*, has also been performed with Louis's approval. In the *Préface* of 1669, after the King had revoked all bans on the performance of *Le Tartuffe*, Molière, reviewing the troubled history of his play, recalled that it had always enjoyed the approval of the King, the Queen, the royal Princes and the King's Ministers.

If *Le Tartuffe* was intended as a satire on Jesuit casuistry and on Jesuit ambitions and their strategies for achieving them, it is clear that the King was pleased to let the Jesuits smart under the satirist's scourge. Perhaps, after a period of hostile relations between France and the papacy following the alleged insult to the French Ambassador to the papal court in 1662—a period which must have posed considerable problems for Jesuits close to the King and also bound by their fourth vow of special loyalty to the Pope— Louis wished to issue a transparent yet indirect reminder to the Jesuits that, in France at least, their first loyalty must be to their King and to the French Church? Perhaps, too, without wishing to quarrel openly with the Jesuits, Louis wished to signal to the many anti-Jesuit factions at court and in France generally that he was firmly in control of his own policies, determined to defend French interests and perfectly able to see through any self-interested plan which the Jesuits at court might propose to him? If so, the King's decision to ban the play in 1664 might well have been a political compromise in which he chose to conciliate the Jesuits by banning the play publicly, while reassuring their opponents by making it clear that he had no objection to private performances and readings. *Le Tartuffe* was performed privately—in the presence of the King and the court—for Monsieur, the King's brother, in 1664, and for *le grand* Condé in 1664, 1665 and twice in 1668; those who missed these performances would have been able to listen to one of the many readings of the play which Molière gave in private *salons*. *Le Tartuffe*, like Pascal's *Lettres provinciales*, enjoyed the success which came from uniting behind it those whose wished to see the Jesuits ridiculed, those, in still greater numbers, who were curious to see a play which had stirred up such a ferment of controversy; and those who relished lively and entertaining satire.

It is hardly surprising that *Le Tartuffe*, a play of such gripping topicality, should have proved so popular with contemporary audiences. What is more remarkable is its continuing success. By stripping the complex political and religious issues behind the play of all inessential details, by understanding the forces he observed at work in the wider society of France and portraying them simply and directly in a coherent and believable domestic comedy, Molière constructed a comic poem which has easily outlived the events and controversies on which it was based. Modern audiences may lose something from sharing none of the partisan feelings which so excited or enraged contemporaries, but they continue to derive pleasure from the poet's telling comic portraits of a hypocrite and a gullible fool, and their effects on family life.

Chronology

1622   Jean-Baptiste Poquelin, first of six children of Jean Poquelin and Marie Cressé, is baptized on January 15.

1631   Jean Poquelin, by purchasing his brother's court appointment, becomes the "tapissier ordinaire de la maison du roi" and thus begins to supply furniture to the Royal family.

1632   Marie Cressé dies. Jean Poquelin remarries the following year.

1636   Jean-Baptiste begins his schooling at the Jesuit College de Clermont. Corneille's *Le Cid* is performed the following year.

1641-42 Law studies in Orleans where Jean-Baptiste is admitted to the bar. His association with the Béjart family begins around the same time that Jean-Baptiste takes over his father's Royal appointment. Richelieu dies in 1642.

1643   Jean-Baptiste transfers this appointment to his brother and forms the stage company Illustre Théâtre with Madeleine Béjart and her brother Joseph. Death of Louis XIII on May 14, 1643. Anne d'Autriche becomes regent.

1644   Jean-Baptiste Poquelin first takes on the pseudonym of Molière.

1656   *Lettres provinciales* by Pascal, a convert to Jansenism, appear.

1659   First performance of *Les Précieuses ridicules*.

1661   Louis XIV marries and assumes personal reign.

1662   *L'Ecole des femmes* has a triumphant success and Molière receives the first Royal pension awarded to an actor. Molière marries Armande Béjart, twenty years his junior, who is either the sister or the daughter of Madeleine.

1664   Molière delivers a private reading of the first act of *Le Misanthrope*. His first born son, Louis, is born and dies in the same year. Molière is the producer for Racine's *Le Thébaïde*.

1665   *Dom Juan* is first presented at the Palais Royal but lasts only 15 performances. Molière's daughter Espirit-Madeleine is baptized.

1666   The King's Players perform *Le Misanthrope* in Paris at the Théâtre Royale with Molière in the role of Alceste. *Le Médecin malgré lui* receives immediate success with its performance at the Théâtre du Palais Royal by the King's Players. Molière's works are collected and translated. His health declines and Molière is unable to perform on stage for several months.

1667   Molière and his wife Armande separate.

1668   *L'Avare* begins a short run in September. The first six books of La Fontaine's *Fables* are published.

1669   First performance of the version in five acts of *Tartuffe* in Paris at the Théâtre de Petit-Bourbon. In its previous versions, Molière originally staged a three-act version of *Tartuffe* at Versailles by command of Louis XIV. The work was banned, later acquired a fourth and fifth act, and was renamed and performed as *L'Imposteur* in 1667. Excommunication was threatened by the Archbishop of Paris to anyone who performed, read, or recited the *Tartuffe* version banned in the same year. Jean Poquelin, Molière's father, dies.

1670   As entertainment for the King, *Le Bourgeous gentilhomme* is performed in Cambourd.

1672   Madeleine Béjart dies after a long illness at the age of fifty-five. At the Théâtre du Palais Royal, the King's Players present the first performance of *Les Femmes savantes*.

1673   Molière falls ill and succumbs on February 17 in his apartment on the Rue de Richelieu. He is enterred on the night of February 21 in the cemetery of Saint Joseph after the intervention of the King with the Archbishop of Paris to permit the burial of the playwright, who died without benefit of the sacraments, in consecrated ground. Much later, in 1817, Molière's remains are moved to Père Lachaise.

Contributors

HAROLD BLOOM is Sterling Professor of the Humanities at Yale University and Henry W. and Albert A. Berg Professor of English at the New York University Graduate School. He is the author of over 20 books, including *Shelly's Mythmaking* (1959), *The Visionary Company* (1961), Blake's *Apocalypse* (1963), *Yeats* (1970), *A Map of Misreading* (1975), *Kabbalah and Criticism* (1975), *Agon: Toward a Theory of Revisionism* (1982), *The American Religion* (1992), *The Western Canon* (1994), and *Omens of Millennium: The Gnosis of Angels, Dreams, and Resurrection* (1996). *The Anxiety of Influence* (1973) sets forth Professor Bloom's provocative theory of the literary relationships between the great writers and their predecessors. His most recent books include *Shakespeare: The Invention of the Human*, a 1998 National Book Award finalist, and *How to Read and Why*, which was published in 2000. In 1999, Professor Bloom received the prestigious American Academy of Arts and Letters Gold Medal for Criticism.

JAMES PATRICK CARMODY is the author of articles such as "Reading Scenic Writing: Barthes, Brecht, and Theatre Photography" and the critical investigation entitled "Molière in America".

GÉRARD DEFAUX, professor of French at Johns Hopkins University works extensively on Marot, as well as Molière, Rabelais and Montaigne. He is the author of *Rabelais agonistes* (1997).

JAMES F. GAINES, professor of French from Mary Washington College in Fredericksburg, VA, has published many studies on Molière along with his investigations on Pierre Du Ryer.

JACQUES GUICHARNAUD, Professor Emeritus from Yale University, has contributed significant, critical studies on French literature over a long and productive career and is the author of *Modern French Theatre from Giraudoux to Genet*.

WILL GRAYBURN MOORE, known for a long and significant career at the University of Oxford, contributed extensively to Molière studies and emphasized to readers of Molière the importance of remembering that Molière's plays were destined to be acted before an audience.

MICHAEL S. KOPPISCH from Michigan State University investigates La Bruyère as well Molière. He is the author of *Dissolution of Character: Changing Perspectives in La Bruyère's 'Caractères'*.

ROBERT MCBRIDE from Queen's University of Belfast has focused his critical investigations on Molière and his contemporary Racine.

RONALD W. TOBIN, from the University of California at Santa Barbara, has written on Pascal and Racine and is the editor and author of *Le Corps au XVIIe siècle*.

H. GASTON HALL has written studies on the theater of La Fontaine, Corneille and Pirandello along with his many publications on Molière including texts on particular plays such as *Molière's 'Le Bourgeous gentilhomme': context and stagecraft*.

JOSEPH I. DONOHUE, JR. from Michigan State University has published articles on Pierre de Marivaux as well as his work on Molière.

PETER H. NURSE from the University of Kent at Canterbury is the author of *Classical Voices: Studies of Corneille, Racine, Molière, Mme de Lafayette* along with many articles on Molière.

DAVID SHAW has also published on the legal aspects in Molière's controversial play 'Tartuffe'.

JULES BRODY, Professor Emeritus from Harvard University, has published many critical studies on Molière and Boileau and has written on Montaigne including *Nouvelles lectures de Montaigne* (1994).

ANDREW CALDER has investigated La Fontaine and La Rochefoucauld along with his studies of Molière and comedy in seventeenth-century French literature.

Bibliography

Albanese, Ralph. *Molière á l'école républicaine: De la critique universitaire aux manuels scolaires (1870-1914).* Stanford: Stanford French and Italian Studies, Anma Libri, 1992.

————."'Tartuffe' Goes to School: The Formation of Academic Discourse in Nineteenth-Century France" in *Approaches to Teaching Molière's 'Tartuffe' and Other Plays.* James F. Gaines and Michael S. Koppisch, eds. New York: Modern Language Association of America, 1995. 19-25.

Bermel, Albert. *Molière's Theatrical Bounty: A New View of the Plays.* Carbondale: Southern Illinois University Press, 1990.

Bray, René. *Molière: Homme de théâtre.* Paris: Mercure de France, 1954.

Brody, Jules. "Esthetique et societé chez Molière" in *Dramaturgie et societe: Rapports entre l'oeuvre theatrale, son interpretation et son public aux XVIe et XVIIe siècles.* Jean Jacquot, Elie Konigson, and Marcel Oddon, eds. Paris: Eds. du Centre National de la Recherche Scientifique, 1968.

————. "'Don Juan' and 'Le Misanthrope', or the Esthetics of Individualism in Molière". *PMLA: Publications of the Modern Language Association of America* 84, (1969): 559-576.

Cairncross, John, ed. *L'humanité de Molière.* Paris, Nizet, 1988.

Calder, Andrew. "Humour in the 1660s: La Rochefoucauld, Molière and La Fontaine". *Seventeenth-Century French Studies* 20, (1998): 125-38.

Canfield, J. Douglas. "The Classical Treatment of Don Juan in Tirso, Molière, and Mozart: What Cultural Work Does It Perform?". *Comparative Drama* 31, no. 1 (1997 Spring): 42-64.

211

Ciccone, Anthony A. *The comedy of language: four farces by Molière*. Potomac, MD: J. Porrua Turanzas, 1980.

Corneille, Pierre. *Three masterpieces : The liar, The illusion, Le cid* . Trans. Ranjit Bolt. London: Oberon, 2000.

Defaux, Gerard. "Un Point de critique et d'histoire litteraire: Molière, 'Les Femmes savantes', et le Florentin". *Papers on French Seventeenth Century Literature* 8, no. 14 (1) (1981): 43-68.

DeJean, Joan. "Classical Reeducation: Decanonizing the Feminine." *Yale French Studies* 75 (1988): 26-39.

Dock, Stephen Varick. *Costume and Fashion in the Plays of Jean-Baptiste Poquelin Molière: A Seventeenth-Century Perspective*. Geneva: Slatkine, 1992.

Edelman, Nathan, ed. *The Seventeenth Century*. Syracuse: Syracuse Univerisity Press, 1961. Vol. 3 of *A Critical Bibliography of French Literature*. David C. Cabenn and Jules Brody, gen. eds.

Fernandez, Ramón. *Molière: The Man Seen through the Plays*. Trans. Wilson Follett. New York: Hill, 1958.

Gaines, James F. *Social Structures in Molière's Theater*. Columbus: Ohio State University Press, 1984.

———. "Caractères, Superstition, and Paradoxes in 'Le Misanthrope'" in *Alteratives*. Warren Motte and Gerald Prince, eds. Lexington, KY: French Forum, 1993.

Gaines, James F. and Michael S. Koppisch, eds. *Approaches to Teaching Molière's 'Tartuffe' and Other Plays*. New York: Modern Language Association of America, 1995.

Gossman, Lionel. *Men and masks: a study of Molière*. Baltimore: Johns Hopkins Press, 1963.

Grene, Nicholas. *Shakespeare, Jonson, Molière: the comic contract*. London: MacMillan, 1980.

Gross, Nathan. *From gesture to idea-esthetics and ethics in Molière's comedy*. New York: Columbia University Press, 1982.

Guicharnaud, Jacques. *Une aventure théâtrale*. Paris: Gallimard, 1963.

———. *Modern French Theatre: from Giraudoux to Genet*. New Haven: Yale University Press, 1967.

Hall, H. Gaston, ed. *The Seventeenth Century: Supplement*. Syracuse: Syracuse University Press, 1961. Vol. 3 of *A Critical Bibliography of French Literature*. Ed. Richard A. Brooks.

———. *Molière's 'Le Bourgeous gentilhomme': context and stagecraft*. Durham: University of Durham, 1990.

Hollier, Denis, ed. *A New History of French Literature*. Cambridge: Harvard University Press, 1989.

Howarth, W. D. *Molière: A Playwright and his Audience*. Cambridge: Cambridge University Press, 1982.

————, ed. *French Theatre in the neo-classical era, 1550-1791*. Cambridge: Cambridge University Press, 1997.

Howarth, W. D. and Merlin Thomas, eds. *Molière: stage and study; essays in honour of W. G. Moore*. Oxford: Clarendon Press, 1973.

Hubert, J. D. *Molière and the Comedy of Intellect*. Berkeley: University of California Press, 1962.

————. "Molière's Theater" in *Le Labyrinthe de Versailles: Parcours critique de Molière a La Fontaine*. Ed. Martine Debaisieux. Atlanta: Rodopi, 1998.

Johnson, Roger, Guy T. Trail, and Editha Neumann, eds. *Molière and the Commonwealth of Letters: Patrimony and Posterity*. Jackson: University Press of Mississippi, 1975.

Koppisch, Michael S. "Molière and the Moralist Tradition". *Papers on French Seventeenth Century Literature* 27, no. 52 (2000): 359-414.

Knutson, Harold C. *Molière: an archetypal approach*. Toronto: University of Toronto Press, 1976.

————. *The triumph of wit: Molière and Restoration comedy*. Columbus: Ohio State University Press, 1988.

La Fontaine, Jean de. *Complete tales*. Trans. Guido Waldman. Manchester : Carcanet, 2000.

Molière. *Oeuvres complètes*. Ed. Georges Couton. 2 vols. Paris: Gallimard, 1971.

————. *Dom Juan and other plays*. Trans. George Graveley and Ian Maclean. Oxford: Oxford University Press, 1989.

————. *Four comedies*. Trans. Richard Wilbur. New York: Harcourt Brace Jovanovich, 1982.

————. *Tartuffe and The Bourgeois Gentleman*. Trans. Stanley Appelbaum. Mineola, NY: Dover, 1998.

————. *The Doctor in spite of himself, and The bourgeois gentleman*. Trans. Albert Bermel. New York: Applause Theatre Book Publishers, 1987.

————. *The Misanthrope and Other Plays*. Trans. Donald M. Frame. New York: New American Library, 1981.

————. *The Misanthrope and Other Plays: A New Selection*. Trans. John Wood and David Coward. New York: Penguin, 2000.

————. *The Miser and George Dandin*. Trans. Albert Bermel. New York: Applause Theatre Book Publishers, 1987.

————. *The School for Wives, and The Learned Ladies*. Trans. Richard Wilbur. San Diego: Harcourt Brace Jovanovich, 1991.

Moore, Will Grayburn. *Molière, A New Criticism*. Oxford: Clarendon Press, 1964.

Muratore, M. J. "Theatrical Conversion in Molière's 'Dom Juan'". *Nottingham French Studies* 34, no. 2 (1995 Autumn): 1-9.

Norman, Larry F. *The Public Mirror: Molière and the Social Commerce of Depiction*. Chicago: University of Chicago Press, 1999.

Nurse, Peter H. "'Tartuffe': Comedy or drame?". *Modern Languages: Journal of the Modern Language Association* 70, no. 2 (1989 June): 118-122.

Pascal, Blaise. *Pensées.* Trans. A. J. Krailsheimer. New York: Penguin, 1986.

Racine, Jean. *Five plays.* Trans. Kenneth Muir. New York: Hill and Wang , 1960.

Shaw, David. "'Tartuffe' and the Law" in *Making Connections.* James Dolamore, ed. Berlin: Peter Lang, 1999.

Tobin, Ronald W. "Fusion and Diffusion in 'Le Bourgeois Gentilhomme'". *The French Review: Journal of the American Association of Teachers of French* 59, no. 2 (1985 Dec.): 234-245.

Wadsworth, Philip A. *Molière and the Italian Theatrical Tradition.* Columbia, SC: French Literature Publications, 1977.

Walker, Hallam. *Molière: Updated Edition.* Boston: Twayne, 1990.

Woshinsky, Barbara. "The Discourse of Disbelief in Molière's 'Dom Juan'." *Romanic Review* 72 (1981): 401-08.

Acknowledgments

"Mise en Scène and the Classic Text" by Jim Carmody. From *Rereading Molière*. © 1993 University of Michigan. Reprinted by permission.

"The Comic at Its Limits" by Gerard Defaux. From *A New History of French Literature*. edited by Dennis Hollier, et. al., Cambridge, Mass: Harvard University Press. © 1989 The President and Fellows of Harvard College. Reprinted by permission.

"Molière, La Fontaine, and Authority." by James F. Gaines. From *Papers on French Seventeenth-Century Literature* 27, no. 53 (2000). © 2000 Gunter Narr Verlag Tübingen. Reprinted by permission.

"Introduction" by Jacques Guicharnaud. From *Molière: A Collection of Critical Essays*. © 1964 Prentice-Hall, Inc. Reprinted by permission.

"Mime" by W. G. Moore. From *Molière: A New Criticism*. © 1949 Oxford University Press. Reprinted by permission.

"Dom Juan's Equal Opportunity Rivalry" by Michael S. Koppisch. From *Papers on French Seventeenth Century Literature* 27, no. 53 (2000). © 2000 Gunter Narr Verlag Tübingen. Reprinted by permission.

"Dom Juan" by Robert McBride. From *The Sceptical Vision of Molière*. © 1977 Robert McBride. Reprinted by permission.

"Rehearsal and Reversal in 'Le Bourgeois Gentilhomme'" by Ronald W. Tobin. From *Tarte à la crème: Comedy and Gastronomy in Molière's*

Theater. © 1990 Ohio State University Press. Updated version appeared in Italian translation as *Tarte à la créme: commedia e gastronomia nel teatro di Moliere* (Rome: Bulzoni, 1999). Reprinted by permission.

"Parody in 'L'Ecole des femmes'" by H. Gaston Hall. From *Comedy in Context: Essays on Molière.* © 1984 University Press of Mississippi. Reprinted by permission.

"Restructuring a Comic Hero of Molière: Le médecin malgré lui" by Joseph I. Donohoe, Jr. From *Approaches to Teaching Molière's 'Tartuffe' and Other Plays.* © 1995 The Modern Language Association of America. Reprinted by permission.

"'Le Misanthrope': philosophical implications" by Peter H. Nurse. From *Molière and The Comic Spirit.* © 1991 Librarie Droz. Reprinted by permission.

"Legal Elements in 'Le Misanthrope'" by David Shaw. From *Nottingham French Studies* 38, no. 1 (1999 Spring). © 1999 The University of Nottingham. Reprinted by permission.

"Love in 'Tartuffe', Tartuffe in Love" by Jules Brody. From *Approaches to Teaching Molière's 'Tartuffe' and Other Plays.* ©1995 The Modern Language Association of America. Reprinted by permission.

"Le Tartuffe" by Andrew Calder. From *Molière: The Theory and Practice of Comedy.* London: The Anthlone Press. © 1993 Andrew Calder. Reprinted by permission.

Index

Abraham, Claude, 109, 112
Aeneid (Vergil), 127
Amants Magnifiques, Les, 28
American Negro Comedians, 49
Amourous Doctor, The, 28
Amorous Quarrel,The, 28
Amphitryon, 28, 42, 51, 161
Animaux Malades de la Peste, Les, 39
Antoine, André 11, 18-22, 24
Apologie, (Montaigne), 105
Arnavon, Jacques, 11, 18, 57

Baroque Theater, 20
Barthes, Roland, 15-16, 18
Baudrillard, Jean, 113
Beckett, 49
Béjard, La, 59
Béjard, Madeleine, 60
Béjart Family, 28, 207
Bentley, Eric, 2
Bernard Dort, (Racine), 14
Besace, La, (La Fountaine), 157
Biancolelli, 63
Blundera, The, 28
Boileau, Nicolas, 33, 40, 107
Bourgeois Gentelhomme, Le, 27, 29, 36,
    55, 64, 107-122, 124, 134, 208
Boutang, Pierre, 43
Braun, Edward, 19
Bray, Rene, 5, 8-9, 12, 57

Brecht, 25
Brody, Jules, 175-182
Burlador de Sevilla, El, (de Molina),
    78-79
"Butterfly of Parnasius", 36

Calder, Andrew, 183-206
"*Cantique de la Vierge*", (DuPerron),132
Carmody, Jim, 5-26
Chappuzeau, Samuel, 134
Chauveau, Francois, 132
Chene et le Roseau, Le, (La
    Fountaine), 40
Chéreau, 8
Cid, Le, (Corneille), 48, 154, 207
*Classiques au Théatre ou la Metamorphose
    Sans Fin, Les*, (Dort), 21
Clinton, Bill, 2
Comic Pastoral, The, 28
Commedia, 6, 63
Commedia dell'arte, 62-63, 78-79
Commédies-ballet, 8, 10, 13, 41, 107,
    116-117, 119
Comtesse d' Escarbagnas, 29, 36, 55
Copeau, 57
Corneille, Pierre, 28-30, 62, 129, 174
Courtesian DéSaubusé, (Bourdonne),
    148
Couton, Georges, 117-118

Critique de L'Ecole des Femmes, 30, 124-
    128, 132-134, 138, 159
Cuisinerfrancois, (La Varenne), 107

*Daily Life in the Theater at the Time of
    Molière*, (Mongredien), 9
Dancourt, Florent, 33
Dante, 2
Darmon, Charles, 41
De Beumarchais, Pierre Caron, 33
Decameron, (Boccaccio), 131
Defaux, Gérard, 27-34, 119
De Marivaux, Pierre Carlet, 33
Depit amoureux, 28, 116
Dernier Molière, Le, (Garapon), 119
Derridean, 15
Des Réaux, Tallemaut, 59-60
De Visé, Jean Donneau, 31, 146
Dictionnaire Francois, (Futetiére),
    107,114
Diderot, Denis, 33
Discourses, (Rousseau), 38
Divertessement, 28, 33, 71
Docteur Amoureux, Le, 28
Dom Garcia de Navarre, 30
Dom Juan, 1-2, 28, 30, 32, 36, 51-
    54,58, 69, 72, 77-105, 118, 137-
    138, 145-146, 148, 183-184, 208
Dom Juan, (Byron), 1
Donohue, Joseph J., Jr., 137-144
Dorante, 107, 114, 116, 119, 121, 124,
    126, 132-133
Dorimène, 114, 119, 121
Dorimond, 79, 81, 93, 102, 124
Dort, Bernard, 14-17, 20-23
Dramaturgie Classique en France, La, 9
Dufresney, Charles, 33
Dullin, 57

Elam, Keir, 15
Elomire Hypocondie, 62
Epitre, (Boileau), 33
Escobar, 194

Fables, (La Fountaine), 37, 39-41, 208
Faucheux, 65, 149, 152
Faucheux, Les, (Bores, The), 29, 115,
    119, 164
Falstaff, 3
Farceur, 11
Faust, (Goethe), 1
Femmes Savantes, Les, 27, 29, 36-38,
    53-55, 111, 113, 124, 128, 130,
    134, 208
Festin de Pierre ou le Fils Criminel, Le,
    (Dorimond), 78
Festin en Paroles, Un (Revel), 107
Fiorelli, 63
Flying Physician, The, 28
*Formation de la Doctrine Classique en
    France, La*, (Bray), 9
Fourberries de Scapin, Les, 28-29, 54, 64,
    164
Force, Pierce, 71
French Revolution, 21
*From Gesture to Idea: Esthetics and Ethics
    in Molière's Comedy*, (Gross), 6

Gaines, James, 35-44
Gauoiserie, 62
George Dandin, 28, 51, 112, 115, 131,
    161
*Genre Burlesque en France au XVII
    Siècle*, (Bar), 127
Gentilhommes, Des (Le Vayer), 100
Geruzez, Eugéne, 127
Gossman, Lionel, 70, 100, 156
Gouhier, 103
"*Grand Siècle*", 12, 18,123, 25
"Grimarest's Biography", 35
Gross, Nathan, 6-8
Guicharnaud, Jacques, 1, 45-58, 155,
    158
Hali, 29
Hall, H. Gaston, 123-135
Hamlet, (Shakespeare), 2, 3, 20
Henry V, 3

Herbert, J.D., 48
Herzel, Roger, 9
Horace, (Corneille), 130, 154, 174
Hotel de Bourgogne, 11, 14, 28, 46
Hotel de Marais, 46
Howarth, W.D., 124

Ibsen, 1
II Convitato de Pietra, (Giliberto), 79
l'Ingratitude, De (Le Vayer), 95, 97, 103
Illustre-Théâtre, 28
Impromptu, 66
Ionesco, 49

Jalousie du Barboriellé, 28
Jarrige, 198
Jasinski, René, 57
Jealousy of Barbouillé,The, 28
Jesuistes mis sur L'Eschafaut, Les, (Jarrige), 198
Jeu de Classiques, Le, (Ubersfeld), 22
Jodelle, 62
Jourdain, M., 11, 113, 115-116, 118, 121
Jouvet, 19, 21-22, 59
Julius Ceaser, (Shakespeare), 22

Knutson, Harold, 119
Koppisch, Micheal, 69-75

La Fountaine, 33, 35-44, 61, 187
La Grange, 123, 163
L'Amour Medecin, 28, 51, 64
Lancaster, Henry C., 9
Lanson, Gustave, 57
Lanson, M., 64-65
Larivey, 62
La Rouchefoucauld, 67, 101, 160
L'Avere, 28-29, 51-52, 54, 61-62 161, 208
Learned Ladies, The, 27

L'Ecole des Cocus ou la Précaution, (Dorimond), 124
L'Ecole des Femmes, 47-50, 54, 56, 60, 67, 111, 114, 123-135, 145-146, 154, 158, 208
L'Ec'ole des Maris, 28, 30, 32, 37, 50, 124, 131
Le Moyne, 192
Lesage, Alain-René, 33
L'Etourdi, 50, 124
L'Etourdi, ou les Contre-Temps, 28, 47
Lettre, (DeVisé), 154
Lettre Sur la Comédie de L'Impostuer, 31
Lettres Provinciales, (Pascal), 185, 187, 190, 207
Le Vayer, Le Mothe, 96, 99-100
Libertin, 77-105
L'Impromtu de Versailles, 30, 60, 65, 138
L'Innocence Persécutré, (Anonymous), 198
Livre de Poche, (Planchon), 20
L'Ovide en Belle Humeur, (d'Assoucy), 127
Loup et L'agneau, Le, (La Fountaine), 39
Louis XIV, 1, 18, 204, 207
Love is the Best Doctor, 28
Love Makes the Painter, 29
Lully, Jean-Baptiste, 28
Lutrin, Le, (Boileau), 129

Magni, Valeriano, 191, 201
Magnificent, The, 28
Malade Imaginaire, Le, 27, 29, 33, 37, 55-56, 65, 113
Mariage Force, Le, 41
Marias, 28
"Mask", 5
Mauriac, Francois, 52
McBride, Robert, 77-105
Médecin Malgré Lui, Le, 28, 51, 137-144, 168, 208

Medecin Volant, Le, 28, 114
Mélicerte, 28, 51
*Membres et L'Estomac, Le*s, (La
    Fountaine), 40
Memoire, (Mahelot), 11
Mémoires Sur la Vie et les Ouvrages, (La
    Seare), 78
Menage, Gilles, 127
"Metadramatic Criticism", 5
Mignard, Pierre, 30
Miller, Jonathan, 16
"Mime", 5, 59-68
Misanthrope, Le, 28, 30-32, 36, 51-57
    62, 118, 127, 131, 135, 137-138,
    145-174, 208
Misanthrope, The, 28
Misanthrope, The, (Shakespeare), 2-3
Miser, The, 28
Miser, The (Shakespeare), 20
Mishaps, The, 28
Molière, (Vendel, Valdermar), 46
Molière: A new Criticism, (Moore), 5
Molière: An Archetypal Approach,
    (Knutson), 119
Molière: Home de Theatre, (Bray), 5, 8
Molère ou les Metamorphoses du Comique,
    (Defaux, Gérard), 119
Molière Tetrelogy of 1978, (Vitez), 11
Mongredien, Georges, 9
Monsieier de Pourceaugnac, 29, 64, 112,
    164
Montaigne, 148
Montia Secreta, (Zaorowski), 188-190
Moore, Will, 5-8, 12, 56, 59-68, 104
Morale, 5, 7
Morail Encomeiene, 33
Muir, Edwin, 158
Murray, Gilbert, 64
Musset, 67
Mutaferraca, 107

Nelson, Robert, 138
Nicomède, 60

Noblese Emprunteé, La, (Erasmus), 134
Nurse, Peter H., 145-162

Odes d'Horace en vers Burlesques, Les
    (Beys), 127
Oedipus, (Shakespeare), 20
Office de la Vierge, (de Saint-Salin), 133
"Ogloriosa Domina", (Racan), 132
Original Castings of Molière's Plays,
    (Herzel), 9

Palais-Royal, 29
Pascal, 56, 104, 187, 190, 193-194,
    196, 201
Pastorale Comique, La, 28
Patin, Grey, 64
Peintures Morales, (Le Moyne), 192,
    196
*Petit Discours Chrétien sur l'Immortalité
    de L'áme,* (Le Vayer), 92
Phaedra, (Racine), 33
Phédre, (Racine), 33
Physician in Spite of Himself, The, 28
Picard, Raymond, 124
Placets, 188, 200, 204-205
Plaideur, Les, (Racine), 173
Planchon, Roger 8, 11, 17-21, 24-25
Plautus, 32
Poquelin, Jean-Babtiste, 45
Praise of Folly, 33
Précaution Inutile, La, (Scarron), 124
*Precieusis, Le*s, 28, 30, 49-50, 64, 130,
    137, 207
*Precious Damsels, Th*e, 28
Préface, 188, 200, 202, 204-205
Princess d'Elide, 28
Princess d'Elide, La, 51
Problémes Sceptiques, (Le Vayer), 95
Psyche, 28-29, 55

Quinault, Philippe, 28

Racine, 1, 14, 29, 33, 52-53, 60, 107,
    129, 187
Racinian Tragedy, 14
Rape of the Lock, The (Pope), 127, 129
Regnard, Jean-Francois, 33
Richelet, 121
Romanticism, 21
Romero, Laurence, 9
Royal Academy of Music, 29

Saint-Evermond, 148, 160
Sarasin, Jean-Francois, 127
Saxe-Meiningen, 19
"Scene", 5
Scherer, Jacques, 8-9
School for Husbands, The, 28
School for Wives, (Jouvet), 10-11
Semiotics of Theatre and Drama, 15
Sennett, Mack, 51
*Sentiments d'ur Hornete et Habile
    Courtisan*, (Saint-Evermond), 148
Sertorius, (Corneille), 129
Sganarelle, 1-2, 30, 55, 61, 115, 124
Shakespeare, 1-3, 20
Shakesperean, 2
Shaw, David, 163-174
Sicilian, The, 29
Sicilien, Le, 51
Sicilien, Le: ou L'Amour Perintre, 29, 51
Siecle de Louis XIV, (Voltaire), 23
Simon, Alfred, 57
Stanislavski, 22
Sweetser, Marie-Odile, 39

Tartuffe, 1,5-6, 11, 18, 27-33, 35, 37,
    41, 51-52, 54-55, 64, 69, 77-79,
    81-82, 85, 87, 91-94, 103-104, 114,
    116, 118, 127-128, 135, 137-138,
    143, 145-146, 148, 171, 175-206,
    208
Tartuffe, (Antoine & Arnavon), 11
Tartuffe, (Jouvet), 8

Tartuffe, (Planchon), 18-19
Terence, 31-32
That Scoundrel Scapin, 28
Theatré Populaire (Dort), 20
"Theatrical Performance", (Carlson),
    15
Tobin, Ronald W., 107-121
Tralage, 63
Travial Théatral, (Dort), 20

Uberfield, Anne, 22-24

Vanité, De la (Montalgne), 148
Vie de Molière, La, (Fernandez), 118
Vie de Monsieur de Molière, (Grimarest),
    45
Vilar, 8, 21
Villiers, 79, 81, 93, 102
Virgile Travesti, Le, 129
Visé, Donneau de, 10
Visionaires, Les, (Desmaret), 131
Vitez, Antoine, 11, 18-19, 21
Voltaire, 115
Von Meiningen, 22
Voiture, 121

Waiting for Godot, 49
World War II, 20-22
Would be Gentleman, The 28